Privacy in the Workplace
Rights, Procedures and Policies

Kurt H. Decker

LRP Publications
Horsham, Pennsylvania

30355165

1/00

LRP Publications
An Axon Group Company
Horsham, Pennsylvania

This publication was designed to provide accurate and authoritative information on the subject matter covered. It is published with the understanding that neither the author nor the publisher is engaged in rendering legal, accounting, or other professional service. If legal advice or other expert assistance is required, the service of a competent professional should be sought.

Library of Congress Cataloging-in-Publication Data

Decker, Kurt H.
    Privacy in the workplace : rights, procedures, and policies / Kurt H. Decker — 1st ed.
      p.   cm.
    Includes index.
    ISBN 0-934753-66-0 : $62.50
    1. Employee rights—United States. 2. Privacy, Right of —United States. 3. Confidential communications—Personnel records—United States. 4. Labor laws and legislation—United States. I. Title.
KF3455.D43 1994
344.73'01—dc20
[347.3041]
                                    9412177
                                       CIP

Printed on acid-free paper in the United States of America.

00 99 98 97 96 95   6 5 4 3 2 1

For Hilary, Christian, and Allison
with love, for providing the moments
where "privacy" is most
cherished, enjoyed, relished,
and understood.

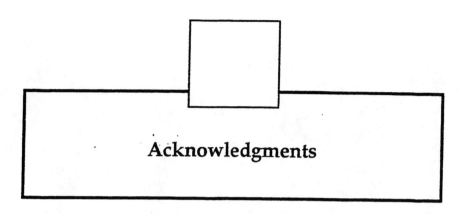

Acknowledgments

In preparing this text, many individuals either provided opportunities or shared their knowledge. Those who should be noted are H. Thomas Felix, II, Esquire, of Montgomery, McCracken, Walker & Rhoads in Philadelphia, Pennsylvania; John M. Skonier, Arbitrator; James Troebliger, Manager of Human Resources of GPU Nuclear Corporation; Dean John Gedid of the School of Law, Widener University; and Dr. Edwin M. Wagner of Saint Francis College.

Kurt H. Decker

Table of Contents

Table of Contents   xv

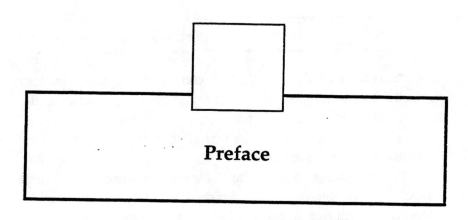

Preface

One of the most rapidly evolving areas of employment law involves workplace privacy. Employers are confronted with new or revised privacy requirements that necessitate regular review of their procedures and policies.

This text sets forth overall principles, procedures, policies, and forms to help employees, employers, human resources professionals, and attorneys to meet these workplace privacy challenges. The following elements of each workplace privacy interest will be reviewed: (1) general principles; (2) procedures relevant in implementing or maintaining the privacy interest; and (3) policies for applying it.

As a beginning point, Chapter 1 gives an overview of employment law and how it relates to workplace privacy. Chapters 2 through 8 cover specific workplace privacy interests that arise during hiring, at the workplace, and outside the workplace by examining privacy issues present in: (1) initial employment contacts; (2) information collection; (3) data verification; (4) records; (5) medical concerns; (6) personal workplace concerns; and (7) employer regulation of employees' activities outside the workplace. Chapter 9 includes an audit procedure which employers can use to evaluate their overall workplace privacy strengths and weaknesses, and Chapter 10 reviews employee disciplinary guidelines to be considered when workplace problems arise. Appendix A is provided as a reference of federal and state constitutional and statutory protections affecting workplace privacy. Appendix B presents in a manual form various policies relevant to workplace privacy. And, finally, Appendix C contains the text of the proposed Privacy for Consumers and Workers Act.

The procedures, policies, and forms contained in this text should be considered only as guidelines. They should not be adopted verbatim or applied without careful evaluation. Many require careful review of applicable legal considerations that are continuously subject to revision. All procedures, policies, and forms should be considered in relation to a particular employer's needs and requirements before being implemented. Once adopted, they should be consistently followed. If they cannot be followed, they should be discontinued or revised to reflect the existing conditions in the workplace. None should be adopted without commitment simply to make the employer look sophisticated or because other employers are doing this.

Introduction to Workplace Privacy

I. Historical Development of Privacy Issues

The concept of privacy within the United States is generally traced to the 1890 *Harvard Law Review* article by Samuel D. Warren and Louis D. Brandeis.[1] Prior to 1890, no claim for damages could be brought in American courts for an invasion of privacy. The Warren and Brandeis article was stimulated by the prying of the press into Warren's private affairs.[2] Warren and Brandeis maintained that even though no prior case law explicitly supported the existence of a right to privacy, it was supported by a reasoned development of common-law principles and society's changing circumstances. Their basic assumption was that the law recognizes innovative causes of action.[3] Warren and Brandeis noted the need for this innovation due to the newly developed methods of invading private and domestic life through photography and newspapers.[4]

The authors recognized that the right to privacy was limited. They proposed rules setting forth its scope within these limited parameters: (1) the right does not prohibit publication of matters of public or general interest; (2) the right does not prohibit communications that are privileged under libel and slander law; (3) there is probably no redress for oral invasions absent actually incurred damages; (4) the right to privacy terminates upon the subject's own publication or consent for another to publish information; (5) truth is not a defense for the invading party; and (6) the absence of "malice" is no defense.[5] Warren and Brandeis also suggested remedies for violation of the right to privacy.[6]

II. Privacy in the Workplace

A. Overview

Today, workplace privacy is a growing concern. Since George Orwell raised the specter of "Big Brother" with his book *1984*, computer technology, electronic communications, court decisions, government intrusion, and the employer's quest to know more about the individuals it employs have eroded employees' sense that their lives are a private matter. These factors have made privacy an increasingly important matter to employees and employers, and the entire workplace is affected.

Privacy concerns the nature and extent of employees' "right to be let alone" or to be free from "unwarranted intrusions."[7] From the moment individuals first confront their employers, privacy rights are placed into issue and may have to be relinquished. As a condition to securing employment, applicants must disclose personal facts about their backgrounds and must continually submit to employer scrutiny that may or may not be performance- or job-related. An employee may, for example, confront a physical examination, polygraph examination, honesty test, psychological evaluation, or even an antibody test for acquired immunodeficiency syndrome (AIDS). Once on the job, physical intrusion may occur through frisking employees as they leave the workplace, even though no reasonable suspicion of theft exists, or through locker searches.

Privacy interests also are implicated when employers conduct routine surveillance and monitoring. Some employers have installed computers to monitor performance of video display terminal operators. Electronic and voice mail is also subject to employer prying. Employers have even been known to operate video cameras in employee restrooms. These probings reveal information about the employee that was previously private and within the employee's exclusive control. Much of this information may have little, if anything, to do with the job or the employee's performance of that job.

Workplace privacy concerns extend to employer efforts to collect personal information. Employers have a legitimate need to know job-related information about their employees, including their abilities, honesty, and prior employment histories, but some employers want to know much more. They mistakenly assert that everything about an employee is relevant to employment, and that it is necessary to examine the "whole person" to determine if employment suitability exists. The employer, even in the absence of a nexus to the job, may want to know, for example, if the employee smokes marijuana at home, is a homosexual, or socializes with the "wrong" kind of people.

Other workplace privacy interests are implicated when employers disclose employment information to third parties, such as prospective employers of current employees. Employers may, perhaps, disclose an employee's confidential medical records or negative private facts to individuals who have no legitimate need for this information. Either type of disclosure may cause embarrassment by subjecting the employee to ridicule from friends or acquaintances or by injuring the employee's reputation and limiting his or her future employment prospects.

Here the issues of "privacy" and "confidentiality" intertwine. Workplace "privacy" is limited to what information should be collected, how much should be maintained, and what should be disclosed. The issue of "confidentiality" concerns the extent to which the employer discloses this information. Confidentiality should guard against unauthorized uses or disclosures of private information, and procedures should exist to ensure its security. Confidentiality requires security controls in oral and written communications and in manual and computerized records.

Today, state and federal legislatures and courts are increasingly concerned about workplace privacy. While employers may have legitimate business or job-related interests that sometimes require infringing on employees' privacy, there are compelling reasons to limit trespass by employers where no legitimate business or job-related reason exists.

B. Definition of "Privacy"

Privacy takes on a variety of meanings in the workplace and encompasses a broad spectrum of employee and employer interests. These interests arise out of the intrusiveness or fairness of how employers collect, maintain, use, and disclose employment information. They relate to employers' regulation of employees' lifestyles both at and outside the workplace.

Sliced another way, these privacy interests arise in relation to: (1) the employee's person, property, or private conversations; (2) the employee's private life or beliefs; (3) the employer's use of irrelevant, inaccurate, or incomplete facts to make employment decisions; and (4) disclosure by the employer of employment information to third parties.[8] These interests can be summarized into five primary themes:

1. *Speech*—What is said about someone, or what someone is free to say to others

2. *Beliefs*—What one privately thinks

3. *Information*—What is collected, maintained, used and disclosed

4. *Association*—With whom one shares parts of one's life

5. *Lifestyle*—How one lives

It is these privacy interests that recur throughout employment as they relate to hiring, the workplace environment, and life outside the workplace.

C. Information and Behavior Privacy

Within the employment relationship there are two basic privacies. One concerns "information privacy" or the employee's interest in controlling the collection, maintenance, use, and disclosure of employment data. The other relates to "behavior privacy" or the employee's interest in participating in activities free from employer regulation or surveillance at and outside the workplace.

Individuals generally are comfortable in relating the more intimate aspects of their lives to a friend. They are secure with the friend's use of what is known or learned, and the friend is trusted to continue to respect them, despite what is confided.

This is different from an employment relationship because employers continually evaluate employee performance and re-evaluate previously formed opinions. Among family and friends the individuals perceive life to be conducted "in private" and to involve "private relations"; that perception promotes a certain openness and comfort. Individuals believe themselves safe from scrutiny and feel secure. That feeling is not present in an employment relationship. There, a sense of potential intrusion is caused by uncertainty over what the employer may know or learn, and how it will use this information. This uncertainty erodes any feeling of comfort on the part of the employee.

D. Privacy Interests at the Workplace

In order to enter into an employment relationship, employees must often relinquish considerable autonomy and control of certain aspects of their lives. Generally, employees are not in a position to negotiate the terms and conditions of employment. Little, if any, negotiation leverage exists unless special or unique skills are present. Employees generally must adhere to the employer's unilateral imposition of terms; if they do not follow or accept these employment terms, they may not be employed. Once hired, employees must conform with the employer's expectations, rules, and procedures that define specific rights and responsibilities of both employees and the employer.

Most employees are wholly dependent upon their employers for their economic well-being and would thus face economic hardship if this relationship were suddenly terminated. Based on the anticipated continuance of the employment relationship, employees generally create various social and financial commitments, such as marriage, children, or the purchase of a home or automobile. Each of these commitments establishes a social or financial reliance in others that, in turn, is dependent upon the employee's economic relationship with the employer. The employer's intrusion into an employee's privacy may disrupt the employment relationship or cause it to be discontinued, both of which impose a financial hardship on the employee.

Absent statutory restrictions, an employer generally can collect, maintain, use, and disclose employment information and thus exert influence on employees' lifestyles.[9] Where an at-will employment relationship exists,[10] an employer generally can terminate an employee who raises an objection to these actions. The employee can therefore accept this relationship, protest and thus confront possible termination, or voluntarily terminate employment. For the employee, none of these options is desirable or realistic because economic loss may result.

Privacy concerns arise, in fact, whether or not an employment relationship is created; they are also present at hiring and after employment terminates. Privacy is affected by how the employer handles: (1) collection of information for hiring decisions; (2) storage, retention, and maintenance of employment information; (3) internal use of information in making decisions after hiring; and (4) disclosure of information to third parties. Accompanying these employment information interests is regulation of employees' lifestyles at and outside the workplace.

In hiring alone, privacy issues can affect an employee amid a myriad of circumstances: applications, interviews, credit checks, and reference checks; blood tests, medical screening, genetic screening, handwriting analysis, and skill testing; exploration of arrest record, criminal convictions, and immigration history; and finger-printing or photograph requirements.[11] Once an employee is in the workplace, privacy concerns create questions regarding employment records including performance evaluations and medical records; employees' health and safety including smoking, employee assistance programs, alcohol and drug abuse, and AIDS; searches, monitoring, and surveillance by camera or electronic means of the workplace or, for example, of union meetings; manipulation of employees' actions through regulation of literature distribution, jury or witness duty, voting time, whistle-blowing, and dress and grooming codes; and employer policies regarding nepotism, hiring of spouses, religious accommodation, language requirements, and privacy misconduct by other employees.[12] On the other hand, privacy may be impacted through employer intrusion into employees' personal associations outside the workplace involving bankruptcy or debtors and union membership, loyalty, conflicts of interest, off-duty misconduct involving noncriminal or criminal activities, and residency requirements.[13] In all of these areas workplace privacy becomes increasingly significant and susceptible to employer breaches for which employees today may seek redress for damages through a variety of litigation theories.

III. Significance of Workplace Privacy

A. Significance for Employees

Employment is generally a close relationship between employee and employer which both parties hope will continue over an indefinite time period. During this relationship many situations arise where the employee's privacy may be compromised.

The earliest employment privacy concerns arise over collection of information on an application form requesting employment, educational, financial, medical, and criminal histories.[14] Despite legal restrictions regarding what may be included on applications, many employers still solicit prohibited information. As the employment relationship continues, more and more written information is collected. Employee records may contain performance evaluations, promotion reports, discipline notices, payroll data, fringe benefit records, pension information, and health insurance data.[15] This employment information may be maintained in a record-keeping system that is either manual or computerized, and access to this information may or may not be controlled.

Information provided by the employee in hopes of creating and maintaining the employment relationship may potentially harm the employee. During the relationship an employee may disclose information for a specific employment purpose only. Years later, prospective employers, credit agencies, government agencies, and others may be granted access to this information without the employee's knowledge or consent. In this situation, the employer's duty to safeguard workplace privacy takes on particular significance.

The employment relationship produces vast amounts of written information which many people use to make decisions affecting employees.[16] The collection, maintenance, use, or disclosure of this information is usually administered unilaterally by the employer, with little or no employee control.[17] Moreover, employment information is often maintained long after the original purpose for its collection expires. Records are written accounts that are not subject to forgetfulness unless they are destroyed, and lengthy retention of information creates further potential for misuse.

Normally, it is the employer who decides to whom information will be disclosed, what information will be disclosed, and under what circumstances it will be provided. Economic circumstances surrounding continued employment may often compel the employee's submission to the employer's information requests and releases. Rarely can an employee verify the accuracy, contents, and use of the information or participate in deciding when, where, and to whom it is disclosed. Consequently, the employee can only surmise what employment information exists. The employer may maintain official as well as unofficial employment records. Identifying errors and finding their sources may be difficult. The employee does not know whether persons with which a confidential relationship is thought to exist have disclosed information to others without the employee's knowledge or prior consent. Through the employer's collection, maintenance, use, and disclosure of employment information, the employee loses substantial control over information the employer possesses.

B. Significance for Employers

Federal and state statutes and their accompanying case law regarding record keeping, disclosure, and privacy interests have made privacy a significant workplace concern which employers must address.[18] Employer reaction to these is complicated by conflicting privacy requirements which restrict employers' operations—record-keeping requirements mandate collection of certain information, but privacy statutes restrict the collection process. Similarly, privacy requirements seek to protect employment information from unwarranted disclosure, while at the same time disclosure statutes require access to the information for certain parties.

Increased governmental regulation of the employment relationship has expanded employer record-keeping obligations. Employers are subject to federal statutes that impose explicit and implicit record-keeping requirements.[19] The Occupational Safety and Health Act of 1970 (OSHA)[20] and the Civil Rights Act of 1964 (Title VII)[21] have the greatest impact. OSHA requires the employer to conduct employee medical examinations and maintain records on employee occupational health,[22] and Title VII requires an annual statement of the racial, ethnic, and gender composition of the employer's workforce.[23] The result is extensive and detailed records for which employee information must be collected.

In addition to these statutory requirements, the employer must collect, maintain, use, and disclose employment information to effectively operate its business. Information from employees is necessary to make decisions for hiring, promotion, training, security, compensation and benefits, retirement, disciplinary actions, termination, and other job opportunities. The employer must balance employees' privacy rights with the employer's need for information to make legitimate and job-related business decisions.

As additional privacy statutes are enacted, the employer must become more cautious in its methods of collection, maintenance, use, and disclosure of employment information. Unaccustomed to outside scrutiny, an employer may be surprised to discover that certain employment information must be disclosed to outside parties; for example, unions may request and obtain employment information.[24] The employer must be knowledgeable about federal and state statutes that specify acceptable and unacceptable information disclosure.[25] Employer familiarity with these requirements is critical to protect employee privacy rights, to limit employer liability, to operate effectively, and to maintain good relations with other organizations.

IV.   Regulation

A. Legislation

There is no comprehensive, nationwide statutory protection of employees' workplace privacy. However, federal and state constitutions and statutes impose certain privacy restrictions.[26] Actions by state legislatures have been more innovative and far-reaching than similar federal responses. States have recognized the need to balance privacy interests against other societal values.

Constitutional protections for personal privacy have historically been safeguards against governmental, rather than private, intrusions. That distinction, however, has disappeared in states whose constitutions protect against both.

While the United States Supreme Court was reviewing a constitutional privacy right,[27] the Freedom of Information Act of 1966

(FOIA)[28] was signed at the federal level to allow the public to "have all the information that the security of the Nation permits."[29] FOIA also exempted certain confidential employment information from public disclosure: "personnel and medical files and similar files the disclosure of which would constitute a clearly unwarranted invasion of personal privacy."[30]

In 1974, the United States Congress debated legislation which would increase the protection of information maintained on individuals by the government. A Senate bill provided for a Federal Privacy Board to oversee the collection, maintenance, and disclosure of information.[31] The House bill focused on federal agency standards for data collection and maintenance.[32] These two bills were combined without a formal conference committee meeting or report into the Privacy Act of 1974.[33]

Under the Privacy Act, an individual has input over the information maintained on the individual by the government, as well as how and by whom it is used.[34] The individual may request the involved agency to correct, amend, or delete any information, and may take legal action against the agency if the request is denied.[35]

The Privacy Act defines an "individual" as "a citizen of the United States or an alien lawfully admitted for permanent residence."[36] Courts have construed this to exclude foreign nationals, nonresident aliens, and corporations.[37] The protected "records" include any document containing "name, or the identifying number, symbol, or other identifying particular assigned to the individual."[38] Subject to twelve exceptions, records may not be released unless pursuant to the written request or prior consent of the individual.[39] Unfortunately, these federal statutes have a minor effect on workplace privacy because activities of most private sector employers are not within their scope.

Other federal statutes and executive orders also have a limited effect on workplace privacy interests.[40] These include the Fair Credit Reporting Act;[41] the National Labor Relations Act (NLRA);[42] the Age Discrimination in Employment Act of 1967 (ADEA);[43] the Vocational Rehabilitation Act of 1973;[44] the Americans With Disabilities

Act;[45] the Civil Rights Statutes (Sections 1981, 1983, 1985, and 1986);[46] Executive Order 11,246 (Affirmative Action);[47] the Omnibus Crime Control and Safe Streets Act;[48] the Bankruptcy Act;[49] the Drug Free Workplace Act;[50] the Hatch Act;[51] whistle-blowing protection;[52] Immigration Reform and Control Act;[53] and the Polygraph Protection Act.[54]

Various states enacted "mini-Privacy Acts" in the 1970s to address the need for increased workplace privacy.[55] In acknowledging employees' right to "be let alone," these statutes regulate the collection, maintenance, use, and disclosure of information about individuals by state and local agencies. Like the Privacy Act, these state statutes generally (1) give an individual the opportunity to know what information the government collects, maintains, and discloses about him or her; (2) permit an individual to correct or amend inaccurate government records; and (3) regulate the collection, maintenance, use, and disclosure of information by the government. Other state responses to privacy concerns in the workplace involve (1) disclosure of credit information; (2) scaled-down versions of the Hatch Act; (3) whistle-blowing; (4) employee access to personnel files; (5) regulation of medical files; (6) fingerprinting and polygraph examinations; (7) employment references; (8) psychological matters; (9) highly communicable diseases; (10) sickle cell anemia; (11) smoking; (12) voting; and (13) use of arrest and conviction records.

B. Judicial Responses

Judicial protection of workplace privacy is generally premised on constitutional, tort, or contract theories. In their constitutions, the federal government and some states provide a limited right to personal privacy or a right to be free from intrusion into one's private affairs.[56] (These rights differ between the federal and state constitutions.) Causes of action, such as invasion of privacy, defamation, false imprisonment, intentional infliction of emotional distress, negligent maintenance or disclosure of employment records, fraudulent misrepresentation, and intentional interference with contractual relations, and public policy also protect workplace privacy interests.

Courts recognize invasion of privacy in four forms: (1) intrusion upon an individual's physical solitude or seclusion; (2) public disclosure of private facts about an individual; (3) public representation of an individual in a false light; and (4) appropriation of an individual's name or likeness.[57]

In the context of workplace privacy, public disclosure of private facts may be asserted by an employee. This tort requires public disclosure—publicity or communication to a large number of persons—of true, embarrassing private facts about the employee.[58] Information contained in personnel files involving performance evaluations, test scores, salary histories, and medical information constitutes "private facts" which, if disclosed by an employer, would form the basis of the tort.[59] Normally, an employer's communication of private facts about an employee will not be to a sufficient number of persons to constitute "public" disclosure.[60] There are indications, however, that as workplace privacy becomes a more prominent issue this cause of action will take on greater importance as more employees seek to have the courts broaden its application.[61] Appropriations of name or likeness without consent may also offer redress where an employer uses an employee's photograph in its advertising without first securing the employee's permission.[62]

Defamation consists of the publication of an untrue statement that holds a person up to ridicule, hatred, or opprobrium.[63] In the employment relationship, defamation may arise when an employer communicates false information about an employee to a third party. Disclosure of negative performance evaluations or reasons for termination may create employer liability.[64] However, employers are protected by a "qualified privilege" which absolves them of liability when the communication is made in good faith, in response to a legitimate inquiry, and within the normal information channels of the employment relationship.[65]

Protection from false imprisonment safeguards the individual's interest in freedom from restraint of movement.[66] False imprisonment occurs in the employment context when an employer or its agent restrains an employee, usually to search or interrogate the employee regarding theft of employer property.[67]

Conduct constituting an intrusion into an employee's privacy must rise to the level of outrageous conduct by the employer for the tort of intentional infliction of emotional distress. This tort redresses only the most extreme workplace privacy invasions; for example, if an employee is terminated for refusing to discontinue a social relationship with another employee outside the workplace which does not adversely affect employee job performance or the employer's business.[68]

The courts also recognize the tort of negligent maintenance of employment records. It is an employer's duty under common law to maintain employment records carefully and to provide accurate employment references. Employees have recovered damages against employers who negligently disclosed to third parties inaccurate employment information.[69]

With the continued modification of at-will employment, public policy may also protect employees' workplace privacy interests. Causes of action have been permitted for an employer's violation of a clear, statutorily-declared policy,[70] and offer protection from employer retaliation for an employee's reporting unlawful or improper employer conduct[71] and for refusing to accede to improper employer demands.[72]

As discussed in later chapters, contracts may form another basis to raise workplace privacy concerns.[73] Contracts include oral and written employment agreements;[74] restrictive covenants,[75] employment handbooks and policies,[76] and collective bargaining agreements.[77]

V. Employment Information: Areas of Concern

A. Collection

"We live, inescapably, in an 'information society.' "[78] Increasingly, employment information must be collected with government agencies, record-keeping organizations, and employers all acting as partners.[79] Concerns arise in the initial collection process, the collection of accurate information, restriction of use to only the collection purpose, and the extent to which disclosure occurs.

An individual provides personal information to assist a potential employer in making its initial hiring decision. This information may be supplemented and verified by tests, interviews, medical screening, references, credit reviews, and a background investigation. Should hiring occur, this information is expanded to accommodate records for wages, benefits, performance evaluations, promotions, attendance, and other employment decisions.

Absent hiring, information is still created about applicants. This information can be extensive, and therefore is considered a valuable resource to entities unrelated to the employment relationship, including government agencies.[80] Confidentiality in the use and disclosure of information is a legitimate concern of both applicants and employees. Correspondingly, the employer's inquiries of applicants and employees should not become intrusive.

The first record of employment information established by an employer is the application form that is used to collect basic employment information. Employers collect information not only directly from an applicant, but also from third parties. It is not uncommon for an employer to request reports from credit agencies or other consumer reporting agencies whose information is frequently based on interviews with friends, neighbors, and relatives.

Employers utilize increasingly sophisticated information collection methods which may intrude upon employees' mental or physical privacy. These methods include psychological testing, polygraph examinations, honesty testing, and electronic storage of personal data. Collection methods should not violate an employee's privacy. Collected information should be disregarded if it is irrelevant to the employment relationship, is confidential, or is likely to be used unfairly in employment decisions.

Other collection methods include fingerprinting, blood tests, physical examinations, and work area surveillance. These generally are valid collection methods because their scope of inquiry is not as broad[81] as that of polygraph and personality tests, which are geared more toward compulsory extraction of incriminating facts.[82] Fingerprinting is "only a means of verifying the required information" and "involves no additional intrusion" into the person's life.[83] A routine physical examination or blood test is likewise not an offensive prying,[84] and photographing employees in work areas can be a reasonable employer method to improve efficiency when recording what is already public.[85]

Employment information should be collected through methods of accepted reliability that seek to discover only job-related facts. In providing employment information, the employee should be able to preserve dignity, prevent personal embarrassment, and foreclose economic harm. These protections, however, must be balanced with the employer's need for facts to ensure efficient decision making.

Employers should not seek private information about employees by requiring them to submit to collection methods which produce anxiety and humiliation suggestive of a criminal interrogation.[86] Employer background investigations should not include interviews with third parties without the employee's knowledge. Informing employees of any investigation is not overly burdensome to the employer.

B. Maintenance and Internal Use

After collecting employment information, the employer begins to use this information internally. This use involves information disclosure within the employer's organization and the subsequent decisions based on that information, including selection and placement; developmental decisions of transfer, promotion, demotion, and training; administration of employee benefits; discipline; and separation by involuntary or voluntary termination of employment.

At times, the employer may need to disclose employment information to the human resources department, payroll department, or supervisory personnel in order for certain employment decisions to be made. However, every decision maker does not need to review or have access to all employment information maintained on an employee. It is unnecessary for a supervisor preparing a performance evaluation to review an employee's medical and financial history. Likewise, a payroll clerk should not review an employee's performance evaluations. In cases such as these, all employment information is not essential for the particular decision each person is making.

Employees have a legitimate interest in restricting the use of their employment information to the purpose for which the employer originally collected it. The employee normally has no right to prevent other uses and, in fact, often times is not aware that information may be used for other purposes. The employer can minimize improper internal use by allowing disclosures only for a "routine use" to designated personnel having a job-related "need to know."[87] The employer should establish standardized routine uses by evaluating whether the information used in any employment decision corresponds with the job-related purpose for which it was collected and the decision to which it applies. For example, routine use at a performance evaluation would include job-related decisions about promotions, wages, or discipline. These information items would not be used for fringe benefit decisions, which clearly are unrelated to the subject of evaluations. Similarly, routine uses for medical information would include decisions regarding employee medical and life insurance plans; it would not be used for employee wage-rate decisions.

Access to employment information should be granted by the employer only on a job-related "need-to-know" basis. Limited access does not hinder an employer's operational efficiency; rather, it minimizes the misuse of employment information and protects the employee.

C. Access to Employees' Personal Information

Employees portray several "roles" in the lives they lead. These roles are acted out within the family, marriage, work, church, politics, and social relationships. In each role, the employee's responses to daily situations may, or perhaps must, differ depending on the needs or requirements of the particular circumstances.

Employees have an interest in maintaining privacy to live in these different roles without having performance in one role placed in conflict with another. Through a process of self-editing, the employee can adjust internal needs for solitude, companionship, intimacy, and general social intercourse with anonymity and responsible participation in society. Employers must refrain from using employment information to which they have access to interfere with employees' rights to live in these roles and alternate between them.

Computer technology enables the employer to administer large volumes of employment information. Through computer programs, employers can transfer and assemble employment information almost anywhere within seconds. Storage capabilities prolong the longevity of employment information, making the potential for improper disclosure and misuse almost as permanent as the information itself. Employers must ensure that access to information is limited to those with an employment-related need, regardless of how the information is maintained.

To safeguard its employees' privacy, the employer should regularly review and purge its records of unnecessary and outdated employment information. Furthermore, employees should be granted access to employment information for correction, supplementation, and deletion.

D. Disclosure to Third Parties

Internal use of employment information is a necessary function, and is permissible as long as the information directly relates to employment decisions. Disclosures to third parties are ordinarily at the discretion of the employer and primarily affect the employee's life outside rather than at the workplace. Frequently, such disclosures involve employment references for a new job or disclosures to credit agencies. The adverse effect of negative disclosure may continue for years. In some instances, employers are statutorily required to disclose information to third parties, including responding to subpoenas and filing reports required by government regulations.

While employer policy and practice have historically provided some confidentiality to employment information, whatever confidentiality exists is generally the result of the employer's voluntary action. Only limited statutory controls exist to preserve confidentiality of employment information. The decision to disclose employment information to third parties depends on the unpredictable and often inconsistent judgment of the employer.

The employee's opportunity to disclose information about him- or herself and to control its use are the linchpin of privacy. The employee should be given opportunities to limit or monitor information disclosures about him or her by the employer to third parties. Random disclosures absent an employee's knowledge or consent should be curtailed.

VI. Employees' Lifestyles

A. Regulation at and Outside the Workplace

Generally, an employee's private activities outside the workplace are within the employee's exclusive purview and are not open to employer scrutiny or regulation. The employment relationship does not install the employer as guardian of the employee's every action. Yet, in certain areas directly affecting the employer's business affairs, the employer is permitted to regulate the employee's lifestyle[88] and actions, even outside the workplace. If an employee's lifestyle adversely affects the employer's business, the employer may properly discipline or terminate the employee.

Lifestyle regulation *at* the workplace may involve dress and grooming standards, spousal employment, consumption of alcohol, smoking, and drug use. Limits on an employee's lifestyle *outside* the workplace may be placed on who the employee may have contact with socially, other employment opportunities that may directly conflict with the employer's business, and the type of image the employee maintains in the community.

Any regulation of employee lifestyle at and outside the workplace should be reasonable and directly related to the employee's position. Regulation should occur only where the employee's lifestyle will have a definitive adverse result on the employer's business affairs. The employer must evaluate each limit on an employee's lifestyle at and outside the workplace on a case-by-case basis.[89]

The reason for an employee lifestyle regulation at or outside the workplace should be readily discernible to a third party as being in the employer's business interest.[90] The lifestyle activity being regulated should be directly job-related and harmful to the employer through immediate financial loss absent the regulation. Speculation regarding possible impact on the employer's affairs is not sufficient reason to restrict the employee's lifestyle.[91]

Endnotes

1   Samuel D. Warren and Louis D. Brandeis, *The Right to Privacy*, 4 HARV. L. REV. 193 (1890).

2   Warren had married into a socially prominent Boston family. He suffered considerable annoyance from the city's newly developed "Yellow Press." The press pried into his and his wife's "blue-blood" social life in detail. Warren took this matter up with Brandeis, his law partner and Harvard Law School classmate.

3   Warren and Brandeis, *supra* note 1, at 193.

4   *Id.* at 195.

5   *Id.* at 214-18.

6   A tort action for damages would exist in all cases with substantial compensation for injury to feelings even absent special damages. Injunctions would rarely issue. Criminal liability could be imposed only through statutory enactment. *Id.* at 219.

7   Public Utils. Comm'r v. Pollack, 393 U.S. 451, 467 (1952).

8   *See* Donald Beaney, *The Right to Privacy and American Law*, 31 LAW & CONTEMP. PROBS. 253, 254 (1966).

9   *See, e.g.;* Hollenbaugh v. Carnegie Free Library, 436 F. Supp. 1328, 1328-30, 1333-34 (W.D. Pa. 1977) (termination of at-will employee discovered to be living in "open adultery" held not to violate constitutional privacy right).

10   The at-will employment relationship gives both the employee and the employer the option to terminate employment at any time, for any or no reason, with or without notice. *See generally* KURT H. DECKER, THE INDIVIDUAL EMPLOYMENT RIGHTS PRIMER Ch. 1 (1991).

11   *See infra* chapters 2, 3, 4, and 5 of this text.

12   *See infra* chapters 4, 5, 6, and 7 of this text.

13   *See infra* chapter 8 of this text.

14   PRIVACY PROTECTION STUDY COMMISSION, PERSONAL PRIVACY IN AN INFORMATION SOCIETY 72-78 (1977) [hereinafter PERSONAL PRIVACY IN AN INFORMATION SOCIETY].

15   *Id.* at 225-26.

16   *Id.* at 13-14.

17   *Id.*

18   *See generally* Appendix A for a list of federal and state statutes affecting workplace privacy.

19   *See, e.g.,* Exec. Order No. 11,246, 3 C.F.R. § 339 (1964-1965), *reprinted as amended* in 42 U.S.C. § 2000e (1988), note originally issued on Sept. 24, 1965; Age Discrimination in Employment Act of 1967, 29 U.S.C. §§ 621-634 (1988); Vocational Rehabilitation Act of 1973, 29 U.S.C. §§ 701-796i (1988); Equal Pay Act of 1963, 29 U.S.C. § 206 (1988); Employee Retirement Income Security Act of 1974, 29 U.S.C. § 1001 (1988); *see also* Appendix A section III for additional federal statutes.

20   29 U.S.C. §§ 651-678 (1988).

21   42 U.S.C. §§ 2000e-1 through 2002-17 (1988).

22   29 C.F.R. § 1904 (1992).

23   Form EEO-1, 29 C.F.R. § 1602.7 (1992).

24   *See, e.g.*, Detroit Edison v. National Labor Relations Bd., 440 U.S. 301 (1979); *see also* Salt River Valley Water User's Assoc'n v. National Labor Relations Bd., 769 F.2d 639 (9th Cir. 1985) (union allowed access to confidential personnel information).

25   *See* Appendix A sections III and IV.

26   *See generally* Appendix A.

27   Griswold v. Connecticut, 381 U.S. 479 (1965) (penumbra of the Bill of Rights); *see also* Roe v. Wade, 410 U.S. 113 (1973) (concept of personal liberty contained in the Fourteenth Amendment); Katz v. United States, 389 U.S. 349 (1967) (Fourth Amendment).

28   5 U.S.C. § 552 (1988).

29   Statement by President Lyndon B. Johnson upon signing Pub. L. No. 89-487 on July 4, 1966. 2 PUB. PAPERS 199 (1967).

30   5 U.S.C. § 552(b)(1)(A)(6) (1988).

31   S. 3418, 93d Cong., 2d Sess. (1974).

32   H.R. 16373, 93d Cong., 2d Sess. (1974).

33   5 U.S.C. § 552a (1988).

34   5 U.S.C. § 552a(e)(1).

35   5 U.S.C. § 552a(d)(3)-(4), 552(d)(2).

36   5 U.S.C. § 552a(a)(2).

37   *See* Raven v. Panama Canal Co., 583 F.2d 169 (5th Cir. 1978), *cert. denied*, 440 U.S. 980 (1979); Dresser Indus., Inc. v. United States, 596 F.2d 1231 (5th Cir. 1979); Oke Corp. v. Williams, 461 F. Supp. 540 (N.D. Tex. 1978).

38   5 U.S.C. § 552a(a)(4) (1988).

39   5 U.S.C. § 552a(b)(1)-(12). *See* Zeller v. United States, 467 F. Supp. 487 (E.D.N.Y. 1979); Local 2407, AFGE v. Defense Gen. Supply Ctr., 423 F. Supp. 481 (E.D. Va. 1976), *aff'd*, 573 F.2d 184 (4th Cir. 1978).

40   *See generally* Appendix A sections III and IV for a brief discussion of these and other federal and state statutes.

41   15 U.S.C. § 1681-1681t (1988).

42   29 U.S.C. §§ 151-169 (1988).

43   29 U.S.C. §§ 621-634 (1988).

44   29 U.S.C. §§ 701-796 (1988).

45   42 U.S.C. §§ 12101-12213 (Supp. 1992).

46   42 U.S.C. §§ 1981, 1983, 1985, 1986 (1988).

47   Exec. Order No. 11,246, 3 C.F.R. § 339 (1964-1965), *reprinted as amended* in 42 U.S.C. § 2000e (1988), note originally issued on Sept. 24, 1965.

48   18 U.S.C. §§ 2510-2520 (1988).

49   11 U.S.C. § 525 (1988).

50   41 U.S.C. §§ 701-707 (1992).

51   5 U.S.C. §§ 1501(5), 7325(a) (1988).

52   5 U.S.C. §§ 1201-1222 (1992).

53   29 U.S.C. §§ 2001-2008 (1988).

54   29 U.S.C. §§ 2001-2009 (1988).

55   *See* Appendix A section IV for state statutes affecting workplace privacy.

56   *See* Appendix A sections I and II. *See also,* Luck v. Southern Pac. Transp. Co., 218 Cal. App. 3d 1, 267 Cal. Rptr. 618 (1990) (private employer's random alcohol and drug testing program violated privacy provisions of California's constitution).

57   WILLIAM PROSSER, HANDBOOK OF THE LAW OF TORTS § 117 (4th ed. 1971).

58   *Id.*

59   *See* Quinones v. United States, 492 F.2d 1269 (3d Cir. 1974) (release of inaccurate personnel file); Bulkin v. Western Kraft East, Inc., 422 F. Supp. 437 (E.D. Pa. 1976) (negligent maintenance of employment records).

60   *See* Kobec v. Nabisco, 166 Ga. App. 652, 305 S.E.2d 183 (1983) (employer's disclosure of employee's attendance record held not to establish tort because of lack of physical intrusion).

61   *See, e.g.,* O'Brien v. Papa Gino's, 780 F.2d 1067 (1st Cir. 1986) (employer-required polygraph test).

62   *See, e.g.,* Colgate-Palmolive Co. v. Tullos, 219 F.2d 617 (5th Cir. 1955).

63   PROSSER, *supra* note 57, § 111.

64   *See* Wendler, Jr. v. DePaul, 346 Pa. Super. 479, 499 A.2d 1101 (1985) (negative employee performance evaluation claimed by employee to be false); Biggins v. Hanson, 252 Cal. App. 2d 16, 59 Cal. Rptr. 897 (1967) (false reasons for employee termination). .

65   PROSSER, *supra* note 57, § 115.

66   *Id.* § 11.

67   Faniel v. Chesapeake & Potomac Tel. Co., 404 A.2d 147 (D.C. 1979); Tocker v. Great Atl. & Pac. Tea Co., 190 A.2d 822 (D.C. 1963); Delan v. CBS, Inc., 111 Misc. 2d 928, 445 N.Y.S.2d 898 (1981).

68   *See* Patton v. J.C. Penney Co., 75 Or. App. 638, 707 P.2d 1256 (1985), *aff'd, rev'd in part*, 301 Or. 117, 719 P.2d 894 (1986).

69   *See* Quinones v. United States, 492 F.2d 1269 (3d Cir. 1974); Bulkin v. Western Kraft E., Inc., 422 F. Supp. 437 (E.D. Pa. 1976).

70   *See* Perks v. Firestone Tire & Rubber Co., 611 F.2d 1393 (3d Cir. 1979) (employee unlawfully terminated for refusing to take a polygraph examination in a state which prohibited its use in employment).

71   *See,* Palmateer v. International Harvester Co., 85 Ill. 2d 124, 421 N.E. 2d 876 (1981).

72   Monge v. Beebe Rubber Co., 114 N.H. 130, 316 A.2d 549 (1974).

73   *See* chapters 2, 7, and 9 of this text.

74   *See, e.g.,* Shebar v. Sanyo Business Sys. Corp., 111 N.J. 276, 544 A.2d 377 (1988) (promise of job "for the rest of his life" to forego rival employer's job offer sufficient to create enforceable contract).

75   *See, e.g.,* Martin Indus. Supply v. Riffert, 366 Pa. Super. 89, 530 A.2d 906 (1987) (covenant void where parties entered into boilerplate noncompetition agreement, contained in form book, that had no geographical limitation inserted and was given worldwide application).

76   *See, e.g.,* Toussaint v. Blue Cross/Blue Shield, 408 Mich. 579, 292 N.W.2d 880 (1980) (employment handbooks may create binding commitment by employer to employees).

77   *See, e.g.,* Klamath County & Operating Eng'rs, 90 Lab. Arb. (BNA) 354 (1988) (Lebak, Arb.).

78   PERSONAL PRIVACY IN AN INFORMATION SOCIETY, *supra* note 14, at 5.

79   *Id.* at 13.

80   For example, form EEO-1 is used by the Equal Employment Opportunity Commission (EEOC) and the Office of Federal Contract Compliance (OFCC) to obtain affirmative action information about the hiring of minorities and women. Form EEO-1, 29 C.F.R. § 1602.7 (1992).

81   *See* Division 241, Amalgamated Transit Union v. Suscy, 538 F.2d 1264 (7th Cir.), *cert. denied*, 429 U.S. 1029 (1976) (requiring blood and urine tests for public bus drivers after any serious accident or suspicion of intoxication is not a violation of the Fourth Amendment because the state had a reasonable objective in furthering public safety, and the actual conditions and the manner of the intrusion were not unreasonable); Miller v. New York Stock Exch., 425 F.2d 1074 (2d Cir.), *cert. denied*, 398 U.S. 905 (1970) (statute requiring fingerprinting of stock exchange workers held constitutional as valid exercise of police power in combatting theft in the securities industry); Thomas v. General Elec. Co., 207 F. Supp. 792 (W.D. Ky. 1962) (taking motion pictures of employee by an employer did not violate the employee's right to privacy when the purpose was to study manufacturing methods and processes); Pitcher v. Iberia Parish Sch. Bd., 280 So. 2d 603, 607-08 (La. Ct. App. 1973), *cert. denied*, 416 U.S. 904 (1974) (requirement that public school teacher submit to annual physical examination is a reasonable interference with the right to privacy).

82   Schmerber v. United States, 384 U.S. 757, 764 (1966).

83   Miller v. New York Stock Exch., 425 F.2d 1074 (2d Cir.), *cert. denied*, 398 U.S. 905 (1970).

84   *See* Breithaupt v. Abram, 352 U.S. 432, 439 (1957).

85   Thomas v. General Elec. Co., 207 F. Supp. 792 (W.D. Ky. 1962).

86   *See, e.g.,* Mansfield v. AT&T, 747 F. Supp. 1329 (W.D. Ark. 1990) (terminating an employee who was questioned without notice for six hours, where she was laughed at and accused of lying, was not given an opportunity to defend herself, was not permitted to smoke or eat, was accused of having a lesbian relationship with a co-employee, was questioned while one employer representative unzipped his pants, and was not permitted to leave until she signed a statement admitting guilt).

87   These phrases are taken from the Federal Privacy Act of 1974. 5 U.S.C. § 552a(a)(7) (1988).

88   *See* Berger v. Battaglia, 779 F.2d 992 (4th Cir. 1986) (police department's attempt to regulate white police officer's off-duty conduct in performing in "blackface" for theater production when this off-duty conduct was considered offensive to the black community).

89   *See* Inland Container Corp., 28 Lab. Arb. (BNA) 312, 314 (1957) (Ferguson, Arb.).

90   *See* Rulon-Miller v. IBM Corp., 162 Cal. App. 3d 241, 208 Cal. Rptr. 524 (1984) (employee's termination for dating employer's competitor violated employee's privacy rights because no legitimate conflict of interest existed).

91   *See* Movielab, Inc., 50 Lab. Arb. (BNA) 632, 633 (1968) (McMahon, Arb.).

Initial Employment Contacts

I. Introduction

Hiring is the human resources function that develops a pool of qualified applicants and selects new employees. This process may create vast information resources for immediate and subsequent workplace privacy intrusions because applicants must disclose considerable personal information during the hiring process. The employer must verify information supplied by applicants, and often this produces even more information. These initial contacts during the hiring process significantly affect applicants' privacy interests in their beliefs, speech, information, associations, and lifestyles. These privacy interests are affected whether or not hiring results.

During the hiring process, the applicant must determine which and how much information needs to be revealed to the potential employer to obtain employment. Typically, newspaper advertisements include some job details that cause interested individuals to evaluate their qualifications before they decide whether or not to apply. Those individuals who do apply generally reveal only information that is necessary to be considered for hiring and not jeopardize other opportunities.

All information disclosed by an applicant may be subject to employer verification. In verifying information, the employer may uncover other data that may or may not be related to the position.

This additional data may be obtained with or without employee knowledge as the employer conducts background and reference checks.

The employer has a duty to collect only information that is relevant to the evaluation of the applicant for the particular position to be filled. This information may be gathered from the application form, interviews, and other hiring procedures. Once the employer has possession of this employee information, privacy concerns are immediately implicated. This chapter examines the workplace privacy principles, procedures, and policies applicable to these initial employment contacts.

II. Advertisements

A. Advertisement Privacy Principles

Advertisements in the help-wanted section of the local newspaper are a common employer recruitment method. Some employers use advertisements to publicize their products, services, or distinctive features. Advertising may motivate applicant interest by educating the reader about unique employer characteristics involving philosophy, product technology, or career opportunities.

Many applicants make their first contact with a prospective employer through these newspaper advertisements. Depending on the content of the advertisement, the applicant may inquire further or may refrain from making an inquiry. When an individual does not apply for employment because he or she believes that it would be futile, privacy interests are affected because the individual has determined that revealing certain personal information may result in an unfair evaluation and thus nonhiring. The employer may be requesting information that is not job-related, and this prevents the applicant from determining whether to exercise the "right to be left alone" or to disclose information that may prejudice employment or other opportunities.[1]

An applicant's determination not to disclose potentially prejudicial information that is unrelated to the job may be no different than the applicant trying to protect himself or herself from an actual physical intrusion. For example, advertisements specifying or relating to an employer preference for a certain race, religion, age, or national origin may invite challenges.[2] The privacy interests of applicants not to disclose this information may be enforced under federal and state fair employment practice statutes[3] or through contractual theories.[4]

Employers are prohibited from using help-wanted advertisements which specify a preference for "male" or "female" applicants unless gender is a *bona fide* occupational qualification. Courts have upheld the constitutionality of statutes prohibiting job advertisements which designate gender.[5]

Generally, advertisements are not employment offers because both the advertiser and the reader understand that employment cannot be finalized without further negotiations. Advertisements are merely requests or invitations by the employer for individuals to identify themselves for possible employment based on the terms and conditions offered by the employer. Advertisements may have legal consequences—those containing specified terms may commit the employer to certain actions. For example, a binding commitment resulted from the following advertisement: "WE WANT enthusiastic, ambitious men to represent us locally. Professional training program w/450 monthly guarantee if qualified. . . ."[6] When the employee's commissions fell below the guaranteed $450 per month, the employee was entitled to the difference.[7] However, in the case of an employee who claimed that the employer's advertisement of a "career opportunity" was binding, the advertisement was considered too general to constitute an offer.[8]

B. Developing an Advertisement

Preparing an effective employment advertisement is an involved process. Several preliminary considerations on the part of the employer can ensure the success of an advertisement:

1. Ensure that the job description and job specifications are correct.

2. Conduct a job analysis if there is doubt about the accuracy of a job description or job specification.

3. Write the advertisement using no technical language so that it can be easily read.

4. Sell the job to prospective applicants by writing advertisements that are appealing in structure and content by considering:

   a. printing style;

   b. borders;

   c. layout; and

   d. factual statements that highlight major features of the job.[9]

1. Minimizing Litigation Risks

To minimize intrusions of applicants' privacy and to reduce the employer's vulnerability to litigation, the employer should consider these guidelines:

1. Advertisements specifying or relating to sex, race, religion, age, national origin, or disability may invite employee privacy challenges under federal and state fair employment practice statutes.[10]

2. Employers are prohibited from using help-wanted advertisements which state a preference for male and female applicants unless sex is a *bona fide* occupational qualification.[11]

3. Advertisements should be worded to avoid creating contractual commitments[12] by not suggesting:

   a. long-term employment,

   b. guaranteed job security,

   c. guaranteed wages or salary, or

   d. career security.

4. The employer should centralize within one department (preferably Human Resources) responsibility for development, writing, and placement of advertisements to ensure consistency.

C. Sample Advertisements

The following advertisements may be used as a guide in developing help-wanted ads that comply with state and federal statutes.

Sample 1

WEST HAMPTON INN

•Porter

•Secretary

•Host/Hostess

Apply in person at 220 East Market Street,

Scranton, Pennsylvania

Equal Opportunity Employer

Sample 2

RADIOLOGY TECHS

REGISTERED AND NEW GRADS

Opportunity to work at Good Samaritan Hospital. The working environment is caring, dynamic, and team-oriented.

Competitive salary and comprehensive benefits.

Interested applicants should call or write:

HUMAN RESOURCES DEPARTMENT

GOOD SAMARITAN HOSPITAL

600 South Street

Allentown, Penna. 18201

(215) 555-1234

Equal Opportunity Employer

III. Applications

A. Application Privacy Principles

The purpose of the application is to elicit job-related information from an applicant to enable the employer to make an informed hiring decision. Applications affect privacy interests in how much non-job-related information an employer can collect regarding an applicant's personal life and experiences.

Privacy interests relating to permissible employer inquiries are implicated by the application and extend throughout and beyond the employment relationship. Statutory regulations do not merely limit the employment information that may be solicited, but require that once this information is collected, the employer use it properly and protect it from unwarranted disclosures. Today, privacy constraints through common law and federal and state fair employment practice statutory protections have been applied to many traditional areas of employer inquiry involving, among other things, age, marital status, pregnancy, and disability.[13]

Applications generally raise privacy concerns related to race, color, sex, national origin, disability, and age. Employer inquiry into areas that are not job-related may affect applicants' privacy by revealing beliefs, speech, association, and lifestyle interests. The employer may unfairly eliminate certain individuals from consideration based on this unrelated information. Therefore, the employer should analyze all applications on the assumption that in subsequent litigation the employer will be required: (1) to defend the use of the information requested; or (2) to explain why the information was collected but not used. Workplace privacy issues may be affected by application questions regarding:

1. Religion
2. Sex
3. Height or weight
4. Age

5. Marital status

6. Arrests

7. Convictions

8. Military discharge

9. Citizenship

10. National origin

11. Race

12. Credit status

13. Names of relatives

14. Disability

Requesting an applicant's clergy as a reference is equivalent to asking an applicant's religion. Sex discrimination may arise through inquiries regarding preschool-aged children and who will care for them during working hours. No employer has ever been able to justify that being married, widowed, divorced, or single has any legitimate relation to job performance.[14] This information has traditionally been used to discriminate against women.

Height and weight requirements may adversely impact various groups (for example, applicants for police and fire services) and therefore may also affect workplace privacy rights.[15] It was once thought that tall police officers were more visible, less often attacked, and more authoritative. This has been proven untrue.[16] Height requirements generally eliminate women[17] and certain national origin groups[18] because on the average these groups generally are much smaller than the typical white male. Weight requirements for physically active jobs or jobs where safety of the individual or the public is a consideration, however, may be job-related.[19]

Inquiries into high school or college training must be necessary for the job in question.[20] An employer cannot require more education than is necessary as a verifiable job requirement.

Convictions cannot be used to arbitrarily deny employment;[21] they can be used only where the conviction is job-related.[22] For example, a recent conviction for theft might bar the applicant from a bank teller position.[23] If the employer inquires into conviction records, it should state on the application that conviction is not an absolute barrier to employment in all cases.

Inquiries regarding financial status also can create problems. Questions concerning home rental or ownership, car ownership, bank accounts, or bankruptcy reveal an applicant's credit rating or history. Such inquiries may affect statutorily protected interests or result in discrimination.

Inquiries indicating a preference for hiring relatives and friends of current employees may indicate an intent to exclude minorities because minorities may not be given notification of job openings or a chance to apply.[24] These employer practices may indicate that minorities are excluded and an intent to maintain this exclusion by hiring relatives and friends of white employees who also are white.

B. Drafting the Application

Initially the employer must determine the information that is needed to select the applicant best suited for a position. This may involve inquiries into education, professional licenses or certifications, previous work experience, special skills, talents, and fluency in a foreign language. The employer's special needs for the position may warrant that certain additional information be collected.

After determining the job-related and general background information that should be collected from the applicant, the employer should draft the remainder of the application to preserve applicant privacy and to limit employer liability. The application should:

1. inform the applicant that employment is at-will;

2. provide for the applicant's acknowledgment that falsification or omission of any information may result in termination if hired;

3. require the applicant's acknowledgement that the information provided is complete and accurate;

4. include a release protecting from defamation the employer and those persons the employer contacts regarding references;

5. inquire only whether the applicant has any physical condition or limitations *that would disqualify him or her from performing the job.* This may require that the applicant's physical condition be examined to determine if reasonable accommodations under federal and state fair employment practice statutes could be made to enable the applicant to perform the job; and

6. not inquire into the applicant's filing for and/or receiving benefits for work-related illnesses or injuries. This may be considered retaliation for the receipt of these benefits.

1. Application Privacy Considerations

The following guidelines will help protect applicants' privacy regarding information collected on the application.

1. Collect only information that is relevant to specific employment decisions.

2. Inform applicants, employees, and former employees of the uses to be made of the collected information.

3. Adopt reasonable procedures to ensure that information provided by the applicant is accurate, timely, complete, and verified.

4. Limit internal and external disclosure of application information.[25]

2. Prohibited Inquiries

Applicants typically are requested to furnish basic information regarding name, address, job being applied for, experience, and education. The application form can provide the employer with

the information needed to adequately compare an applicant's qualifications to the job specifications. However, an improperly struc-
tured application can cause problems for the employer. Employers
should use this standard to determine whether an inquiry should
be made: "How does this inquiry ensure a job-related selection?"
Inquiries should not be made if they are not obviously job-related.

Some employers include on their applications potentially improper questions regarding an applicant's age, birth date, marital
status, and other personal information. Some inquiries that may
be difficult for employers to justify and that could encourage complaints under fair employment practice statutes include:

1. Eye color

2. Hair color

3. Height

4. Weight

5. Gender

6. Credit record

7. Personal financial information

8. Garnishment record

9. Marital status

10. Spouse's name

11. Spouse's employment status

12. Number of children

13. If applicant has children under age 18

14. Religious practices which limit availability for Saturday and
    Sunday work

15. Citizenship of a country other than the United States

16. Arrests

17. Disability

18. Bonding refusal[26]

Sometimes employers seek this information in conjunction with affirmative action reporting requirements. In that case, the employer is advised to put these inquiries on a tear-off sheet attached to the application to minimize improper use or disclosure of this information.[27]

C. Application Forms and Accompanying Documents

The employer should prepare its application with the objectives of gathering the information necessary to make job-related hiring decisions and providing a foundation for defending against privacy-related litigation that may arise if hiring does not result or if termination subsequently occurs. Careful drafting of the application by the employer will minimize litigation exposure and intrusions of employee privacy.

Comprehensive Application and Employment Agreement

Please Print

Date _____

Name_____

Street Address_____

City_____

State_____Zip Code_____

Business Telephone ( )_____

Home Telephone ( )_____

How were you referred?   [ ] Newspaper   [ ] School   [ ] On my own   [ ] Company Employee   [ ] Agency   [ ] Other

Name of referral source:_____

Type of Work Desired

Indicate the position for which you are applying._____

_____

What is your minimum weekly salary requirement?_____

Date available to begin work:_____

Do you have any commitments to another employer which might affect your employment with us?_____

_____

Educational Data

Name, Street, City, State, and Zip Code for each School	Type of Course or Major	Graduated?	Degree Received

High School_____

College_____

Graduate School_____

Trade, Business, Night, or Correspondence_____

Other_____

Military Experience

Were you in the U.S. Armed Forces? [ ]Yes   [ ]No

If yes, what Branch?_____

Rank at Separation:_____

Briefly describe your duties._____

_____

Employment History

List previous employers. Begin with present or most recent employer (use other side of this application if necessary). May we contact these employers?   [ ] Yes   [ ] No

Employer_____   Supervisor's Name_____

Address_____   Your Job Title_____

_____   Describe your duties._____

Telephone_____   _____

Your Salary: _____

Start_____   _____

End_____   _____

Explain your reason for leaving.

_____

_____

_____

_____

Employer_____   Supervisor's Name_____

Address_____   Your Job Title_____

_____   Describe your duties._____

Telephone_____   _____

Your Salary: _____

Start_____   _____

End_____   _____

Explain your reason for leaving.

_____

_____

_____

Employer_____   Supervisor's Name_____

Address_____   Your Job Title_____

_____   Describe your duties._____

Telephone_____   _____

Your Salary: _____

Start_____   _____

End_____   _____

Explain your reason for leaving.

_____

_____

_____

General Information

Have you previously applied for employment with this Company?

[ ] Yes   [ ] No

If yes, when?_____

Have you previously been employed by the Company or its subsidiaries?   [ ] Yes   [ ] No

If yes, when?_____

Please include any other information you think would be helpful in considering you for employment, including additional work experience, articles or books published, activities, and accomplishments. Exclude all information indicative of age, sex, race, religion, color, national origin, and disability.

_____

_____

_____

_____

Employment Agreement

Should I be employed by the Company, I agree to conform to the Company's rules and regulations, and agree that my employment and compensation can be terminated at any time, for any or no reason, with or without notice at the option of either the Company or myself.

I certify that the information provided on this application is true, correct, and complete to the best of my knowledge and agree that falsified information or omissions of significant information may disqualify me from further consideration for employment and may result in termination if discovered at a later date should hiring occur.

I authorize persons, schools, current employer, previous employers, and organizations named in this application to provide the Company with any relevant information that may be required. I further release all parties providing information from any and all liability or claims for damages whatsoever that may result from the release, disclosure, maintenance, or use of this information.

This application has been read by me in its entirety.

_____   _____

Date   Signature

Note: The following application was designed to solicit as little information as possible by the employer. The burden of information disclosure rests entirely on the applicant, who must make the choices regarding what information to reveal:

General Application

Please send one copy of this form with a resume outlining your qualifications to (*Employer's Name and Address*)

_____

_____

_____

Name:_____ Date:_____

Current Position:_____

Current Employer:_____

Ultimate Employment Goal?_____

_____

Next Employment Step?_____

_____

Why?_____

_____

_____

Are You Willing To Relocate?_____

To Where?_____

Why?_____

_____   _____

Date   Signature

Employment Contract Disclaimer[28]

In consideration of my potential employment, I agree to conform to the Company's rules and regulations and agree that my employment and compensation can be terminated at any time, for any or no reason, with or without notice at the option of either the Company or myself. I understand that no manager or representative, other than the Company President or _____ (Name), has authority to enter into any agreement with me for employment for any specified time period, or to make any agreement contrary to this document. Any agreement for employment for any specified time period must be in writing and signed by the Company President.

_____   _____

Date   Signature

Information Release Form

I authorize schools, references, prior employers, and physicians or other medical practitioners to provide my record, reason for leaving employment, and all other information they may have concerning me to the Company, and I release all parties providing information from any and all liability or claims for damages whatsoever that may result from the release, disclosure, and use of this information.

_____   _____

Date   Signature

1. Affirmative Action Information

Note: Employers are mandated by federal and state fair employment practice statutes to collect certain information for statistical and affirmative action purposes.[29] The following inquiries should be included on the application in a manner which allows the inquiries and the resulting information to be separated from the application. This will prevent the information provided by the applicant from being used improperly during the hiring process.

Affirmative Action Information

To aid in the Company's commitment to provide equal employment opportunities to all applicants, applicants are asked to voluntarily provide the following information. This section will be separated from the application and maintained in a separate file.

[ ] Male   [ ] Female

Your Age Group

1. Under 21   5. [ ] 50-59

2. [ ] 21-29   6. [ ] 60-69

3. [ ] 30-39   7. [ ] 70 and over

4. [ ] 40-49

Please check the one box which best describes you.

1. [ ] Aleut   11. [ ] Japanese

2. [ ] American-Indian   .   12. [ ] Korean

Specify tribe:_____   13. [ ] Mexican, Mexican-Amer-
                                        ican, Chicano

3. [ ] Asian Indian   14. [ ] Puerto Rican

4. [ ] Black   15. [ ] Samoan

5. [ ] Chinese   16. [ ] Spanish/Hispanic

6. [ ] Cuban   17. [ ] Vietnamese

7. [ ] Eskimo   18. [ ] White

8. [ ] Filipino   19. [ ] Other, not listed

9. [ ] Guamanian/Chamorro   Specify:_____

10. [ ] Hawaiian

Check any major disability of which you have a record and which
may have impeded your securing, retaining, or advancing in employment:

1. [ ] Hearing   5. [ ] Developmental

2. [ ] Sight   6. [ ] Orthopedic (amputations)

3. [ ] Speech   7. Other disability

                                    Specify: _____

4. [ ] Physical   8. [ ] No disability

Are you a veteran, spouse of a 100% disabled veteran, or a widow or widower of a veteran?

[] Yes   [] No

Only applicants who check Yes will be verified for veterans preference points in examinations which allow the addition of these points.

IV. Interviews

A. Interview Privacy Principles

Unlike the written inquiry of the application, the interview is primarily oral, although a written record may be created by the interviewer. After the initial interview, others may be conducted prior to the final hiring decision. At each interview, the applicant's privacy interests may be affected because each employer decision maker attempts to refine the information initially requested by obtaining additional information to set the applicants apart from each other.

Because of the prohibitions contained in federal and state fair employment practice statutes,[30] employers must take special care during applicant interviews. The employer may not use an applicant's race, color, sex, age, national origin, religion, marital status, or disability as a basis for an employment decision, unless the employer is hiring pursuant to goals and timetables contained in its affirmative action plan.[31] Similarly, an interviewer is not permitted to ask an applicant questions related to these areas nor may a former employer be asked these questions during a written or telephone reference check.

B. Procedures to Minimize Litigation Risks

The employer's objective in conducting interviews is to gain maximum information about an applicant and at the same time refrain from any statements or questions that may lead to liability. To this end, the employer should use:

1. well-prepared interviewers who:

    a. become well-informed prior to the interview by reviewing

        (1) applications,

        (2) resumes, and

        (3) other pertinent information about the applicants;

    b. know what further job-related information should be obtained from the applicants during interviews;

    c. know what information to convey about the employer; and

    d. know what information to convey about the particular job for which the applicants have applied;

2. interviewers who are not only knowledgeable about the employer's advantages and benefits but who also are aware that certain statements should not be made to "sell" applicants on the employer, such as:

    a. specifying and promising definite employment terms and conditions greater or different than the employer's oral or written policies, thereby avoiding creating a binding commitment; and

    b. asking questions that could be considered discriminatory or intrusive—only job-related inquiries should be made.

C. Interview Inquiry Policy

The following list contains examples of impermissible interview inquiries and their acceptable counterparts. The employer should use this list to train all personnel involved in the interview process.

Interview Inquiry Policy[32]

Unacceptable	Acceptable

Age[33]

Unacceptable	Acceptable
1. What is your age?	1. Interviewer should state that hiring is subject to verification that applicant meets legal age requirements.
2. When were you born?	2. If hired, can you show proof of age?
3. During what dates did you attend or complete elementary or high school?	3. Are you over eighteen years of age? If under eighteen, can you, after hiring, submit a work permit?

Arrest and Criminal Record[34]

Unacceptable	Acceptable
1. Do you have an an arrest record?	1. Have you ever been convicted of a felony or, within the previous two years, a misdemeanor which resulted in imprisonment? Note: This question should be accompanied by a statement that a conviction will not automatically disqualify the applicant from consideration for the available position.

Unacceptable	Acceptable

Birthplace and Citizenship[35]

Unacceptable	Acceptable
1. Where is your birthplace? Where is your spouse's birthplace or that of your relatives?	1. Can you, prior to employment, submit verification of your legal right to work in the United States?
2. Are you a U.S. citizen?	2. Interviewer should state that proof of U.S. citizenship is required after employment.
	3. Interviewer should state that applicant is required to produce naturalization, first papers, or other legally acceptable documents prior to employment.

Bonding[36]

Unacceptable	Acceptable
1. Any questions regarding refusal or cancellation of bonding	1. Interviewer should state that, based on the position, bonding may be a condition of hiring.

Military Service[37]

Unacceptable	Acceptable
1. General questions regarding military service that pertain to date or type of discharge	1. Questions regarding relevant skills acquired during applicant's U.S. military service
2. Questions regarding service in a foreign military	

Unacceptable	Acceptable

Name[38]

Unacceptable

1. What is your maiden name?

Acceptable

1. Have you ever used or been known by another name?

2. Is any additional information regarding a name change or use of an assumed name or nickname necessary to check on your work or education record? If yes, please explain.

National Origin[39]

Unacceptable

1. Questions regarding nationality, lineage, ancestry, national origin, descent, or parentage of applicant, applicant's parents, or spouse

2. What is your mother tongue?

3. What language do you commonly use?

4. How did you acquire the ability to read, write or speak a foreign language?

Acceptable

1. Languages applicant reads, speaks, or writes if this information has a job-related purpose

Notice in Case of Emergency[40]

Unacceptable

1. Name and address of relative to be notified in case of accident or emergency

Acceptable

1. After hiring: "Name and address of person to be notified in case of accident or emergency."

Unacceptable	Acceptable

Organizations and Activities[41]

Unacceptable	Acceptable
1. List all organizations, clubs, societies, and lodges to which you belong.	1. List job-related organizations, clubs, professional societies, and other associations to which you belong. Omit those indicating or referring to your race, color, religion, national origin, ancestry, sex, age, or disability.

Physical Condition/Disability[42]

Unacceptable	Acceptable
1. Questions regarding applicant's general condition, state of health, or illness	1. Interviewer should state that offer of employment may be made contingent on applicant passing a job-related physical examination.
2. Do you have any disabilities?	2. Are you able to perform the tasks of the job with or without accommodation? If no, what can be done to accommodate your limitation?
3. Questions regarding receipt of worker's compensation.	

Race and Color[43]

Unacceptable	Acceptable
1. Questions regarding applicant's race or color	1. Statement that photograph may be required after employment

Unacceptable	Acceptable

Race and Color—*Cont.*

Unacceptable	Acceptable
2. Questions regarding applicant's complexion or color of skin, eyes, or hair	
3. Requirement that applicant affix a photograph to application	
4. Requesting applicant, at his or her option, to submit a photograph	
5. Requiring a photograph after the interview but before employment	

References[44]

Unacceptable	Acceptable
1. Questions to applicant's former employers or acquaintances which elicit information specifying the applicant's race, color, religion, national origin, ancestry, disability, medical condition, marital status, age, or sex	1. By whom were you referred for a position?
	2. Can you provide names of persons willing to provide professional and/or character references?

Unacceptable	Acceptable

Religion[45]

1. Questions regarding applicant's religion	1. Interviewer should explain the regular days, hours, or shifts to be worked.
2. What religious days do you observe?	
3. Does your religion prevent you from working weekends or holidays?	

Marital Status and Family[46]

1. Questions regarding applicant's marital status	1. Interviewer should explain employer policy regarding work assignment of related or married employees.
2. Number and/or ages of children or dependents	2. Do you have any relatives currently employed by the Company? If so, list their names and positions held.
3. Name(s) of spouse or children of applicant	
4. Questions regarding pregnancy, childbearing or birth control	
5. Questions regarding child care	

V. The Hiring Process

A. Hiring Privacy Principles

To protect workplace privacy interests and limit employer liability, an employer's overall hiring procedure should address the three main components of hiring—advertisements, applications, and interviews. The overall hiring procedure should ensure that only relevant or job-related information necessary for employment decisions is collected, maintained, and used. Likewise, the sensitivity of this information should be preserved through confidentiality procedures in effect prior to and during employment and after employment terminates. Confidentiality should be maintained to minimize privacy-related claims that may arise out of violations of federal or state fair employment practice statutes[47] and tort[48] or contractual[49] litigation.

B. Hiring Procedures

In developing an overall hiring procedure, the employer should consider the following steps that will help preserve applicants' privacy.

1. Determine the interviewer.
2. Determine who will review employment records.
3. Collect information only from verifiable sources.
4. Collect information by legally acceptable methods.
5. Obtain information only from reliable consumer reporting agencies and regularly reevaluate the selection of these agencies.
6. Maintain confidentiality of all information that is collected.
7. Exercise caution when checking references.
8. Inform applicants what information will be maintained if they are or are not hired.

9. Inform applicants of the uses to be made of collected information.

10. Adopt procedures to assure the accuracy, timeliness, and completeness of the collected information.

11. Permit new employees to review, copy, correct, or amend this information.

12. Limit internal use of information and inform new employees of the information that will be collected.

13. Limit external disclosures, especially disclosures made without employee authorization, to specific inquiries or requests to verify information.

14. Provide for a regular internal review of hiring procedures.[50]

1. Minimizing Litigation Risks

Due to the high cost of litigation and the changing character of the at-will employment doctrine, employers should attempt to minimize their litigation risk by structuring hiring procedures and policies to meet certain objectives.

1. Interviewers should be properly trained to prevent them from making improper or exaggerated promises to applicants.

2. Personnel policies, handbooks, and manuals should be examined to ensure they contain no promises that the employer is unable or unwilling to keep. Remove any language that might imply that employment is other than at-will.

   a. Avoid terms like "permanent employee."

   b. Change "probationary period" to "initial review period," or completely discontinue use of this concept.

   c. Include in each employee handbook a statement that:

      (1) policies are subject to unilateral change without notice;

(2) the handbook does not create a binding employment contract, thereby preserving the at-will nature
of the employment relationship; and

(3) work rules or list of termination causes contained
in any employer publication are not all-inclusive.

3. Every applicant should be required to sign a written acknowledgment that any employment with the employer is
at-will. This acknowledgment should be:

a. a part of the actual application and

b. a statement that the application has been read in its
entirety.

C. Useful Documents

Pre-Employment Checklist

The Company asks that you complete the following checklist
before reporting for employment. It is important that the Company
orient you to its procedures and policies. By signing in the given
place, you are acknowledging that the corresponding topic has
been fully explained and questions have been answered to your sat-
isfaction.

Topic	**Employee Signature**
1. The date on which my employment begins has been established.	_____
2. The rate of compensation is understood.	_____
3. I understand that occasionally I may be requested to perform various tasks unrelated to my position.	_____

Topic	Employee Signature

4. I understand that my supervisor will introduce me to my fellow employees and personnel in other departments with whom I may have contact.

_____

5. I have answered accurately and completely all questions on my Employee's State Withholding Allowance Certificate (W-4).

_____

6. I have answered accurately and completely all questions on my IRS Employee's Withholding Allowance Certificate (Federal W-4).

_____

7. I have answered accurately and completely all questions on my Employment Eligibility Verification (Form I-9).

_____

8. I have completed my Employee Information Sheet.

_____

9. I have received and read a copy of the Employee Handbook—Book Number_____.

_____

10. I have received and read a copy of the Group Insurance Benefits Booklet. I also have received and completed an enrollment card for these benefits.

_____

Topic	**Employee Signature**
11. I have received and read a copy of the Company-paid, weekly income insurance plan.	_____
12. I have received and read a copy of the plan summary for the profit sharing program and have been informed of the date on which I become eligible to participate and the benefits I can derive through participation in the plan.	_____

_____

Date

_____

Employee Signature

_____

Supervisor's Signature

Hiring Policy

Section 1. PURPOSE. It is the Company's intent to hire only qualified employees. Selection will be based on qualifications, skill, training, and ambition displayed by the applicant.

Job openings not filled from within the Company's workforce will be filled by referrals, walk-ins, or advertisement respondents. Active files for recent applicants are maintained by the Human Resources Department as required by law. These will be reviewed when the Company seeks new employees. The Manager requesting additional employees will submit to the Human Resources Department a written request which identifies the position and necessary qualifications.

Section 2. GENERAL PROCEDURE. Prior to employing an individual, the Company must take certain preliminary steps to ensure uniformity of personnel practices and compliance with federal and state employment statutes. The following procedure will be followed:

a. reception of applicant;

b. preliminary interview and screening by the Human Resources Department;

c. completion of application;

d. testing of applicant;

e. interview by the prospective supervisor;

f. verification of references provided by applicant;

g. preliminary selection of qualified applicants by the Human Resources Department after consultation with the prospective manager;

h. final selection by the supervisor and Human Resources Department; and

i. hiring of selected applicant.

Section 2a. RECEPTION. The applicant will be met in the lobby of the Human Resources Department where literature and information on the Company will be available. Each referred applicant, walk-in, or advertisement respondent should be told to initially report to this area. It is the Company's policy to treat each applicant with the same consideration given to a customer. Each applicant, whether or not hired, can spread goodwill for the Company or give it a bad name based on the treatment he or she receives. The Company's policy is to maintain a good image to continue attracting qualified applicants.

Section 2b. PRELIMINARY INTERVIEW AND SCREENING. A short, preliminary interview of each applicant by the

Human Resources Department staff will identify the most promising applicants and those who are not qualified.

Section 2c. APPLICATION. After the preliminary interview, all applicants are given an application to complete. The questions used on this application are in compliance with federal and state fair employment practice statutes and regulations. The application also includes clauses covering falsification of records and an agreement to submit to medical testing if a job offer is made. Both clauses are signed by the applicant. The applicant is asked at this time for information required by the Immigration Reform and Control Act of 1986. If the applicant cannot comply with requirements of this Act, he or she will not be considered for employment. Once it is obtained, this information will be separated from the application.

Section 2d. SKILL TESTING. All applicants who are approved as possible candidates, whether they are walk-ins, advertisement respondents, or referrals from employees, will be subject to skill testing. An outside agency will conduct the skill testing to ensure that the Company adheres to federal and state fair employment practice statutes which require that the overall selection process show no evidence of adverse impact on minority groups.

Section 2e. INTERVIEW WITH PROSPECTIVE MANAGER. If an applicant's test results meet the standards set for the position, an interview with the prospective manager is scheduled. The time of the interview will be mutually convenient for both supervisor and applicant. The purpose of this interview is: (a) to assess the applicant; (b) to describe the job and working conditions to the applicant by touring the area in which he or she will work; and (c) to create goodwill for the Company whether or not the applicant is hired. To accomplish these objectives, the supervisor must be alert, perceptive, free from prejudice, even-tempered, and able to keep accurate records. Managers also must avoid any question or conduct that violates federal and state fair employment practice statutes. After the interview, the applicant will be told that he or she will be contacted by the Human Resources Department.

The manager does not have the authority to offer the job to the applicant. A checklist will be given to the manager to ensure that certain points are covered during the interview. The manager will return the application with the completed interview checklist to the Human Resources Department for determination of whether to continue the hiring procedure.

Section 2f. REFERENCE VERIFICATION. If the interview proves positive, the Human Resources Department will check references with former employers, schools, and other information sources listed by the applicant. The applicant must sign a consent form to be given to previous employers who otherwise might be unwilling to provide information on the applicant.

Section 2g. PRELIMINARY SELECTION. A preliminary selection will be made by the Human Resources Department and the manager after they are satisfied that qualified applicants are available. If no qualified applicants are available, other applicants will be sought.

Section 2h. FINAL SELECTION. A final selection will be made by the prospective manager and the Human Resources Department after they are satisfied that a qualified applicant is available. All participants in the selection must agree on wages, terms, and employment conditions for the new employee.

Section 2i. HIRING OF APPLICANT. The Human Resources Department will contact the selected applicant and offer employment. Details of the wages, terms, and employment conditions will be discussed. If the applicant accepts, the Human Resources Department will set up a time for the employee to sign in and begin the Company's orientation program.

Section 3. REJECTED APPLICANTS. In most circumstances, a number of applicants will be interviewed for a particular position. There may be times when more than one applicant will progress through the interview procedure, but only one will be chosen. If other applicants would have been eligible for the position, these approved applicants will be retained by the Human Resources Department in a special referral file to be considered for additional openings that might occur in the same department or in other departments or shifts. As openings develop, these applicants will be referred to managers for consideration with additional new applicants as required by the manager to make a quality selection.

Section 4. APPLICABILITY. Anyone being hired as a full-time employee is subject to this hiring policy. Employees hired on a temporary basis through outside temporary services are subject to this hiring policy.

Endnotes

1   Public Utils. Comm'r v. Pollack, 393 U.S. 451, 467 (1952).

2   *See* Hailes v. United Airlines, 464 F.2d 1006 (5th Cir. 1972) (sex discrimination found where employer advertised for flight attendants under "Help Wanted—Females" heading in newspaper).

3   *See* Appendix A sections III.F and IV.H.

4   *See, e.g.,* Willis v. Allied Insulation Co., 174 So. 2d 858 (La. 1965) (terms of advertisement created binding, contractual commitments on the part of employer).

5   Pittsburgh Press Co. v. Pittsburgh Comm'n on Human Relations, 413 U.S. 376 (1973) (help-wanted advertisements designating a desired gender of applicants were discriminatory).

6   Willis v. Allied Insulation Co., 174 So.2d 858 (La. 1965).

7   *Id.*

8   Horizon Corp. v. Weinberg, 23 Ariz. App. 215, 531 P.2d 1153 (1975).

9   DONALD MYERS, HUMAN RESOURCES MANAGEMENT: PRINCIPLES AND PRACTICE 186-87 (2nd ed. 1992).

10   *See, e.g.,* Hailes v. United Air Lines, 464 F.2d 1006 (5th Cir. 1972).

11   *See, e.g.,* Pittsburgh Press Co. v. Pittsburgh Comm'n on Human Relations, 413 U.S. 376 (1973).

12   *See, e.g.,* Willis v. Allied Insulation Co., 174 So. 2d 858 (La. 1965).

13   *See* Appendix A sections III.F and IV.H for a list of federal and state fair employment practice statutes affecting applications.

14   Sprogis v. United Air Lines, 444 F.2d 1194 (7th Cir.), *cert. denied,* 404 U.S. 991 (1971) (employer policy requiring flight attendants to be unmarried constituted sex discrimination).

15   *See, e.g.,* Horace v. City of Pontiac, 624 F.2d 765 (6th Cir. 1980) (females); Officers for Justice v. Civil Serv. Comm'n, 395 F. Supp. 378 (N.D. Cal. 1975) (females, Asians, and Latinos).

16   Dothard v. Rawlinson, 433 U.S. 321 (1977).

17   *See* Blake v. City of Los Angeles, 595 F.2d 1367 (9th Cir.), *cert. denied,* 446 U.S. 928 (1980).

18   Lum v. New York City Civil Serv. Comm'n, 10 Fair Empl. Prac. Cas. (BNA) 365 (S.D.N.Y. 1975).

19   *See* Jarrell v. Eastern Airlines, Inc., 430 F. Supp. 884 (E.D. Va. 1977), *aff'd,* 577 F.2d 869 (4th Cir. 1978); Leonard v. National Airlines, Inc., 434 F. Supp. 269 (S.D. Fla. 1977).

20   Griggs v. Duke Power Co., 401 U.S. 424 (1971).

21   Green v. Missouri Pac. R.R., 523 F.2d 1290 (8th Cir. 1975).

22   Carter v. Gallagher, 452 F.2d 315 (8th Cir. 1971), *cert. denied,* 406 U.S. 950 (1972).

23   *See, e.g.,* Carter v. Maloney Trucking & Storage, Inc., 631 F.2d 40 (5th Cir. 1980) (an employer's refusal to rehire a former employee who had murdered one of its employees found to be a legitimate nondiscriminatory action).

24   *See, e.g.,* United States v. Carpenters Local 169, 457 F.2d 210 (7th Cir.), *cert. denied,* 409 U.S. 851 (1972) (family relation criterion for union membership excluded minority group members from carpenters trade with predominantly white membership and contributed to finding that Title VII of the Civil Rights Act of 1964 was violated); United States v. Iron Workers, Local 1, 438 F.2d 679 (7th Cir.), *cert. denied,* 404 U.S. 830 (1971) (union that has only white members can effectively preclude nonwhites from membership by giving preference in admissions to relatives of members).

25   Privacy Protection Study Commission, Personal Privacy in an Information Society Appendix 3, Employment Records (1977).

26   For a more detailed discussion of prohibited inquiries under fair employment practice statutes, *see* section IV.C of this chapter, *infra*.

27   For an example of a form, *see* section III.C.1 of this chapter, *infra*.

28   *See, e.g.,* Novosell v. Sears, 495 F. Supp. 344 (E.D. Mich. 1980) (application disclaimer that no employment contract was intended to be created was enforceable to preserve at-will employment relationship).

29   *See* Appendix A sections III.F.5.

30   *See* Appendix A sections III.F and IV.H for a list of federal and state fair employment practice statutes affecting interviews.

31   *See* Exec. Order No. 11,246 (Affirmative Action), 3 C.F.R. § 339 (1964-1965), *reprinted as amended in* 42 U.S.C. § 2000e (1988), note originally issued on Sept. 24, 1965.

32   These interview principles also apply to applications. See section III of this chapter, *supra*.

33   *See, e.g.,* Goodyear Tire & Rubber Co., 22 Fair Empl. Prac. Cas. (BNA) 755 (W.D. Tenn. 1979) (age discrimination because maximum applicant age of 40 for tire builders was not a bona fide occupational qualification).

34   *See, e.g.,* Gregory v. Litton Sys., Inc., 316 F. Supp. 410 (C.D. Cal. 1970), *aff'd with modification not here relevant,* 472 F.2d 631 (9th Cir. 1972) (race discrimination against black employee where arrest record not relevant to position applied for and individual had not been convicted).

35   *See, e.g.,* Smith v. Union Oil Co., 17 Fair Empl. Prac. Cas. (BNA) 960 (N.D. Cal. 1977) (national origin discrimination).

36   *See, e.g.,* United States v. Chicago, 459 F.2d 415 (7th Cir. 1977) (disqualifying applicants based on credit checks).

37   *See, e.g.,* EEOC Dec. 74-25, 10 Fair Empl. Prac. Cas. (BNA) 260 (1973) (4.2% of whites and 7.5% of blacks receive general discharges; 2.6% of whites and 5.2% of blacks receive undesirable discharges).

38   *See, e.g.,* Allen v. Lovejoy, 553 F.2d 522 (6th Cir. 1977) (sex discrimination in requiring married women, but not married men, to change their surnames to that of their spouses on personnel forms).

39   *See, e.g.,* Rogers v. Equal Employment Opportunity Comm'n, 454 F.2d 234 (5th Cir. 1971), *cert. denied,* 406 U.S. 957 (1972).

40   Prior to hiring, employer inquiries into emergency notification information may constitute sex discrimination by revealing marital status or

national origin information indicated by an ethnic name. However, this information can be obtained after hiring.

41   *See, e.g.,* Abrams v. Baylor College of Medicine, 581 F. Supp. 1570 (S.D. Tex. 1984) (religious discrimination in denying applicant a position in Saudi Arabia because applicant was Jewish).

42   *See, e.g.,* Bentivegna v. Department of Labor, 694 F.2d 619 (9th Cir. 1982) (disqualification of all uncontrolled diabetics for construction positions could not be justified by an alleged risk of injury and therefore constituted discrimination based on disability).

43   *See, e.g.,* Cal. Lab. Code § 1051 (West 1971) (California statute prohibiting employers from requesting a photograph of an applicant or employee as a condition of employment).

44   *See, e.g.,* Smith v. Union Oil Co., 17 Fair Empl. Prac. Cas. (BNA) 960 (N.D. Cal. 1977) (national origin discrimination in recruitment and hiring).

45   *See, e.g.,* Compston v. Borden, Inc., 424 F. Supp. 157 (S.D. Ohio 1977) (religious discrimination occurred where Jewish plaintiff was subjected to supervisor's anti-Jewish slurs).

46   *See, e.g.,* Phillips v. Martin Marietta Corp., 400 U.S. 542 (1971) (sex discrimination regarding pre-school children).

47   *See* Appendix A sections III.F and IV.H for a list of federal and state fair employment practice statutes affecting hiring.

48   *See, e.g.,* Slohada v. United Parcel Serv., 193 N.J. Super. 586, 475 A.2d 618 (App. Div. 1984), *rev'd on other grounds,* 207 N.J. Super. 145, 504 A.2d 53 (1986) (inquiry by employer into extramarital sexual activities could give rise to tort liability if the employee were terminated for those activities).

49   *See, e.g.,* Toussaint v. Blue Cross & Blue Shield, 408 Mich. 579, 292 N.W.2d 880 (1980) (employer liable for interviewer's statement that the employee would be employed as long as he did his job).

50   *See* PRIVACY PROTECTION STUDY COMMISSION, PERSONAL PRIVACY IN AN INFORMATION SOCIETY 231-238 (1977).

3

Verification of Employee Data

I. Introduction

After an application is accepted, employers must verify the information provided by the applicant. An employer may decide to verify this data with or without the individual's consent or knowledge. This verification procedure affects the applicant's privacy interests present in speech, beliefs, and associations by producing information other than what the employee may have knowingly revealed.

This verification is the step in the employee selection process in which the employer checks the accuracy of the data that was supplied. Almost every qualification an applicant offers for consideration can be verified. The employer has many sources of verification available to it, such as previous employers, schools, military records, certifying or licensing bodies, and public records (documents from courts, law enforcement agencies, licensing bureaus, and tax assessors).

Some verification sources are more objective than others. Verifying a college degree can be accomplished by contacting the college registrar who will simply confirm or deny that a degree was earned. A driver's license can be checked with the state motor vehicle bureau in a similar manner. This type of verification is documented and can be objectively proved or disproved. Other sources, however, sometimes provide more subjective verification. Previous employers may give inaccurate information because of their fear of liability that may arise if they release defamatory information about a former employee. Previous employers may be more cooperative when the information request is accompanied by a release signed by the applicant detailing what information may be disclosed.

Accuracy of information supplied by applicants can be increased substantially by advising applicants that the information they furnish will have a direct bearing upon their hiring and that all information will be carefully verified. These simple steps will help to decrease the number of inconsistencies between information given by applicants and that obtained through verification.

Employers can use outside companies whose services include verification of job experience, work performance, attendance, training, education, criminal convictions, motor vehicle driving records, and military records. These companies also conduct applicant background searches and provide comprehensive reports by reviewing workers' compensation claims, credit bureau records, and bankruptcy filings. Results from interviews with co-workers and neighbors are used to determine an applicant's reputation regarding honesty, alcohol use, or drug abuse. Employers must be aware, however, that wrongful collection and disclosure of this information by these outside companies can create liability for employers that use their services.

Some of the information received as a by-product of the verification process may be irrelevant to the position the applicant is seeking. To safeguard the applicant's privacy interests and minimize the employer's exposure to litigation, procedures and policies must be developed to counteract these privacy problems. This chapter reviews workplace privacy interests raised by the employer's verification of employment data through credit checks, review of arrest records and criminal convictions, fingerprints, photographs, immigration requirements, and reference checks.

II. Credit Checks

A. Credit Check Privacy Principles

One of the most serious violations of workplace privacy rights is also the most common—employers' accumulation and disclosure of personal, often intimate, information solicited from credit bureaus. Often an employer will desire information about an individual in addition to what was learned from applications, interviews, or references. These employer needs may be fulfilled by credit information.

For most people today, credit is a part of everyday life. When in need of credit, individuals look most frequently to banks, savings and loan associations, credit unions, and retailers. To these and other credit grantors, recorded information is essential to establish and maintain credit relationships. Grantors pass on this information to credit bureaus that in turn provide employers with much more than an applicant's general financial background. A credit bureau's records can disclose much about an individual's beliefs, lifestyle, and associations. For example, an individual's lifestyle may be revealed through information about expenditures on possessions, eating habits, and travel history. Also, the individual's religious beliefs may be disclosed by a listing of donations to a specific church. In addition to employment history, an employer may request a credit bureau to obtain information regarding an applicant's reasons for leaving previous employment and whether a prior employer would rehire the individual and records concerning education, grades, and class rank.

Individuals applying for credit consent to certain privacy intrusions and expect certain information to be collected. At the time of credit application, the individual is concerned only with obtaining the credit, and he or she may reveal information that is unnecessary or irrelevant. Later, when the individual can assess the impact of the information disclosure, the credit process has been completed and the information recorded for potential future disclosure. The employer's awareness of the circumstances surrounding the credit application will enable it to more accurately evaluate information provided by credit bureaus.

Once an employer has received a credit report, it may use this information to appraise an applicant or employee for hiring, promotion, reassignment, or retention. However, sometimes credit

information is obtained for purposes that are not job-related because the employer wishes to know more about an employee's
general background. Every instance of collection, maintenance, use,
and disclosure of credit information raises significant workplace
privacy concerns by potentially revealing data that is irrelevant
in the employment context. Generally, personal finances are not
relevant to the job applied for or currently held and may disclose
an adverse financial situation that may prejudice the employer's
decisions. Federal and state statutes place restrictions on the credit
information that may be used for employment purposes.[1] Additionally, use of credit data that is not job-related violates federal and
state fair employment practice statutes.[2]

   Under the federal Civil Rights Act of 1964 (Title VII),[3] courts
have concluded that an employer's requirement that all job applicants maintain a good credit record had a disproportionate impact
on nonwhites[4] because census figures and other statistics show that
a disproportionate number of nonwhites live below the poverty
level. Similarly a bank's requirement that job applicants have a
good credit record had an adverse impact on nonwhite applicants
when statistics revealed that 35.4 percent of the nonwhite persons
in the local geographic area were below the poverty level compared
with 10.3 percent of the area's white population.[5] Requiring that
applicants and employees have a good credit record may have to
be justified by a legitimate, job-related business necessity.[6] A bank's
credit checks on successful job applicants were justified where
checks were done on blacks and whites alike because, for employment of tellers, a legitimate job-related business purpose was
served.[7] Conversely, a general background investigation that included inquiries into financial histories of applicants for police
officer candidates violated Title VII because a disproportionate
number of minority applicants were disqualified and the investigation yielded results that were not job-related.[8]

   In addition to these examples of employee claims, employers
may face potential litigation for other actions regarding credit reports. An employer may be liable if it obtains information from a

credit agency that it was not legally permitted to request from employees directly. Moreover, denying employment based on information that is not job-related or information believed or known to be false may open the employer to litigation based on a wrongful refusal to employ. Refusal of employment based on undesirable information in a credit report may be insufficient to withstand challenges of noncompliance with federal and state fair employment practice statutes even if the information is correct. Finally, employers that hire an outside investigative firm may be liable for illegal acts of that firm even if those acts are beyond the scope of the contract between the two.[9]

Considering these and other potential claims, an employer must act to limit its susceptibility to litigation. The results of credit investigations should be restricted to job-related information and should be used only for positions involving access to highly confidential or classified information or where the handling of money is involved.

B. Precautionary Procedures

Employers should take the following steps to ensure that the privacy interests of applicants and employees are preserved during a credit investigation and in any subsequent use of the information collected.

1. Select a reputable credit agency and periodically review the choice.

2. Notify the applicant or employee that a credit check will be performed, and indicate:

   a. the types of information expected to be collected that are not collected on the application and each area of inquiry regarding character, general reputation, and mode of living;

   b. the techniques that may be used to collect the information;

    c. the sources that are expected to provide the information;

    d. the employer's procedure by which the individual may gain access to any record resulting from investigation;

    e. the procedures the individual may use to correct, amend, or dispute any collected record;

    f. the parties to whom and circumstances under which information about the individual may be disclosed without employee authorization and the information that may be disclosed; and

    g. the possibility that information in any report prepared by a consumer-reporting agency may be retained by that organization and subsequently disclosed to others.

3. Obtain written consent of the applicant or employee for undertaking a credit check.

4. Limit credit checks to job-related information and purposes.

5. Provide written certification to employees that credit information will be used only for job-related purposes.

6. Not share with potential creditors the information received regarding an applicant or employee.

7. Consider credit information highly confidential and sensitive.[10]

C. Credit Check Documents

Credit Check Policy

Section 1. DEFINITIONS. For the purposes of this policy, the following definitions will apply:

    a. *Consumer report.* Any report containing information relating to an individual's credit record, or the manner of obtaining credit directly from a creditor of the individual or from a consumer reporting agency. A consumer report also will include information pertaining to an individual's character, general reputation, personal characteristics, or mode of living obtained through personal interviews with neighbors, friends, or associates of the subject of the report, or others with whom he or she is acquainted who may have knowledge concerning any of these items.

b. *Consumer reporting agency.* Any person or organization who, for monetary fees or dues, regularly engages in assembling or evaluating information to be used by employers for employment purposes.

c. *Individual.* A person who has applied for employment with or who is currently employed by the Company.

Section 2. PROCUREMENT. The Company will request a consumer report only for legitimate employment purposes which must be job-related.

Section 3. WRITTEN PERMISSION. The Company will procure a consumer report only after receipt of written permission from the individual.

Section 4. INFORMATION INSPECTION. The Company will, upon request and proper identification of any individual, allow the inspection of any and all consumer reports maintained regarding that individual.

Section 5. CONFIDENTIALITY. The Company will maintain all consumer report information in strict confidence and will not disclose it absent the individual's written permission.

Credit Check Consent Form

I hereby authorize (*Company's Name*) to conduct a job-related credit check, provided that information requested by the Company is related to the position for which I am applying or currently hold.

_____   _____

Date   Applicant or Employee Signature

III. Arrest Records

A. Arrest Record Privacy Principles

Many employers believe that the arrest histories of applicants or employees are critical or at least relevant to employment. However, employers must exercise caution when using arrest information for employment decisions because improper use of this information may violate employees' privacy rights. Employers must realize that arrest indicates only that a law enforcement agency believed that there existed probable cause to arrest an individual for some offense; it does *not* reflect guilt or that the person actually committed the offense.

Employers are not permitted to refuse employment or to terminate employees because of arrest records without evidence that the offense is related to the employer's business.[11] An applicant's rejection based solely on this arrest record may violate federal and state fair employment practice statutes[12] or state statutes[13] which prohibit the collection or use of arrest information.

B. Procedural Considerations

When an employer uses arrest records for employment decisions, it should ensure that the use is not prohibited by state or federal statute. Other considerations include:

1. differentiation between arrest and conviction;

2. the frequency and severity of arrests;

3. the age of the applicant or employee at the time of arrest;

4. elapsed time since an arrest;

5. the whole individual—his or her aptitudes, abilities, interests, and education level obtained—rather than only this one aspect of personal history; and

6. the nature of the job and its relation to the employability of those with arrest records.[14]

C. Arrest Record Policy

Arrest Record Policy

Section 1. DEFINITIONS. An "arrest" indicates only that a law enforcement officer believed that probable cause existed to detain an individual for possible involvement in wrongdoing. Arrest does not indicate guilt.

A "conviction" includes a plea, verdict, or finding of guilt regardless of whether sentence is imposed by a court.

Section 2. COLLECTION. The Company will not ask an applicant or employee to disclose, through any written form or verbally, information concerning an arrest, detention or disposition of charges that did not result in conviction or information concerning a referral to and participation in any pretrial or post-trial diversion program. The Company will not seek this information from any other source.

Section 3. USE. In determining any employment condition including hiring, promotion, termination, apprenticeship, or any other training program leading to employment, the Company will not utilize as a factor any record of arrest or detention that did not result in conviction or any record regarding a referral to and participation in any pretrial or post-trial diversion program.

Section 4. EXCEPTION. The Company may ask an applicant or employee about an arrest for which the applicant or employee has been released on bail or on his or her own recognizance pending trial.

IV. Criminal Conviction Records

A. Conviction Privacy Principles

Unlike arrest records, which indicate only a suspicion of involvement, conviction records show that guilt and accountability have been finalized. A conviction is a judgment by society that an individual's actions were improper, but this judgment does not give to employers or others unrestricted access to or use of conviction information.

Privacy concerns of employees with criminal convictions may be adversely impacted by how an employer uses and to whom it discloses conviction information. For example, an employer may take legitimate employment actions based on criminal convictions when it correlates the circumstances, the gravity of the offense, and the time elapsed since the conviction to the nature of the job.

To protect the privacy interests of those convicted of crimes, employers use of conviction records is regulated by federal and state fair employment practice statutes.[15] In addition, federal laws restrict the use of conviction information in the employment context because of a discriminatory affect on protected groups. For example, under the federal Civil Rights Act of 1964 (Title VII),[16] an employer cannot automatically deny employment based on a conviction record because of an adverse impact on blacks and other minorities. In one case, an employer's policy of automatically terminating employees convicted of crimes was found to discriminate against blacks because they are convicted at rates in significant excess of their percentage of the general population.[17] Title VII also protects against discrimination by national origin. For example, in the southwest United States, automatically excluding applicants with criminal convictions may be national origin discrimination because in that area the Spanish-surnamed population has a conviction rate disproportionate to that of whites.[18]

B. Determining Proper Use of Conviction Records

To ensure compliance with federal and state statutes, the employer must consider all job-related circumstances of a conviction before determining that hiring or continuing employment of an individual would be inconsistent with the safe and efficient operation of its business. These circumstances include:

1. the relationship between each conviction and the responsibilities of the position;

2. the nature and number of convictions;

3. the facts surrounding each offense;

4. the length of time between conviction and the employment decision;

5. the employment history of the applicant or employee before and after the conviction; and

6. the rehabilitation efforts of the applicant or employee.

The first factor, the relationship between a conviction and the job, is an important consideration. This relationship must be close and clearly established. Sufficient relationship existed between conviction and job where an employer:

1. terminated a hotel's bellman for convictions of theft and receiving stolen goods;[19]

2. refused to hire an applicant for a custodial job which required possession of a master set of keys because of a felony robbery conviction;[20]

3. refused to employ persons convicted of violent crimes where violent altercations occasionally occurred among employees during work hours on employer property;[21]

4. terminated a public auditorium utility worker because of a criminal record for rape, assault and battery, drunkenness, and a firearms offense;[22]

5. terminated an apartment manager who had unsupervised access to apartments and rent receipts because of three convictions for theft-related offenses.[23]

Disqualification from employment can not be justified if the relationship between conviction and job is not a close one. Remoteness existed where an employer:

1. refused to hire an applicant for mechanic position because of a gambling conviction;[24]

2. terminated a utility operator in a manufacturing plant who was convicted of unlawful delivery of marijuana;[25]

3. failed to hire an applicant as crane operator because of an armed robbery conviction.[26]

Rehabilitation, a good work record, and the remoteness in time of the conviction can be used to overcome job disqualifications due to convictions. The business necessity defense was not effective where an employer:

1. rejected a bus driver applicant based on a burglary conviction because six years had passed since the conviction and the applicant's subsequent work history and rehabilitation efforts were documented through positive recommendations from previous employers, community leaders, and parole and police officers;[27]

2. failed to hire an applicant for a photographer position which would have required money-handling, due to a forgery conviction because six years had elapsed between the conviction and the application for the job, and the applicant had cooperated with authorities at the time of the conviction, had been steadily employed following his conviction, and had continued his education;[28]

3. refused to rehire a crane operator/welder because of a six-year-old murder conviction where the applicant had worked

for the employer for sixteen years before the conviction without disciplinary or violent incidents and where the violent crime was inconsistent with the applicant's established behavior;[29]

4. failed to hire an applicant as a truck driver or dockman because of a thirteen-year-old conviction for driving on a revoked license and two drunkenness convictions where the most recent conviction occurred four years prior to the job application.[30]

However, in some situations job-relatedness considerations can outweigh evidence of the individual's rehabilitation, good work record, or the remoteness in time of the conviction. Business necessity prevailed where an employer:

1. terminated a truck driver because of a drunk driving conviction, even though the offense occurred off-duty in the employee's private vehicle and the driver had an otherwise clean criminal and work record;[31]

2. terminated a delivery person for a drug manufacturer because of convictions for larceny, receiving stolen property, and an illegal weapons offense, even though the employee's work record was good;[32]

3. refused to hire an applicant as a kitchen helper because of eleven convictions, six of which were theft-related, with the most recent occurring only six months before the job rejection, despite the applicant's consistent efforts to find work since his prison release;[33]

4. failed to hire an applicant for a bill collector position which involved entry to customers' homes because of a murder conviction, even though the applicant had worked satisfactorily for the employer for four years before the conviction and the crime was not consistent with the employee's established behavior before or after the murder.[34]

An interesting caveat to federal and state statutory restrictions on employers' use of conviction information is the area of negligent hiring. Although an employer is limited in what conviction information it may collect and use in employment decisions, the same employer may be liable for negligent hiring if it employs someone with a criminal conviction who adversely affects or injures another employee during the employment relationship.[35]

Employers must consider only legitimate, job-related circumstances of a conviction before determining that employment would be inconsistent with safe and efficient business operations. These circumstances include:

1. the job and its responsibilities;

2. the nature and number of convictions;

3. the facts of each conviction;

4. individual's age at the time of the conviction;

5. geographic location of the offense;

6. the length of time between a conviction and the employment decision;

7. employee's work history before and after the conviction;

8. the individual's efforts at rehabilitation; and

9. the possibility that the particular conviction would prevent job performance in an acceptable businesslike manner.

C. Criminal Conviction Record Policy

Criminal Conviction Record Policy

Section 1. CONVICTION. A "conviction" includes a plea, verdict, or finding of guilt regardless of whether sentence is imposed by a court.

Section 2. USE OF CONVICTION RECORD. The Company may consider as a possible justification for the refusal, suspension, revocation, or termination of employment any conviction when the conviction directly relates to:

a. the applicant's potential performance in the job applied for or

b. the employee's performance in the job the employee currently holds.

Section 3. JOB-RELATEDNESS OF CONVICTION.   To determine if a conviction is job-related, the Company will consider, among other things:

a. the job and its responsibilities;

b. the nature and number of convictions;

c. the facts of each conviction;

d. age at the time of the conviction;

e. the geographic location of the offense

f. the length of time between a conviction and the employment decision;

g. employment history before and after the conviction;

h. the individual's efforts at rehabilitation; and

i. any possibility that the particular conviction would prevent job performance in an acceptable, businesslike manner.

Section 4. EXCLUDED CONVICTIONS.   The Company will not consider:

a. convictions which have been annulled or expunged;

b. convictions of penal offenses for which no jail sentence may be imposed; or

c. convictions of misdemeanors if the period of twenty years has elapsed since the date of conviction and if there has been no subsequent arrest or conviction.

V. Fingerprinting

A. Fingerprinting Privacy Principles

Fingerprinting is generally considered by courts to be a valid employer method for verifying information about applicants and employees.[36] Although its primary use is verification, fingerprinting is regulated by some states to limit abuse of applicants' or employees' workplace privacy.[37] For example, some states prohibit an employer from requiring as an employment condition that an applicant or employee be fingerprinted for the purpose of furnishing information to a third party where this information could be used to the detriment of the applicant or employee.[38] The employer's access to fingerprint data can by used as a means to obtain other information about the individual; for example, the person's arrest record.

B. Use of Fingerprinting

If employers use fingerprinting in the hiring process, its purpose should be limited to:

1. verification of employee's identity for receipt of an employee benefit or where an employee's identity is in doubt and

2. compliance with immigration requirements.

C. Fingerprinting Policy

Fingerprinting Policy

The Company will not require, as a condition to securing or retaining employment, that an applicant or employee be fingerprinted where fingerprints could be used to the detriment of the applicant or employee in a non-job-related situation.

VI. Photographs

A. Photograph Privacy Principles

Ordinarily, the mere taking of someone's photograph without consent is not considered an invasion of privacy. Most individuals do not object to having their photograph taken; it is not until the photograph is published that privacy interests are affected.

Historically, employers have been permitted to photograph employees while performing their jobs even if the employees object, but only if a legitimate business purpose is being served.[39] Examples of justifiable business purposes include the improvement of workplace safety or identification of employees who are violating employer rules.

While photographing employees on the job is often acceptable, photographing applicants during the hiring process has raised objections. Rules and regulations promulgated by the Equal Employment Opportunity Commission (EEOC) have consistently cautioned employers against using identification procedures which produce information that is not essential to personnel actions.[40] While requiring a photograph prior to hiring is not automatically an act of discrimination, the requirement does create the opportunity for the employer to use a photograph in a discriminatory manner. Additionally, photographs can provide information that is otherwise protected from inquiry by the employer and not readily available from an application; for example, race, sex, national origin, color, disability, and age. For these reasons, federal and state fair employment practice statutes prohibit employers from photographing applicants during the hiring process.

Informing applicants that they may affix a photograph to an application at their option or at any time prior to hiring is illegal in many states. California is just one state which prohibits an employer from requiring that an applicant or employee be photographed for the purpose of furnishing information to a third party as a condition to securing or retaining employment where this could be used to the applicant's or employee's detriment.[41] In the event that employees' photographs are used for legitimate business purposes, new employees should sign a consent form at hiring permitting certain uses of their photographs.

B. Procedural Safeguards

To ensure that privacy interests of applicants and employees are preserved and to comply with federal and state requirements employers should:

1. not require photographs on applications or at interviews;

2. use photographs only for legitimate business purposes, for example, monitoring of job performance; and

3. obtain employee consent when photographs are used in employer literature or advertisements.

C. Photograph Documents

Photograph Policy

The Company will not require, as a condition to securing or retaining employment, that an applicant or employee be photographed if photographs could be used to the detriment of the applicant or employee in a non-job-related manner.

Photograph Consent Form

The Company may use my name, picture, or likeness for any advertising, publicity, or other legitimate business purpose regardless of whether or not I am employed by the Company at the time it is used. The legitimate use of my name, picture, or likeness will not be considered an invasion of privacy, defamation, intentional infliction of emotional distress, or a violation of any other property right that I may have. I understand that I will receive no additional consideration, compensation, or benefit if my name, picture, or likeness is used. Any negatives, prints, or other material for printing or reproduction in connection with the use of my name, picture, or likeness will remain the property of the Company. This consent is given in consideration of my employment.

_____   _____

Date   Employee Signature

                                        _____

                                        Witness

VII. Immigration Requirements

A. Immigration Privacy Principles

The Immigration Reform and Control Act of 1986 (IRCA)[42] attempts to curtail illegal immigration into the United States. One objective of the Act is to prevent illegal aliens from securing employment. To this end, IRCA requires employers to collect and maintain particular information about every applicant and employee. In addition, IRCA requires employers to ask all applicants for specific written verification establishing that they can be legally employed in the United States. Employers who knowingly hire or recruit an illegal alien are subject to civil and criminal penalties.

A second objective of IRCA is to deter employers from discriminating against applicants because of their national origin. It is an unfair immigration-related employment practice to discriminate against any individual in hiring, recruitment, or termination because of that individual's national origin or citizenship status.

The collection of age, national origin, or other data required by IRCA may create workplace privacy problems because the information could be used in a discriminatory manner. Employers should collect the required IRCA information only after the applicant pool has been narrowed to a select group of candidates being seriously considered for hiring. This will minimize privacy intrusions because the employer will avoid obtaining sensitive applicant data unnecessarily. Once collected, the information should be maintained separately from the newly hired employees' personnel files to prevent disclosures that could have a discriminatory impact. Information regarding applicants who are not hired should be retained with the application. These precautions will minimize workplace privacy challenges arising out of federal or state fair employment practice statutes.[43]

B. Immigration Procedures and Form I-9

The Immigration Reform and Control Act (IRCA) requires employers to hire only United States citizens and aliens who are authorized to work in the United States. The Employment Eligibility Verification Form (Form I-9) was developed for verifying that persons are eligible to work under the IRCA guidelines. IRCA requires employers to:

1. ensure that all employees complete Form I-9 within three days after they begin working;

2. check specific documents which establish employee identity and eligibility to work;

3. properly complete the employer portion of Form I-9;

4. retain Form I-9 for at least three years after hiring date if an individual is employed for less than three years;

5. retain Form I-9 for one year after an individual leaves employment if the person is employed for more than three years; and

6. present Form I-9 for inspection to an officer of the Immigration and Naturalization Service (INS) or Department of Labor (DOL) upon request.

1. Acceptable Documents for Verifying Employment Eligibility

All employees must comply with IRCA by providing a document or documents that establish: (1) identity and (2) eligibility for employment in the United States. IRCA designates certain documents which are acceptable as proof of these two conditions.

Some documents establish both identity and employment eligibility. These are listed on Form I-9 under List A, "Documents that Establish Identity and Employment Eligibility."

If a person does not provide a document from List A, he or she must provide one document that establishes identity and a separate document that establishes employment eligibility. To establish identity, the person must provide one document from List B. To establish employment eligibility, one of the immigration documents in List C must be furnished. Lists A, B, and C are summarized below.

If an employee is unable to provide the required document or documents within three days of hiring, he or she must at least produce within three days a receipt showing that he or she has applied for the document. The employee must produce the document itself within 21 days of hiring.

List A

Documents that Establish Identity and Employment Eligibility:

1. United States Passport

2. Certificate of United States Citizenship (INS Form N-560 or N-561)

3. Certificate of Naturalization (INS Form N-550 or N-570)

4. Unexpired foreign passport which:

   a. contains an unexpired stamp which reads: "Processed for I-551. Temporary Evidence of Lawful Admission for

permanent residence. Valid until Employment authorized" or

b. has attached thereto a Form I-94 bearing the same name
as the passport and containing an employment authorization stamp, as long as the period of endorsement has
not yet expired and the proposed employment is not in
conflict with any restrictions or limitations identified on
Form I-94

5. Alien Registration Receipt Card (INS Form I-151) or Resident
Alien Card (INS Form I-551), provided that it contains a
photograph of the bearer

6. Temporary Resident Card (INS Form I-688)

7. Employment Authorization Card (INS Form I-688A)

List B

Documents that Establish Identity:

For individuals 16 years of age or older:

1. State-issued driver's license or state-issued identification
card containing a photograph or, if the driver's license or
identification card does not contain a photograph, identifying information should list name, date of birth, sex, height,
color of eyes, and address

2. School identification card with photograph

3. Voter's registration card

4. United States Military card or draft record

5. Identification card issued by federal, state, or local government agencies

6. Military dependent's identification card

7. Native American tribal documents

8. United States Coast Guard Merchant Mariner Card

9. Driver's license issued by a Canadian government authority

For individuals under age 16 who are unable to produce one of the documents listed above:

1. School record or report card

2. Clinic, doctor or hospital record

3. Day-care or nursery school record

List C

Documents that Establish Employment Eligibility:

1. Social Security Number card other than one which has printed on its face: "not valid for employment purposes"; card must be issued by the Social Security Administration— reproductions are not acceptable

2. An original or certified copy of a birth certificate issued by a state, county, or municipal authority and bearing an official seal

3. Unexpired INS employment authorization

4. Unexpired re-entry permit (INS Form I-327)

5. Unexpired Refugee Travel Document (INS Form I-571)

6. Certification of Birth issued by the Department of State (Form FS-545)

7. Certification of Birth Abroad issued by the Department of State (Form DS-1350)

8. United States Citizen Identification Card (INS Form I-197)

9. Native American tribal documents

10. Identification Card for use of Resident Citizen in the United States (INS Form I-179)

2. Detecting Counterfeit Documents

Employers must carefully examine for legitimacy all documents presented by applicants for identification and employment eligibility. To ensure that only legitimate documents are accepted, employers should:

1. be familiar with the information contained in the documents;

2. determine whether the information pertains to the individual presenting the document (for example, a conflict exists if the person appears to be 18 and the ID says 45);

3. look for alterations of an official document through methods such as erasures or photograph substitutions. Official documents are never altered, they are replaced;

4. check that the document is squarely cut;

5. check that printing and engraving are parallel with the edges of the document;

6. view documents as suspect if printing and engraving are dull, unclear, broken, or blurred;

7. not deny employment to someone based on a suspect document, instead, contact the local INS office for verification of the document number; and

8. check if the state employment agency has a process to verify an applicant's documents through the INS and if the agency will issue a letter of certification to potential employers that can serve as proof of an individual's employment eligibility.

C. Immigration Policy

Immigration Policy

The Company will not discriminate against any individual other than an unauthorized alien in decisions regarding hiring, disciplining, terminating, recruiting, or other employment actions because of that individual's national origin or, in the case of a citizen or intending citizen, because of citizenship status.

VIII. References

A. Reference Privacy Principles

Similar to credit checks and fingerprinting, reference checks represent another employer method of compiling and verifying the most complete and accurate information about applicants. In gathering reference information, employers may infringe upon an applicant's privacy by uncovering speech, belief, association, and lifestyle interests that are not job-related. For example, an employer might learn from a reference that an applicant is homosexual. Unrelated information frequently is collected or disclosed absent the employee's knowledge. It often involves former employers who may be solicited without the employee's knowledge or consent.

In addition to checking references of applicants, employers must provide references for its current and former employees. Detailed reference requests from other employers often present a risk of litigation by the involved employees. Therefore, many employers limit their responses to verifying only dates of employment, job titles, and salaries of former employees.

Employers must be aware of common law, such as claims for invasion of privacy and defamation, and federal and state fair employment practice statutes which regulate references.[44] In addition to fair employment practice statutes, defamation may impose employer responsibility as it affects the employee's privacy interest in his or her reputation. Defamation encompasses any false and unprivileged communication, either oral or written, that injures the employee. If the communication is made with malice, the employer may be subject to punitive damages.

Employees who claim that a previous employer's reason for termination was false may assert that the employer "defamed" them if this allegedly false reason is repeated in a reference to a prospective employer.[45] However, employers have a legitimate need to exchange information about former and prospective employees without fear of litigation. A qualified privilege for employment references has been recognized. This qualified privilege extends to employers who issue references in good faith or without any malice or reckless disregard for truth. For example, the doctrine of qualified privilege protected a federal official from liability for truthfully remarking to a prospective employer than a former employee had used excessive leave and had trouble with other employees.[46]

This qualified privilege may be lost, however, if the reference includes information that was extraneous to job performance or if the circumstances indicate it was motivated by personal animosity. Loss of the qualified privilege is illustrated by a case involving a former hospital employee. The employee claimed that he had been defamed by the hospital's statement to a prospective employer that he had been terminated "for cause." The former employer maintained that stating it had acted with "cause" could not be defamatory. However, the statement's defamatory meaning had to be tested against the average reader's understanding because "for cause" could be, and in this case was, interpreted to imply incompetence.[47]

A viable defamation claim was found against an employer that had stated to prospective employers only that its employee had "suddenly resigned." The employer argued that the phrase "suddenly resigned" was incapable of any defamatory meaning. This phrase was found to suggest to a prospective employer that the party who resigned did so under suspicion of wrongdoing.[48]

The "name, rank, and serial number" approach to employment references may not absolve an employer from liability. In one case, an employer adopted a policy of refusing to discuss former employees with prospective employers. Although the employer explained to four employees that it was terminating them for gross insubordination, a charge which the employer knew to be false, the employer did not state this reason to any other person or directly to any prospective employer. When the employees sought other employment, they encountered questions from prospective employers about their prior employment. The employees repeated the employer's stated grounds for termination. Because the employees' publication of reasons for their terminations should have been reasonably foreseeable to the former employer and because the employer knew the reasons were false, the employees received a nearly one million dollar jury award of compensatory and punitive damages.[49]

B. Reference Checking Procedures

Proper reference checking is time-consuming. It demands personal involvement and extends beyond having someone make telephone calls to references listed on an application. Possible approaches to reference checking include:

1. meeting with the applicant's references. This method is the most preferable because:

   a. people are more willing to be open in a face-to-face conversation and

   b. it provides the opportunity to interpret facial expressions and body language which, in addition to words, may indicate how the reference actually feels about the applicant's prior work performance;

2. using the telephone; and

3. checking references by mail.

When checking references provided by applicants, employers should:

1. obtain the applicant's written permission to check references;

2. check references before making the final job offer;

3. undertake a more extensive investigation if a discrepancy exists between information as provided by the applicant and reference;

4. be skeptical of all subjective evaluations given by references, especially those that do not include specific acts or behavior that can be verified; and

5. view silence of the reference as an indication of need for further investigation. A former employer may attempt to avoid wrongful termination litigation by negotiating with an employee a settlement that prohibits the employer from giving unfavorable references to future employers.

C. Providing References

In providing references, employers should:

1. review federal and state statutes regarding what information can be disclosed absent an employee's consent;

2. require the human resources staff to distribute procedures and policies to employees regarding:

   a. content of information which may be disclosed,

   b. circumstances under which disclosure may occur, and

   c. persons eligible to receive information;

3. ensure that the accuracy of the information is substantiated by factual records; and

4. instruct all personnel not to discuss another employee's performance with persons outside the Company.

D. Reference Documents

Reference Policy

Absent the written consent of an employee or a former employee, the Company will not provide information, except name, job title, and employment dates, regarding current or former employees unless required by federal or state law or court order. All requests for employee information must be referred to the Human

Resources Department. Supervisors or other employees are not permitted to respond to a reference request. Telephone inquiries will not be answered. Only written inquiries from the person seeking the information will be considered if such inquiry is on that person's letterhead with his or her name and title.

Information Release Form

I hereby authorize the Company to release the following information regarding my employment with the Company to (*Company's Name, Person, and Title*):

Information List

_____

_____

_____

_____   _____

Date   Employee Signature

Endnotes

1   *See* Appendix A sections III.E and IV.G for federal and state statutes that affect credit.

2   *See* Appendix A sections III.F and IV.H.

3   42 U.S.C. §§ 2000e to 2002-17 (1988).

4   EEOC Dec. No. 74-02, 6 Fair Empl. Prac. Cas. (BNA) 830 (1973).

5   EEOC Dec. No. 72-0427, 4 Fair Empl. Prac. Cas. (BNA) 304 (1971).

6   *See* United States v. Chicago, 549 F.2d 415 (7th Cir. 1977) (credit check for police officer not job-related).

7   EEOC v. American Nat'l Bank, 21 Fair Empl. Prac. Cas. (BNA) 1595 (E.D. Va. 1979).

8   United States v. Chicago, 549 F.2d 415 (7th Cir. 1977).

9   *See* Ellenberg v. Pinkerton's Inc., 125 Ga. App. 648, 188 S.E.2d 911 (1972) (one who employs a private investigator may not be insulated from wrongful acts committed by the investigator).

10   *See* PRIVACY PROTECTION STUDY COMMISSION, PERSONAL PRIVACY IN AN INFORMATION SOCIETY 250-251 (1977).

11   *See, e.g.,* Gregory v. Litton Sys., Inc., 316 F. Supp. 401 (C.D. Cal. 1970), *aff'd with modifications not here relevant,* 472 F.2d 631 (9th Cir. 1972) (employer inquiries into arrest record are prohibited).

12   *See* Appendix A sections III.F and IV.H.

13   *See* Appendix A section IV.B.

14   *Id.*

15   *See* Appendix A sections III.F and IV.H.

16   42 U.S.C. 2000e-1 through 2002-17 (1988).

17   EEOC Dec. No. 80-28, 26 Fair Empl. Prac. Cas. (BNA) 1812 (1980).

18   EEOC Dec. No. 78-03, EEOC Dec. (CCH) ¶ 6714 (1977).

19   Richardson v. Hotel Corp. of Am., 332 F. Supp. 519 (E.D. La. 1971), *aff'd mem.,* 486 F.2d 951 (5th Cir. 1972).

20   EEOC Dec. No. 76-50, EEOC Dec. (CCH) ¶ 6636 (1975).

21   EEOC Dec. No. 76-84, EEOC Dec. (CCH) ¶ 6662 (1976).

22   EEOC Dec. No. 78-35, 26 Fair Empl. Prac. Cas. (BNA) 1755 (1978).

23   EEOC Dec. No. 79-40, EEOC Dec. (CCH) ¶ 6778 (1979).

24   EEOC Dec. No. 71-2682, 4 Fair Empl. Prac. Cas. (BNA) 25 (1971).

25   EEOC Dec. No. 80-18, 26 Fair Empl. Prac. Cas. (BNA) 1802 (1980).

26   EEOC Dec. No. 80-20, 26 Fair Empl. Prac. Cas. (BNA) 1805 (1980).

27   EEOC Dec. No. 78-10, EEOC Dec. (CCH) ¶ 6715 (1977).

28   EEOC Dec. No. 80-16, 26 Fair Empl. Prac. Cas. (BNA) 1799 (1980).

29   EEOC Dec. No. 80-17, 26 Fair Empl. Prac. Cas. (BNA) 1800 (1980).

30   EEOC Dec. No. 76-53, EEOC Dec. (CCH) ¶ 6638 (1975).

31   EEOC Dec. No. 79-13, EEOC Dec. (CCH) ¶ 6744 (1978).

32   EEOC Dec. No. 79-47, EEOC Dec. (CCH) ¶ 6782 (1979).

33   EEOC Dec. No. 79-61, EEOC Dec. (CCH) ¶ 6795 (1979).

34   EEOC Dec. No. 79-5, EEOC Dec. (CCH) ¶ 6736 (1978).

35   Henley v. Prince George's County, 305 Md. 320, 503 A.2d 1333 (1986) (young boy sexually assaulted and murdered by former inmate employed as carpentry instructor where employer failed to check employee's background).

36   *See* Miller v. New York Stock Exch., 427 F.2d 1074 (2d Cir.), *cert. denied*, 398 U.S. 905 (1970) (statute requiring fingerprinting of stock exchange employees held constitutional as valid exercise of police power in combatting theft in securities industry).

37   *See* Appendix A section IV.I for state fingerprinting statutes.

38   *See* Appendix A section IV.I.

39   *See, e.g.,* Thomas v. General Elec. Co., 207 F. Supp. 792 (W.D. Ky. 1962) (permissible to take motion pictures in the workplace to study plant layout and evaluate employee job performance).

40   29 C.F.R. §§ 1607.1-.18 (1993).

41   Cal. Lab. Code § 1051 (West 1971).

42   Pub. L. No. 99-603, 100 Stat. 3359 (1986) (codified in scattered sections of 7 U.S.C.; 8 U.S.C.; 18 U.S.C.; 20 U.S.C.; 29 U.S.C.; 42 U.S.C.

43   *See* Appendix A sections III.F and IV.H.

44   *See* Appendix A sections III.F and IV.H for state statutes and federal state fair employment practice statutes that regulate references.

45   *But see* Montgomery v. Big B., Inc., 460 So. 2d 1286 (Ala. 1984) (employer not liable for defamation because alleged false job reference was not made public).

46   Jefferson v. Ashley, 643 F. Supp. 227 (D. Or. 1986).

47   Carney v. Memorial Hosp., 64 N.Y.2d 770, 485 N.Y.S.2d 984 (1985).

48   Klages v. Sperry Corp., 118 L.R.R.M. (BNA) 2463 (E.D. Pa. 1984).

49   Lewis v. Equitable Life Assurance Soc'y, 361 N.W.2d 875 (Minn. Ct. App. 1985).

4

Workplace Records

I. Introduction

Employment records, usually referred to as personnel files, generally contain employees' personal, employment, and medical histories. Personal history concerns past wage record, education, training, and work experiences. Employment history details an employee's current work record regarding wages, promotions, disciplinary actions, commendations, sick days, vacation days, positions held, and performance evaluations. Medical history contains information about the employee's physical and psychological health.

Employers use this information in most employment decisions including hiring, placement, transfer, promotion, demotion, training, compensation, discipline, termination, and provision of fringe benefits. Employment records contain a vast amount of information on individuals, and information accumulates as the employment relationship continues. Some of this information may be unrelated to workplace issues and may be used and disclosed by the employer with no prior notice to or knowledge of employees. For these reasons the privacy and integrity of employment records are of concern to both employees and employers.

This chapter reviews policies and procedures employers use to create and maintain useful employment records while protecting the privacy interests of employees regarding the information which is collected and how it is used. Specifically, this chapter will address the personal and medical information components of employment records.

II. Employment Records

A. Employment Record Privacy Principles

Employers use many methods to access, collect, and maintain information for employment records. Employee privacy is affected as employers, unaware of legal restrictions, use detailed application forms, interviews, and questionable information collection devices such as polygraph examinations, honesty tests, and credit checks.

Federal and state statutes regulate certain aspects of the employment record.[1] Generally, these statutes set forth the employment information that employers may collect. Also, these statutes require employers to honor employees' requests for access to review their records and to copy record contents.[2]

These requirements give employees access to records employers have used to determine employment qualifications, promotion, compensation, or disciplinary action up to and including termination. Employers are required to maintain personnel files at the work location of employees or to make them available at that location upon reasonable notice.

In providing employment information, the employee relinquishes control of sensitive personal information and the opportunity to verify the accuracy of information that may be developed from these disclosures. The possibility of collecting inaccurate employment information exists because each employer has its own record-keeping system that may not have the necessary safeguards to ensure accuracy. Some statutes permit employees to place a counterstatement in their record when information is incorrect or challenged.

Employers frequently receive requests for employment information from other employers, social workers, insurance companies, credit bureaus, government officials, and union business agents. Although the employee initially revealed information to obtain employment or to maintain it, disclosure may occur for a purpose unrelated to employment that is against the employee's best interest.

In some situations, state constitutions prohibit disclosure of personnel files to third parties.[3] For example, employee requests to review personnel files of co-workers may violate the co-workers' guaranteed privacy rights.[4] The employer, as the custodian of private information, cannot waive employee privacy rights that are constitutionally protected.[5]

In addition to statutory and constitutional protections, several tort theories allow challenges to employers' use and disclosure of employee records. Invasion of privacy,[6] defamation,[7] intentional infliction of emotional distress, negligent maintenance or disclosure of employment records,[8] fraudulent misrepresentation, and public policies are all applicable to workplace privacy issues. For example, invasion of privacy may result through employer actions which place an employee in a false light[9] or which publicly disclose personal, private facts contained in employment records.[10]

Defamation can be readily applied to privacy problems arising out of employers' disclosure of employment information. Defamatory information tends to harm the reputation of another or to deter others from wanting to associate or deal with a person. Employers have a "conditional privilege" to communicate information about their employees. This privilege recognizes the need of employers to discuss unfavorable information about their employees as long as they do it in a business-related context and the information is not false.

Internal documents concerning employee performance are subject to this conditional privilege.[11] Secretaries who type or receive mail as part of their duties are entitled to this privilege.[12] Employees performing human resource functions are likewise protected.[13] Similarly, a conditional privilege applies to performance evaluations sent by an employee's supervisor to the supervisor's superior.[14] When the conditional privilege applies to employer communications, the employee receiving the information about another employee has a duty not to disclose this information to anyone who is not legitimately entitled to receive it. This duty arises out of and is directly related to the employee's job functions.

If disclosure of the employment record is not necessary to the employer's functioning, the conditional privilege may not apply.[15] Employers may not reveal to co-workers the reason for an employee's discipline or termination in order to improve employee morale or to eliminate rumors.[16] Disclosure of information in these circumstances does not serve a legitimate employer duty corresponding with any legal, moral, or social interest.[17]

Disclosure to parties not involved in the employment relationship may also be protected by conditional privilege; for example, communications between an employee's former employer and a prospective employer.[18] This privilege, however, should not be exceeded. Disclosures should not embellish the seriousness of employee misconduct or add unnecessary derogatory information.[19] Liability will result if the former employer's disclosures are false.[20]

Employers may be insulated from defamation claims by statutes or collective bargaining agreements. Some state statutes provide that employers' disclosures about an employee to a state's unemployment compensation department are privileged.[21] A termination notice required by a collective bargaining agreement and released only to those directly involved with the grievance arbitration process is privileged.[22] The employee's union membership constitutes consent to release this information.[23]

Intentional infliction of emotional distress may result if sensitive personal information is disclosed in a manner that under the circumstances would be considered outrageous. Negligent maintenance or disclosure of employment records also may trigger employer liability.[24]

Contractual litigation theories also are applicable to employment record privacy. Workplace privacy interests regarding employment records may receive protection in employment contracts, restrictive covenants, employment handbooks and policies, and collective bargaining agreements through statements contained in these documents. For example, arbitrators have found that employees must be informed of entries made by employers in the employee's personnel file where a collective bargaining agreement required these disclosures.[25]

B. Employment Record Procedures

A comprehensive employment record policy will protect the privacy interests of employees and, consequently, will limit employers' vulnerability to litigation. The following elements should be included in a policy:

1. A uniform system of collection, maintenance, access, use, and disclosure of employment information

2. Preservation and protection of employee privacy

3. Review of employment information currently collected

4. Fair treatment of applicants, employees, and former employees through information collection procedures that:

   a. Limit collection to information that is job-related

   b. Inform what records will be maintained

   c. Assure accuracy, timeliness, and completeness of information

   d. Ensure that information retention conforms to applicable law

   e. Permit review, copying, correction, or amendment of information with a corresponding notation made in the file describing any employment action

   f. Limit internal use

   g. Inform of the uses to be made of information

   h. Restrict access to information to individuals with a need to know and to those who are authorized outside of the employer; for example, law enforcement officials or government agencies

i. Limit external disclosures to specific inquiries or requests to verify information

j. Include with the employment application a waiver authorizing the employer to disclose employee file contents to those whom the employee grants access; for example, future employers seeking references

k. Contain a privacy clause

l. Provide for a regular policy compliance review by the Human Resources Department.[26]

1. Employment Record Inspection

Although statutes grant employees the right to inspect their personnel files, this right is not absolute; some exceptions do apply. Statutes prohibit an employee from inspecting any records relating to the investigation of a possible criminal offense by the employee. Also, reference letters maintained by employers may not be reviewed by employees.[27] Employers are entitled to impose reasonable restrictions upon employees' access to their personnel files. These restrictions may take various forms including:

1. requiring employees to submit written requests to inspect their personnel files;

2. allowing inspection only by appointment;

3. allowing inspection only during regular business hours but on employees' own time;

4. allowing inspection only in the presence of a representative of the employer;

5. limiting frequency of inspection;

6. permitting employees to make a written request to amend or correct information; and

7. permitting employees whose amendment or correction requests are refused to include a written explanation in their file.[28]

2. Employment Record Retention

Certain federal statutes require that employers collect, maintain, and disclose specific items of employment information. The following list is not exhaustive, but includes those statutes most relevant to this discussion.

Civil Rights Act of 1964 (Title VII)[29]

Records to be Retained	Time Period
A. Any personnel or employment record made or kept by an employer, including applications, having to do with hiring, promotion, demotion, transfer, layoff, termination, pay rates, compensation terms, and selection for training or apprenticeship	A. Six months from the date of making the record or taking the personnel action involved, whichever occurs later
B. Personnel records relevant to a discrimination charge or action brought by the Attorney General against the employer, including records relating to the charging party and to all other employees holding similar positions, applications or test papers completed by the unsuccessful, charging applicant and by all other candidates for the same position	B. Until final disposition of the charge or action

Records to be Retained	Time Period

Civil Rights Act of 1964 (Title VII)—*Cont.*

C. For apprenticeship programs:

C.

1. A chronological list of names and addresses of all applicants, dates of application, sex, and minority group membership or a file of written applications containing the same information; other records pertaining to apprenticeship applicants, including test papers and interview records

1. Two years or the period of the successful applicant's apprenticeship, whichever is later

2. Any other record made solely for completing apprenticeship report EEO-2 or similar reports

2. One year from due date of the report

D. Employers with 100 or more employees must file a copy of Employer Information Report (EEO-1)

D. Current report must be retained indefinitely

Age Discrimination in Employment Act (ADEA)[30]

A. Payroll records containing each employee's name, address, date of birth, occupation, rate of pay, and compensation earned per week

A. Three years from date of employment termination

Records to be Retained	Time Period
Age Discrimination in Employment Act (ADEA)—*Cont.*	
B. Personnel records relating to:	B. One year from the date of the personnel action to which the record relates, except applications and other applicant pre-employment records for temporary jobs, which must be retained for only 90 days
1. Job applications, resumes, or other replies to job advertisements, including applications for temporary positions and records pertaining to failure or refusal to hire	
2. Promotion, demotion, transfer, selection for training, layoff, recall, or termination	
3. Job orders submitted to an employment agency or union	
4. Test papers in connection with employer-administered aptitude or other employment tests	
5. Physical examination results considered in connection with a personnel action	
6. Job advertisements or notices to the public or employees	

Records to be Retained	Time Period
Age Discrimination in Employment Act (ADEA)—*Cont.*	
regarding openings, programs, or opportunities for overtime work	
C. Employee benefit plans, written seniority or merit rating systems	C. Period during which plan or system is in effect plus one year
D. Personnel records, including the above, relevant to an enforcement action against the employer	D. Until final disposition of the action

Vocational Rehabilitation Act of 1973[31]

For contractors and subcontractors of the federal government:	
A. For disabled applicants and employees, complete and accurate employment records as required by the Act. The Department of Labor suggests that this requirement may be met by annotating the application or personnel form of the disabled applicant or employee to indicate each vacancy, promotion, and training program for which he or she was considered, including a statement of reasons for any rejection that	A. One year from date of application

Records to be Retained   **Time Period**
Vocational Rehabilitation Act of 1973—*Cont.*

compares the disabled individual's qualifications to those of
the person selected, as well as
any accommodations considered. Descriptions of accommodations actually under-
taken also should be attached.

B. Records regarding com-   B. One year from date of complaints and actions taken   plaint
against the employer by an employee or applicant under the
Act

Americans With Disabilities Act[32]

A. Similar to those required by   A. To meet minimum consid-
the Civil Rights Act of 1964 (42   erations for this statute, apply
U.S.C. §§ 2000e-1 through   the retention requirements of
2002-17 (1988))   the Civil Rights Act of 1964 (42
                                   U.S.C. §§ 2000e-1 through
                                   2002-17 (1988))

Executive Order 11246 (Affirmative Action) (as amended September 24, 1965)[33]

For contractors and subcontractors of the federal government:

A. Written affirmative action   A. Not specified
programs and supporting doc-
umentation, including re-
quired utilization analysis and

Records to be Retained   Time Period
Executive Order 11246 (Affirmative Action) (as amended
September 24, 1965)—*Cont.*

evaluation; other records and
documents relating to compliance with applicable Equal Employment Opportunity (EEO)
nondiscrimination and affirmative action requirements, including   records   and
documents on nature and use
of tests, test validations, and
test results as required; and
compliance with construction
industry EEO plans and requirements

Occupational Safety and Health Act of 1970[34]

A. Log & Summary of Occupational Injuries and Illnesses,
briefly describing recordable
causes of injury and illness, extent and outcome of each incident, and summary totals for
calendar year. (Effective Jan. 1,
1983 the following industries
are exempt: retail trade, finance, insurance, real estate,
and service.)

A. Five years following the
end of the year to which the
records correspond

B. Supplementary   Record,
containing more detailed information for each occurrence of
injury or illness

B. Five years following the end
of the year to which the records
correspond

Records to be Retained   **Time Period**
Occupational Safety and Health Act of 1970—*Cont.*

C. Complete and accurate records of all employee medical
examinations required by law

C. Duration of employment
plus 30 years, unless a specific
OSHA standard provides a different time period

D. Records of any personal or
environmental monitoring of
employees' exposure to hazardous materials

D. Thirty years from date of
employment termination

Immigration Reform and Control Act of 1986[35]

A. Employment Eligibility
Verification Form (Form I-9)
must be completed by employers for all new employees hired
after November 7, 1986. This
form must be completed
within three days of hiring.

A. Three years after the employee's hiring or one year
after employment termination,
whichever is later

3. Employment Record Confidentiality

Initially, employers should ascertain if employees have a reasonable expectation of confidentiality of their employment information. When this reasonable privacy expectation exists, employers
should not release information without first obtaining employees'
consent or authorization. In determining a response to each request
for information in employees' records, employers must balance the
requestor's need for the data against employees' privacy interests
in maintaining the confidentiality of the information. Factors to
consider include:

1. The originator of the request

2. The purpose of the request

3. Any existing agreement between employees and employer regarding third-party requests for this information

4. The feasibility of restricting disclosure to only job-related information

5. The accuracy of the information

6. The possible effect on employees if the information is released

7. A statutory or other duty requiring or prohibiting disclosure of the information

C. Employment Record Policies

Employment Records: Basic Policy

Section 1. EMPLOYEE.   An "employee" is any person currently employed by the Company, any person subject to recall after layoff or leave of absence with a right to return to a position with the Company, or a former employee who has terminated services within the preceding year.

Section 2. OPEN RECORDS.   The Company, upon an employee's request which the Company may require to be in writing, will permit the employee to inspect any personnel documents which are, have been, or are intended to be used in determining that employee's qualifications for employment, promotion, transfer, additional compensation, and termination or other disciplinary action, except as provided in Section 9 (EXCEPTIONS). The inspection right encompasses personnel documents in the possession of a person, corporation, partnership, or other association having a contractual agreement with the Company to keep or supply a personnel record. An employee may request all or any part of his or her records, except as provided in Section 9 (EXCEPTIONS). The Company will grant at least two inspection requests by an employee in a calendar year when requests are made at reasonable intervals, unless otherwise provided in a collective bargaining agreement. The Company will provide the employee with the inspection opportunity within seven working days after the employee makes the request, or, if the Company can reasonably show that the deadline cannot be met it will have an additional seven working days to comply. The inspection will take place at a location reasonably near the employee's place of employment and during normal working hours. The Company may allow the inspection to take place at a time other than working hours or at a location other than where the records are maintained if that time or place would be more convenient for the employee. If an employee demonstrates that he or she is unable to review his or her personnel record at the employing unit or other location, the Company may, upon the employee's written request, mail a copy of the requested record to the employee. Nothing in this policy will be construed as permission for an employee to remove any personnel records or any part of these records from the place where they are made available for inspection. The Company retains the right to protect its records from loss, damage, or alteration to ensure their integrity.

Section 3. COPIES.   The employee may obtain a copy of the information or part of the information contained in the employee's personnel record. The Company may charge a fee for providing a copy of the information, with this fee limited to the actual cost of duplicating the information.

Section 4. PERSONNEL RECORD INSPECTION BY DESIGNATED REPRESENTATIVES.   An employee who is involved in a current grievance against the Company may designate in writing a representative of the employee's union or collective bargaining unit or another agent to inspect the employee's personnel record which may have a bearing on the grievance's resolution, except as provided in Section 9 (EXCEPTIONS). The Company will allow the designated representative to inspect that employee's personnel record in the same manner as provided under Section 2 (OPEN RECORDS).

Section 5. PERSONNEL RECORD CORRECTION. If the employee disagrees with any information contained in the personnel record, removal or correction of that information may be mutually agreed upon by the Company and the employee. If an agreement cannot be reached, the employee may submit a written statement explaining his or her position. The Company will attach the employee's statement to the disputed portion of the personnel record. The employee's statement will be included whenever that disputed portion of the personnel record is released to a third party as long as the disputed record is a part of the file. The inclusion of any written statement attached to the record without further comment or action by the Company will not imply or create any presumption of Company agreement with its contents.

Section 6. DISCLOSURE OF DISCIPLINARY ACTION: WRITTEN NOTICE.

a. The Company will not disclose a disciplinary report, letter of reprimand, or information regarding other disciplinary action to a third party, to a party outside of the Company's organization, or to a party who is not involved with a labor organization representing the employee, without written notice to the employee as provided in this section.

b. The employee will receive written notice of disclosure by first-class mail at the employee's last known address. Notification will be mailed on or before the day the information is disclosed.

c. This section will not apply if:

1. the employee has specifically waived written notice as part of a written, signed employment application with a previous employer;

2. the disclosure is ordered to a party in a legal action or arbitration; or

3. information is requested by a government agency as a result of a claim or complaint by an employee or as a result of a criminal investigation of the employee by the agency.

Section 7. REVIEW OF RECORD PRIOR TO RELEASE OF INFORMATION. The Company will review a personnel record before releasing information to a third party and will delete disciplinary reports, letters of reprimand, or other records of disciplinary action which are more than four years old, except when the release is ordered to a party in a legal action or arbitration.

Section 8. RECORD OF NONEMPLOYMENT ACTIVITIES. The Company will not gather information on or keep a record of an employee's associations, political activities, publications, communications, or nonemployment activities unless the employee submits the information in writing or authorizes the Company in writing to keep or gather the information. This prohibition will not apply to activities that occur on the Company's premises or during the employee's working hours which interfere with the performance of the employee's legitimate job duties or the duties of other employees; activities which constitute criminal conduct or may reasonably be expected to harm the Company's property, operations, or business, regardless of when and where activities occur; or activities which could cause the Company financial liability. Any record which is kept by the Company as permitted under this section will be part of the personnel record.

Section 9. EXCEPTIONS. The right of the employee or the employee's designated representative to inspect his or her personnel records does not apply to:

a. reference letters for that employee;

b. any portion of a test document, however, the employee may see a cumulative total test score for either a section of or the entire test document;

c. materials used by the Company for management planning, including but not limited to judgments, external peer review documents or recommendations concerning future salary increases and other wage treatments, management bonus plans, promotions and job assignments, or other comments or ratings used for the Company's planning purposes;

d. information of a personal nature about an individual other than the employee if disclosure of the information would constitute a clearly unwarranted invasion of the other person's privacy;

e. records relevant to any pending claim between the Company and the employee which may be discovered in a judicial proceeding; or

f. investigatory or security records maintained by the Company to investigate criminal conduct by an employee or other activity by the employee which could reasonably be expected to harm the Company's property, operations, or business or could by the employee's activity cause the Company financial liability, unless and until the Company takes adverse personnel action based on information in the records.

Section 10. ADMINISTRATION.   The Director of Human Resources or an authorized representative will administer and enforce the provisions of this policy.

Section 11. COMPLAINTS.   If an employee alleges that he or she has been denied his or her rights under this policy, he or she may file a complaint with the Human Resources Department. The Human Resources Department will investigate the complaint and attempt to resolve the complaint by conference or conciliation.

Employment Records: Comprehensive Policy

Section 1. PURPOSE.   To establish policies and procedures for the collection, maintenance, access, use, and disclosure of employee information.

Section 2. OBJECTIVES.   To provide a uniform system for the collection, maintenance, access, use, and disclosure of employee information and to preserve and protect the personal privacy of all wage and salaried employees.

Section 3. PERSONNEL RECORDS.

a. An employment record will be established for each employee upon hiring.

b. Official employment records for current employees will be maintained by the Human Resources Department.

c. Documents maintained in official employment records are classified as permanent or temporary, as defined below and in Section 6 (TYPE OF INFORMATION KEPT).

　　1. "Permanent information" is formal documentation of a person's current employment status and employment history. Permanent information will remain in the official employment record when an employee transfers or terminates.

　　2. "Temporary information" is information which does not make a significant contribution to a person's employment record or which becomes outdated or inaccurate with the passage of time. Temporary information is to be retained for four years unless otherwise indicated and then is to be removed in accordance with Section 8 (REVIEW OF RECORDS).

d. The following information is specifically prohibited from being placed in official employment records:

　　1. Arrest records upon acquittal or when formal charges have been dropped

　　2. Investigative material regarding a civil, criminal, or administrative investigation of alleged wrongdoing by an employee which resulted in the employee's acquittal

3. National origin identification

4. Racial identification, except data used in support of the Company's Affirmative Action Program

5. Political affiliation

6. Religious affiliation

7. Financial information and

8. Written criticisms of which an employee is not aware.

Section 4. RECORD ACCESS.

a. Official employment records will be secured in locked file cabinets during nonwork hours. Operating instructions for computer terminals in which records are stored will be accessible only to persons designated by the Human Resources Department, and terminals will be secured during nonwork hours.

b. Only the Human Resources Department and its designees will have access to official employment records, to data maintained in the computer system files, and to computer-produced reports.

c. The following individuals will have access to all information in official employment records and to information on the computer system when needed in the performance of their duties, provided that requests for access are made to the Human Resources Department:

1. President

2. Division heads and their designees

3. Affirmative Action Officer

4. An employee's department director

5. An employee's immediate supervisor and those in direct chain of command above the immediate supervisor

d. Employees and persons with written permission of employees have the right to review official employment records. Reviews must be conducted in the presence of a Human Resources Department staff member at times amenable to both, and an employee may have a representative present. Employees may request copies of documents in their employment records; however, they are not permitted to alter, remove, add, or replace any documents. The Human Resources Department may charge reasonable fees when requested to provide copies of all materials contained in the official employment record or when frequent requests for copies of materials are received from the same employee.

e. Employees have a right to submit rebuttals to any material in their official employment record. Rebuttals will be acknowledged by the Human Resources Department. Rebuttals and acknowledgments will become part of the official employment record in the same permanent or temporary category as the material being rebutted. If rebuttals are submitted by inactive employees, both the acknowledgment and rebuttal will be included in the former employee's official employment record.

Section 5. RESPONSIBILITIES.

a. The Director of Human Resources is required to maintain a record of all employees and to develop standards for the establishment and maintenance of employment records.

b. Department directors are to ensure that necessary procedures and safeguards are implemented in accordance with this policy.

c. Human Resources officers will be the custodians of personnel records. Custodians will disclose and withhold employee information in accordance with this policy and will ensure that information under their control is not accessible to unauthorized persons.

d. The Human Resources Department will store and control official employment records of inactive employees until each individual's 75th birthday. At that time, the folders and all contents are to be burned or shredded.

e. The Human Resources Department will audit the implementation of this policy and review complaints and appeals arising from it.

f. The Human Resources Department will review all subpoenas and other written judicial orders seeking information.

g. All personnel having access to official employment records, to data maintained on the computer files, or to computer-produced reports, directly or through someone else, are to disclose and withhold information in accordance with this policy and are to ensure that information under their control is not accessible to unauthorized persons.

Section 6. TYPE OF INFORMATION KEPT.

a. This list does not include all information appropriate for maintenance in official employment records. Questions regarding the appropriateness of maintaining other data should be referred to the Human Resources Department. The following types of information are permanent and must be included in official employment records as long as records are maintained:

1. Latest employment application

2. Last five annual performance evaluations

3. Employee benefits records

4. Significant training records

5. Absence and leave records

6. Employee requests and Company responses concerning voluntary retirement, voluntary separation, transfer, demotion, and leaves of absence other than vacation, illness, or personal days

7. Notifications to employees regarding appointment, promotion, demotion, involuntary retirement, resignation by reason of abandonment of position, layoff, reassignment, transfer, salary changes (except general pay increases), termination, suspension, disciplinary notices, and temporary assignment to a higher job classification

8. Employee-initiated acknowledgments of temporary employment or unusual employment conditions, such as the certificate required of minors

9. Authorizations for current payroll deductions including, but not limited to, group life insurance, retirement, medical/hospital insurance, workers' compensation, federal and state withholding tax, earned income tax, union dues, credit union, and tax-sheltered annuities

10. Letters of commendation, cost reduction awards, management improvement awards, awards for excellence, professional organization or society awards, and any other form of official recognition given an employee that relates to his or her duties and responsibilities

b. The following types of information are temporary and are to be purged from official employment records in accordance with Section 7b:

1. Reference letters

2. Letters of caution, reprimand, admonishment, or warning

3. Employee confirmations of oral reprimands

4. Nonpermanent performance evaluations

5. Professional affiliations

6. Out-service and in-service training of limited significance to an employee's development

7. Records of periodic health examinations required by federal or state regulations

c. Only the following employee information may be maintained by departments not maintaining official employment records:

1. Name and home address

2. Social security number

3. Job classification and title

4. Job description, performance objectives, and performance standards

5. Data necessary to verify payrolls

6. Attendance records

7. Emergency telephone numbers

8. Copies of last five performance evaluations

d. Supervisors' or managers' notes and records on matters involving discipline or performance on specific work assignments may be maintained separately from the official employment record and are not subject to employee access.

e. If a personnel action is amended, only information concerning the amended action is to be maintained. The original personnel action and any rescinded personnel actions are to be removed from an official employment record.

Section 7. REQUEST FOR INFORMATION.

a. Requests for employment information are to be handled as follows:

1. An employee's home address may be furnished to police or court officials upon written request showing that an indictment has been returned or a complaint, information, accusation, or other writ has been filed against the

employee and the home address is needed to serve a summons, warrant, or subpoena.

2. An employee's social security number and home address may be furnished to taxing authorities upon written request.

3. Medical information may be furnished:

   (a) to medical personnel to aid treatment when needed by an employee who is not able to provide the information; and

   (b) to a federal or state investigative agency when requested information is required to verify adherence to regulations.

4. Any information available to an employee from his or her own official employment record may be released to a third party upon written authorization by the employee.

5. The Director of Human Resources is to be notified immediately of the receipt of any subpoena or other written judicial order seeking information not listed in Section 7a.1. The Human Resources Department, in conjunction with the Company's Legal Counsel, will determine the response to a subpoena or judicial order. Should a subpoena appear to be relevant to the legal proceeding and not to be overly broad in scope, the Company will, absent a compelling policy or legal reason to the contrary, make the requested records available. However, before the Company complies with a subpoena, the employee will be given an opportunity to consult with a private attorney to seek to have the subpoena quashed. Should the Human Resources Department be unable to contact the employee, it will mail notification of the subpoena to the employee's last known address, using certified mail with return receipt requested.

6. Federal and state law enforcement and investigative agencies may be provided, upon request, information deemed under the law as a public record. Requests from these agencies for employment information are to be honored only if the requested information is determined to be relevant to the investigation or audit and is within the statutory authority of the requesting agency. Questions concerning the release of this information should be referred to the Director of Human Resources.

7. Following the release of nonpublic information to a federal or state investigative agency due to a subpoena or otherwise, the Human Resources Department will notify the employee in writing of the information that was released.

8. Replies to inquiries from a prospective employer concerning specific reasons for an employee's employment separation are to indicate only whether the separation was voluntary or involuntary. Particular circumstances or issues involved in an involuntary separation are to be disclosed only with the employee's written authorization or when authorized by the Human Resources Department.

b. Requests by employees to review official employment records will be responded to as follows:

1. Employees will be advised that they may choose to travel to the location where the official employment record is maintained. Travel expenses or unpaid leave will not be authorized for this purpose.

2. Upon request, the contents of an employee's official employment record may be duplicated and forwarded to the employee for review. The Human Resources Department will attach a signed statement to the file certifying

that the entire contents of the record were copied and
sent to the employee.

3. Employees may be charged reasonable fees for the cost
   of reproducing material in their official employment records.

Section 8. REVIEW OF RECORDS.   Official employment records will be reviewed at least once every two years or when an
employee transfers or is terminated. Information within the files
will be maintained in chronological order. Temporary information
four years old or older will be removed. Oral and written reprimands will be maintained for two years if no similar incidents
occur. Employees will be notified when documents are removed
from their folders and will be given ten calendar days to request
these documents. Documents not needed for current or pending
disciplinary or grievance actions or not requested by employees
will be destroyed.

Section 9. ACCESS TO INACTIVE RECORDS.   The Human
Resources Department will provide access to inactive official employment records to positively identified former employees or persons with letters of authorization from former employees.

Section 10. ADMINISTRATION.   The Human Resources Department will review compliance with this policy. Department directors will be advised of areas of noncompliance and any corrective
action required. If any procedure in this policy conflicts with provision in a collective bargaining agreement which is otherwise lawful,
the provision of the collective bargaining agreement will control.

III. Medical Records

A. Medical Record Privacy Principles

Medical records may contain sensitive employee personal details regarding an employee's age, life history, family background,

present and past health or illness, disabilities, mental and emotional health or illness, treatment, accident reports, laboratory reports, and other scientific data from various sources. They may also contain medical providers' notes, prognoses, and reports of the patient's response to treatment.

Employers may face requests for employees' medical records for many legitimate purposes. These records may be important to legal actions, public health evaluation, occupational health research, and other health care provider use.

However, improper disclosure of this medical information by the employer could cause the employee embarrassment or humiliation. Disclosure could also damage the employee's relationships with family members or co-workers. Disclosure could infringe upon the employee's privacy rights by affecting his or her associations and lifestyle. Courts have partially acknowledged that employees do have a privacy interest regarding their medical records.[36] Confidentiality of medical records is protected under federal and state privacy statutes.[37] One such statute is the Americans with Disabilities Act of 1991 which requires that employee medical records be kept confidential and separate from other employee records.[38]

Various states restrict disclosure of medical information in the custody of health care providers and strictly limit the use and disclosure of employee medical information by the employer.[39] Employers should not collect, maintain, use, disclose, or knowingly permit employees to use or disclose medical information which the employer possesses, without the written authorization of the affected employee permitting this use or disclosure.

B. General Procedural Considerations

It is an employer's responsibility to establish appropriate procedures to ensure the confidentiality of its employees' medical information and to protect this data from unauthorized collection, maintenance, use, and disclosure. These procedures should dictate the actions of the employer and all employees who handle medical records in the course of their duties. Employers should develop general procedures which:

1. prevent the employer from seeking medical information directly from an employee's physician or hospital records without consent of the employee, except in emergency situations;

2. restrict employee access to medical records to managers with a legitimate job-related interest in obtaining the information;

3. instruct employees who are custodians of medical files on confidentiality requirements of state and federal law;

4. provide for a security system for computer terminals which store medical files; and

5. provide for amendment or correction of information.

1. Authorization for Disclosure

Prior to releasing any information contained in employees' medical files, employers should receive written permission from the employees. Employee authorization for disclosure of medical records should:

1. be handwritten by the employee;

2. be separate from any other language on the same page;

3. be signed and dated by the employee;

4. state the names of persons authorized to disclose the information;

5. state the names of persons authorized to receive the information;

6. state the limitations on the use of medical information by those authorized to receive it;

7. provide a date after which the employer is no longer authorized to disclose the information; and

8. provide the employee with a copy of the authorization.

2. Confidentiality of Records

When faced with a request for employee medical information, employers must determine if the need for the information outweighs the employee's interest in keeping the information confidential. Employers must evaluate:

1. the identity of the person making the request;

2. the purpose of the request;

3. the information contained in the record;

4. any existing agreement between the employer and employee regarding third-party requests for the information;

5. the potential effect on the employee if disclosure occurs;

6. the effect of disclosure on the physician-patient relationship;

7. safeguards against inadvertent or accidental disclosure of information other than that requested;

8. statutory or public interest reasons requiring disclosure;

9. the employer's statutory or other duty prohibiting disclosure; and

10. the effect of restricting disclosure to only necessary information.[40]

C. Medical Record Policies

Medical Record Collection Policy

Section 1. AUTHORIZATION FOR COLLECTION OF MEDICAL INFORMATION. Each employee will be required to sign an authorization for the Company to obtain medical information from the employee. The Company will provide a copy of the completed authorization to the employee upon demand. The Company will disclose any limitations on the use of the information to the person to whom it is communicated. The Company will honor any cancellation or modification of the authorization by the employee upon receipt of written notice.

Section 2. LACK OF MEDICAL RECORD AUTHORIZA-TION. If an employee refuses to execute an authorization, the Company will not discriminate against the employee in terms or conditions of employment on the basis of that refusal. However, discipline or termination may be appropriate if the Company is unable to ascertain an employee's ability to perform a job function due to a physical condition because the employee refuses to release medical information. When drug or alcohol use is suspected, the Company has the right to discipline an employee based on other information available to it if the employee refuses to be tested for use of these substances.

Section 3. NO AUTHORIZATION REQUIRED. The Company is not required to obtain employee authorization for release of medical records in the following circumstances:

a. the information is compelled by judicial or administrative process;

b. the information is relevant in a lawsuit, arbitration, grievance, or other claim or challenge to which the Company and employee are parties and in which the employee has placed in issue his or her medical history, medical or physical condition, or treatment;

c. the information is necessary for administering and maintaining employee benefit and workers' compensation plans and for determining eligibility for paid and unpaid leave from work for medical reasons; and

d. the information is needed by a provider of health care.

Section 4. EMPLOYEE REQUEST FOR CORRECTION OR AMENDMENT.

a. Upon the request of an employee for correction or amendment of medical information maintained by the Company, the Company will:

    1. disclose the source of the medical information to the employee or to a person designated by the employee;

    2. make the correction or amendment within a reasonable time period if the source of the information concurs that it is inaccurate or incomplete; and

    3. establish a procedure for an employee to present supplemental information to the employer's medical record of the employee, provided that the source of the supplemental information also is included.

Medical Record Release Policy

Section 1. RELEASE.   The Company will provide medical information that it has collected or maintained regarding an employee upon the written request of the employee, former employee, or his or her designated representative. This information extends to any medical report arising out of any physical examination by a physician or other health care professional and any hospital or laboratory tests or examinations which are required by the Company as a condition of employment or arising out of any injury or disease related to the employee's employment. However, if a physician concludes that presentation of all or any part of an employee's medical record directly to the employee will result in serious medical harm to the employee, the physician will so indicate on the medical record, and a copy will be given to a physician designated in writing by the employee.

Section 2. COST REIMBURSEMENT.   The Company may require the employee, former employee, or his or her designated representative to pay the reasonable cost of furnishing medical report copies.

Endnotes

1   *See, e.g.,* Privacy Act of 1974, 5 U.S.C. § 552a (1988); Pa. Stat. Ann. tit. 43, §§ 1321-1324 (Purdon 1991) (Pennsylvania's statute regulating personnel file inspection). *See* Appendix A sections III.O and IV.E for federal and state statutes affecting employment records.

2   *See* sources cited *supra* note 1.

3   Board of Trustees of Stanford Univ. v. Superior Court, 119 Cal. App. 3d 516, 174 Cal. Rptr. 160 (1981) (interpreting California Constitution).

4   *Id.*

5   *Id.*

6   Quinones v. United States, 492 F.2d 1269 (3d Cir. 1974) (release of inaccurate personnel file information to outside third party); Bulkin v. Western Kraft E., Inc., 422 F. Supp. 437 (E.D. Pa. 1976) (negligent maintenance of employment records by maintaining incorrect data).

7   *See, e.g.,* Wendler v. DePaul, 346 Pa. Super. 479, 499 A.2d 1101 (1985) (negative employee performance evaluation); Biggin v. Hanson, 252 Cal. App. 2d 16, 59 Cal. Rptr. 897 (1967) (reasons for employee termination).

8   Quinones v. United States, 492 F.2d 1269 (3d Cir. 1974); Bulkin v. Western Kraft E., Inc., 422 F. Supp. 437 (E.D. Pa. 1976).

9   *See* Anderson v. Low Rent Hous. Comm'n, 304 N.W.2d 239 (Iowa 1981) (recovery permitted against public employer for presenting employee in false light).

10   Bratt v. International Business Machs., 392 Mass. 508, 467 N.E.2d 126 (1984) (disclosure of employee's medical information); *contra* Eddy v. Brown, 715 P.2d 74 (Okla. Sup. Ct. 1986) (employer did not invade privacy of employee by disclosing employee psychiatric problems to a limited number of co-workers).

11   Molinar v. Western Elec. Co., 525 F.2d 521 (1st Cir. 1975), *cert. denied,* 424 U.S. 978 (1976).

12   Gaines v. Cuna Mut. Ins. Soc'y, 681 F.2d 982 (5th Cir. 1982).

13   Andrews v. Mohawk Rubber Co., 476 F. Supp. 1276 (E.D. Ark. 1979).

14   Keddie v. Pennsylvania State Univ., 412 F. Supp. 1264 (M.D. Pa. 1976); Chow v. Alston, 2 Haw. App. 480, 634 P.2d 430 (1981).

15   Caslin v. General Elec. Co., 608 S.W.2d 69 (Ky. 1980).

16   Haddad v. Sears Roebuck & Co., 526 F.2d 83 (6th Cir. 1975).

17   Drennen v. Westinghouse Elec. Co., 328 So. 2d 52 (Fla. 1976).

18   Zuschek v. Whitmoyer Lab., Inc., 430 F. Supp. 1163 (E.D. 1977), *aff'd*, 571 F.2d 573 (3d Cir. 1977); Sholtes v. Signal Delivery Serv., Inc., 548 F. Supp. 487 (W.D. Ark. 1982).

19   *See* Andrews v. Mohawk Rubber Co., 476 F. Supp. 1276 (E.D. Ark. 1979).

20   Pirre v. Printing Devs., Inc., 468 F. Supp. 1028 (S.D.N.Y. 1979); Stumpges v. Parke Davis & Co., 297 N.W.2d 252 (Minn. 1980).

21   *See, e.g.,* N.Y. Lab. Law § 537 (Consol. 1983 & Supp. 1986); *see also* Clegg v. Bon Temps, Ltd., 114 Misc. 2d 805, 452 N.Y.S.2d 825 (1982).

22   Macy v. Transworld Airlines, Inc., 381 F. Supp. 142 (D. Md. 1974).

23   DeLuca v. Reader, 227 Pa. Super. 392, 323 A.2d 309 (1974).

24   *See, e.g.,* Quinones v. United States, 492 F.2d 1269 (3d Cir. 1974) (release of inaccurate personnel file); Bulkin v. Western Kraft E., Inc., 422 F. Supp. 437 (E.D. Pa. 1976) (negligent maintenance of employment records).

25   Singer Co., 85 Lab. Arb. (BNA) 152 (1985) (Yarowsky, Arb.).

26   *See* PRIVACY PROTECTION STUDY COMMISSION, PERSONAL PRIVACY IN AN INFORMATION SOCIETY 235, 237-38 (1977), [hereinafter "PERSONAL PRIVACY IN AN INFORMATION SOCIETY"].

27   *See, e.g.,* Pa. Stat. Ann. tit. 43, §§ 1321-1324 (Purdon 1991) (Pennsylvania's statute regulating personnel file inspection).

28   PERSONAL PRIVACY IN AN INFORMATION SOCIETY, Employment Records, Appendix 3, 35-43.

29   42 U.S.C. §§ 2000e-1 through 2002-17 (1988).

30   29 U.S.C. §§ 621-634 (1988).

31   29 U.S.C. §§ 701-796 (1988).

32   42 U.S.C. §§ 12111-12117 (Supp. II 1990).

33   Exec. Order No. 11,246, 3 C.F.R. § 339 (1964-1965), *reprinted as amended* in 42 U.S.C. § 2000e (1988), note originally issued Sept. 24, 1965.

34   29 U.S.C. §§ 651-678 (1988).

35   Pub. L. No. 99-603, 100 Stat. 3359 (codified in scattered sections of 7 U.S.C.; 8 U.S.C.; 18 U.S.C.; 20 U.S.C.; 29 U.S.C.; and 42 U.S.C.

36   *See* United States v. Westinghouse Elec. Corp., 638 F.2d 570, 577 (3d Cir. 1980) (explicitly recognizing employee's constitutional right to privacy of medical records).

37   *See* Appendix A section IV.P for state statutes affecting medical records.

38   42 U.S.C. §§ 12111-12117 (Supp. II 1990).

39   *See, e.g.,* Md. Ann. Code art. 100, § 95A(a)-(e) (1979) (Maryland statute protecting privacy of medical records). *See* Appendix A section IV.P for other state statutes offering similar protection.

40   PERSONAL PRIVACY IN AN INFORMATION SOCIETY at 263.

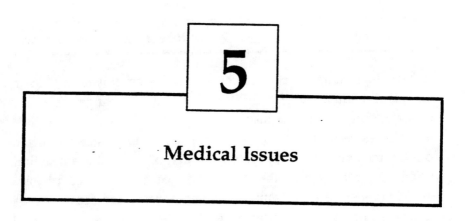

5

Medical Issues

I. Introduction

The growing awareness of alcohol and drug abuse and the uncertainty over acquired immunodeficiency syndrome (AIDS) have brought added attention to employees' interests in the privacy of workplace medical issues. Employees and employers are increasingly confronted with serious questions regarding how medical privacy issues should be balanced—what information should the employer collect or not collect, what information should the employer disclose or not disclose, what information are employees required to provide? This chapter reviews medical privacy concerns in the workplace arising out of physical examinations, smoking, employee assistance programs, alcohol and drug abuse, and AIDS.

II. Physical Examinations

A. Physical Examination Privacy Principles

As part of the hiring process, employers have a right to require an individual to undergo a physical examination after an employment offer is made.[1] Situations also arise that may require physical examinations during the employment relationship.[2] It is important that the medical information obtained by the employer as a result of these physical examinations be kept confidential and is disclosed only for legitimate job-related purposes. The employer must maintain confidentiality to prevent prejudice from affecting the employee's workplace opportunities.

Unless restricted by a collective bargaining agreement, employers may require employees to undergo physical examinations under legitimate job-related circumstances. For instance, physical examinations are permissible if the employer needs to verify the improved health of an employee who desires to return to work following an accident, sick leave, or extended layoff. The employer may also require an examination if an employee applies for a job which demands greater physical effort than his or her current position.[3]

It has been acknowledged, however, that the employer's right to require physical examinations "is not an absolute one exercisable at the whim" of the employer and that examinations "cannot be arbitrarily insisted upon without reasonable grounds."[4] Unreasonable requests for physical examinations could expose employers to liability under federal and state fair employment practice statutes.[5]

B. Physical Examination Procedures

To ensure that proper medical information is obtained when physical examinations are necessary, the employer should use the following guidelines:

1. Establish relationships with one or more physicians who:
   a. understand the physical requirements of all jobs which require testing;
   b. are able to provide a quick conclusion regarding employment eligibility;
   c. are familiar with paperwork required by the employer; and
   d. provide ready access for communication with the human resources staff.
2. Retain the services of a physician on retainer.

C. Physical Examination Policies

Depending on the employer's workplace needs, various types of physical examination policies may be required. These policies may deal with physical examinations of an applicant after an employment offer has been extended, physical examinations of an employee after an accident or illness to determine current readiness to return to work, and the procedure for how conflicting medical evidence can be reconciled.

Physical Examination Required

To determine medical fitness for employment, the Company may require physical examinations of employees by a Company-employed physician when it deems an examination is advisable for the health and safety of both the employee and his or her co-workers. The Company may also require applicants to undergo physical examinations by an outside physician at the Company's expense after an offer of employment has been made. Should an employee be found medically unfit to work at his or her assigned job, the Company will furnish the employee a copy of the physician's report or a physician's statement. Any applicant or employee may also be examined at his or her own expense by a self-selected physician, and the physician's report may be submitted to the Company for consideration.

Physical Examination after Accident or Sickness

Section 1. PHYSICAL EXAMINATION REQUIRED. If an employee has been absent because of accident or sickness, the Company may require a physical examination by a Company-employed physician before the employee may return to work. If it is determined by the examining physician that the sickness or accident may subject the employee to other or continued sickness or accidents, he or she will not be allowed to return to work.

Section 2. RESULT DISPUTES. Should the employee disagree with the decision of the Company's physician, he or she may be examined by a physician of his or her own choosing, provided that notification of this intent is given to the Company within three (3) calendar days after the Company has denied the right to return to work. Any costs incurred because of this examination will be paid by the employee.

If the employee's physician indicates that the employee is able to return to work, the Company must be notified in writing by the physician making the determination. The notification must be given to the Company no later than thirty (30) calendar days from the date the employee has been notified that he or she has been denied the right to return to work.

If the matter still cannot be resolved, the Company's and the employee's physicians will select a third physician to whom they will submit their respective findings. The third physician will examine the employee and make a determination concerning the employee's status. Any expense incurred by the third physician will be shared equally by the Company and the employee. The finding of the third physician will be considered by the Company in determining whether the employee should return to work.

Physical Examination Information Available to Employee's Physician

Employee's physical examinations will be arranged by the Company only when necessary and only after the employee is notified of the specific reasons for the examination. Copies of the physical examination reports and medical treatments will be maintained by the Company in its Medical Department and will be available to the employee's physician, if authorized in writing by the employee.

Confidentiality of Physical Examination Results

The Company will maintain as confidential the results of all physical examinations. Results will be furnished only to the employee's designated physician upon the employee's written authorization. It is understood by employees that the Company may use or supply physical examination results in response to subpoenas or requests to the Company by any governmental agency authorized by law to obtain these reports and in arbitration or litigation of any claim or action involving the Company.

Dispute of Physical Examination Results:
Medical Arbitrator

Section 1. DEFINITION. For the purposes of this policy, "individual" will refer to either a current Company employee or an applicant for a position with the Company.

Section 2. PHYSICAL EXAMINATIONS REQUIRED. After an employment offer has been extended, an applicant must meet certain health and physical fitness standards as determined by a physical examination by a Company-designated physician. After employment, periodic physical examinations may be offered or required to aid an employee to improve health or to enable the Company to ensure its employees' health.

Section 3. RESULTS. Upon request, an individual will have the opportunity to discuss the results of his or her physical examination with the Company's physician. Upon the individual's request, the information will be made available to his or her personal physician.

Section 4. RESULT DISPUTES. Should the Company's physician determine that an individual cannot perform the job for which hired or currently held because of an existing medical condition, and should a dispute arise between the Company's physician and the employee's personal physician regarding this determination, a complaint may be filed by the individual with the Human Resources Department.

If the Human Resources Department cannot resolve the complaint, the individual, the Company's physician, and the individual's personal physician will exchange X-rays, laboratory test reports, and physical examination reports within ten (10) calendar days of the date the complaint was filed with the Human Resources Department.

If, after exchanging X-rays and reports, final agreement cannot be reached regarding the medical findings and conclusions, the individual may, within fourteen (14) calendar days after the exchange, refer the dispute to the Company's President who will attempt to resolve the problem by examining all available medical evidence.

If a dispute still exists regarding the individual's medical condition after review of the records by the Company's President, the dispute may be presented to an impartial medical arbitrator selected by mutual agreement of the parties in accordance with the following:

a. Within fourteen (14) calendar days following referral of the dispute to the Company's President, all X-rays and reports will be forwarded to the medical arbitrator.

b. Within fourteen (14) calendar days thereafter, the medical arbitrator will conduct whatever physical examination of the individual is deemed necessary and appropriate, and will meet with the two physicians and any additional medical experts to discuss the findings.

c. Within fourteen (14) calendar days thereafter, the medical arbitrator will submit a written determination to the Company and the individual.

d. Any of the time limits provided herein may be extended by the mutual, written agreement of the parties.

e. The charges and expenses of the medical arbitrator will be paid equally by the Company and the individual.

f. The determination of the medical arbitrator will be final and binding on the parties involved.

III. Smoking

A. Smoking Privacy Principles

Mounting evidence of the harmful effects of smoking on the health, productivity, and morale of smokers and nonsmokers has led to increased public concern over the ramifications of this habit. This concern, combined with changing social attitudes toward smoking, is reversing the notion that smoking is an acceptable public practice. Increasingly, smoking is becoming an activity that individuals must confine to their own homes. Recent laws enacted by state and local legislatures have restricted or totally prohibited smoking in many public gathering places. Regulation or deliberate non-regulation of smoking aggravates the conflict between the privacy rights of smokers and nonsmokers, and this conflict extends to the workplace.

As the arbiter of workplace activities, the employer is caught in the middle of this conflict. On the one hand, the employer can not infringe on the rights of smoking employees by regulating a personal-choice activity. On the other hand, the employer has a right and a responsibility to secure a healthy and safe work environment. Employers who permit or fail to regulate workplace smoking may be challenged by nonsmoking employees who claim that their lifestyle choice is being affected. Awards for unemployment,[6] disability,[7] and medical treatment[8] have been made to nonsmokers, and union grievances under collective bargaining agreements are increasingly challenging employers to confront this issue.[9] In addition to the health risk posed by smoking, employers also must consider its effect on sensitive technical equipment and the possible safety hazard it presents.[10]

While discrimination against smokers is not prohibited by federal and state fair employment practice statutes,[11] it certainly affects the privacy interests of those who choose to smoke. Employers that do not hire smokers or that attempt to restrict smoking outside the workplace use smoking as a non-job-related criteria that controls employment distribution. By not confining employment standards to criteria that are directly related to the workplace, employers could deny employment opportunities based on applicants' activities outside the workplace unless it can be established that the health of other employees is a valid job-related criteria. Employers that restrict smoking during off-duty hours are, in effect, using the employment incentive to control how employees act at home, and therefore are deciding what can be done by employees in private. This could give the appearance of discrimination if statistics establish that certain minority, national origin, or age groups smoke more than others.

Employees' privacy interests in obtaining a smoke-free working environment may be enforced through statutory, tort, and contractual litigation theories. Statutory remedies may exist under federal and state fair employment practice statutes which include protection for the disabled.[12] For example, under the federal Vocational Rehabilitation Act of 1973,[13] disabled individuals include those who are unusually sensitive to tobacco smoke.[14] Hypersensitivity to smoke limits a major life activity by preventing an individual from working in any environment that is not smoke-free. Employers, however, are not required to provide a *completely* smoke-free environment; a reasonable accommodation in separating smokers from nonsmokers or offering an alternative job in a non-smoking area is sufficient.

As yet, constitutional privacy protections of smokers have been found inapplicable.[15] However, nonsmokers have successfully obtained court orders stopping employers from permitting smoking in the workplace.[16] These injunctions have been granted when courts have found an employer duty to provide a workplace environment that is reasonably free of recognized hazards, including tobacco smoke.[17]

When determining a policy for smoking in the workplace, employers must balance the privacy rights of both smokers and nonsmokers. The optimal policy will provide for reasonable accommodation which satisfies both groups. If accommodation is not possible, courts strongly support the prevalence of the rights of nonsmokers.[18]

B. Procedural Guidelines

The employer should consider the following guidelines as a basis for developing workplace smoking procedures:

1. Determine if the smoking policy will be a total prohibition.
2. Review federal and state statutes and regulations which restrict or prohibit smoking in the workplace.[19]
3. Consult employees for their input.
4. Meet with the employees' union to discuss the smoking policy.
5. Communicate the policy to all employees.
6. Require all employees to follow the policy.
7. Offer smoke cessation classes for employees who want to stop smoking.
8. Designate smoking and nonsmoking areas.
9. Improve ventilation to minimize the health hazard of smoking.
10. Separate from smokers those employees who have a medically proven reaction to smoke but do not terminate them.
11. Implement a reasonable smoking ban in areas where smoking presents a safety hazard due to the presence of paints, chemicals, or explosives.
12. Investigate employees' complaints of policy violations.

C. Smoking Policy

Smoking Policy

Section 1. PURPOSE AND BACKGROUND. This policy is designed to promote employee health and safety and the performance of Company business. It is not intended to totally prohibit smoking on the Company's premises but does restrict smoking to certain areas.

Smoking poses a significant risk to the health of smokers and nonsmokers. It can damage sensitive technical equipment and can be a safety hazard. In sufficient concentrations, second-hand smoke can be an annoyance and potential health risk to nonsmokers and may be harmful to individuals with heart and respiratory diseases or allergies to tobacco smoke.

Smoking is a habit that involves elements of psychological and physiological addictions. Many smokers who desire to eliminate smoking from their lives require assistance. It is not a dependency that can be eliminated completely by prohibition or restriction by others. This policy is intended to assist employees in finding a reasonable accommodation between those who do not smoke and those who do, and it demonstrates the Company's desire to improve the health of all employees.

Section 2. POLICY. It is the Company's policy to respect the rights of nonsmokers and smokers in Company buildings and facilities. When these rights conflict, the Company and its employees will endeavor to find a reasonable accommodation. When an accommodation is not possible, the nonsmokers' rights will prevail.

Section 3. PROHIBITED AREAS. Smoking is not permitted:

a. in areas with sensitive equipment or computer systems or where records and supplies would be exposed to hazard from fires, ashes, or smoke;

b. in areas where combustible fumes can collect (as in garage and storage areas), areas where chemicals are used, and all other designated areas where an occupational safety or health hazard might exist;

c. in confined areas of general access, such as libraries, medical facilities, cashier waiting lines, elevators, restrooms, stairwells, copy rooms, lobbies, waiting rooms, and fitness centers;

   d. in areas of Company premises which are frequently visited by customers, such as public offices and customer service areas; and

   e. in other locations the Company may designate where smoking specifically is not permitted.

Section 4. WORK AREAS. In work areas where space is shared by two or more persons, an effort will be made to accommodate individual smoking preferences to the degree reasonably possible. When requested, managers and supervisors will make a reasonable attempt to separate persons who smoke from those who do not.

Employees may designate their private offices as smoking or nonsmoking areas. Visitors to private work areas should honor the employees' wishes.

In Company vehicles, including Company-sponsored van pools, smoking will be permitted only when there is no objection from one or more of the occupants.

Section 5. AREAS OF COMMON USE. Smoking will not be permitted during meetings and in enclosed locations, including conference rooms and classrooms. Breaks and appropriate access to outside areas may be scheduled to accommodate the needs of smokers.

In enclosed common-use locations, including cafeterias, dining areas, employee lounges, and auditoriums, smoking sections will be identified if there is adequate ventilation and the locations are not normally used by customers. Smoking is permitted only in these designated sections of common-use locations. Smoking is permitted in corridors. Employees and visitors are expected to honor the smoking and nonsmoking designations and to be considerate of nonsmokers in their vicinity.

IV. Employee Assistance Programs (EAPs)

A. EAP Privacy Principles

Employee assistance programs (EAPs) aid employees and their families to recognize and overcome personal problems that interfere with employees' work performance. EAPs are an extension of the performance evaluation process and may identify problems including job dissatisfaction, supervisor or co-worker conflicts, job performance anxiety, alcohol or drug abuse, emotional problems, marital problems, gambling problems, and financial difficulties.

EAPs can be developed by the employer or contracted through agencies that provide these programs. Generally employers use three types of EAPs. The first type involves the employer hiring an in-house EAP counselor who meets with individual employees and, when appropriate, refers them to other specialists for further assistance with their problems. The second type of EAP utilizes outside specialists who come to the employer's place of business to consult with employees. These EAP providers also may recommend that the employee seek more specialized treatment. The final EAP type consists of a relationship between the employer and an off-premises EAP provider to which the employees are given access.

Critical to the success of any EAP is confidentiality.[20] Employees must be certain that the sensitive, non-work-related information they share with the EAP counselor will be kept confidential. With this assurance, employees will feel comfortable seeking assistance and freely discussing their problems, allowing the EAP to benefit employees. Counselors share information with the employer only if it is job-related and if it presents a threat to others.

Confidentially is not merely a desirable aspect of an EAP, it is a duty imposed on EAP counselors and employers. Counselors are governed by the code of ethics adopted by the professional organization to which they belong. For example, ethical obligations of confidentiality are imposed on EAP providers by the Code of Ethics of the Employee Assistance Professional Association, which states: "I respect the privacy of all people I serve and I will maintain the confidential nature of all my professional relationships, regardless of pressures to the contrary."[21] Employers are subject to federal and state statutes which impose a confidentiality duty on information that is obtained.[22] Employer representations to employees, whether oral, written, or implied, may also create a confidentiality duty.

Despite these constraints, the employer's duty of confidentiality must be balanced with the duty to disclose information. Under certain circumstances, an employer may be required to disclose confidential information obtained from an EAP provider in situations which present a threat or hazard to the workplace and those in it.[23]

EAPs require considerable planning and administration on the part of employers, who must act to ensure that the program functions effectively to prevent employee problems and to identify, treat, and rehabilitate those employees who are troubled.

B. Implementing an EAP

In developing an EAP, employers should address the following issues:

1. Provision of the EAP by an outside agency or the employer by considering:

   a. Location of the EAP which would be most convenient to employees

   b. Qualifications of the outside agency's EAP staff

   c. Cost of malpractice liability insurance to cover an in-house counselor

2. Communication of EAP services by:

   a. Educating employees on available services

   b. Training managers, supervisors, and union representatives to help employees utilize services

V. Alcohol and Drug Use

A. Alcohol and Drug Use Privacy Principles

Employers are developing programs for employees who use or abuse alcohol and drugs. In addition to helping employees overcome their addictions, these programs strive to increase workplace productivity and safety. Medical testing procedures are a significant part of these programs.

Regardless of the benefits that testing may provide through increased productivity and workplace safety, it presents important workplace privacy considerations. By its very nature, medical testing of any type intrudes upon the employees' physical integrity. When tests are administered to detect alcohol or drug use, intrusiveness increases in complexity and degree. Like all other individual rights, however, employees' physical workplace privacy is not absolute. It must be balanced against competing employee and employer interests and objectives.

Public employers that implement alcohol and drug programs are subject to privacy limitations under the United States Constitution[24] and certain state constitutions.[25] For example, random testing by a school district of its teachers was found to be an unconstitutional search and seizure.[26] The school district needed a reasonable suspicion that the teachers were using drugs before they could be tested. Additionally, random searches conducted by the state without reasonable suspicion are generally permitted only when: (1) the privacy interests implicated are minimal; (2) the government's interest is substantial; and (3) safeguards are provided to ensure that the individuals' reasonable privacy expectations are protected. In this case, the school district required that probationary teachers be tested for drugs as a condition of receiving tenure. This reasoning did not satisfy the three requirements listed above because the school district could not show that it had a reasonable suspicion that these teachers used drugs.

Because random alcohol and drug tests are increasingly considered to be searches under federal and state constitutions, public

Section 3. ALCOHOL AND DRUG ABUSE COVERAGE. For the purposes of the EAP, alcohol and drug abuse is defined as the continuing use of alcoholic substances or drugs that definitely and repeatedly interferes with health or job performance. The Company views alcoholism and drug abuse as significant problems for the addicted employee, his or her family and co-workers, and the work environment. However, the Company recognizes alcohol and drug abuse as treatable diseases and will offer assistance to any employee who voluntarily seeks it. An employee with an alcohol or drug abuse problem will receive the same care and consideration that is extended to employees suffering from any other disease.

Section 4. JOB PERFORMANCE. The Company recognizes job performance as the principal indicator of a need for EAP services. Employees whose deteriorating job performance does not respond to normal corrective action will be referred to the EAP by the supervisor if the supervisor believes that the employee's poor job performance is caused by a medical, emotional, or behavioral problem.

Section 5. SUPERVISOR PARTICIPATION. Supervisors should understand that they are not expected to be qualified to diagnose alcoholism, drug abuse, or other personal problems or to make judgments about the causes of any behavioral problem.

Section 6. EMPLOYEE RESPONSIBILITY. The employee has a responsibility to the employer to accept any EAP diagnosis and to comply with the prescribed treatment. An employee's refusal to accept diagnosis and treatment will be handled in the same way that similar refusals are handled for other illnesses if the result of the refusal is a continued deterioration of job performance.

Section 7. CONFIDENTIALITY. All records and activities generated by the EAP will be preserved in accordance with Company policies on privacy and confidentiality of sensitive records.

3. Procedures for referral of employees by managers, supervisors, and/or union representatives

4. Procedures for employees and their families to seek help directly

5. Coordination of the EAP with medical and disability benefit plans

6. Protection of confidentiality by:

   a. Coding records to prevent inadvertent identification of those who are enrolled

   b. Limiting access to records

   c. Keeping EAP records separate from employee personnel or medical records

C. EAP Policy

Employee Assistance Program

Section 1. PURPOSE. The Company has always been concerned with the health and well-being of its employees. Out of this concern, the Company has developed an Employee Assistance Program (EAP) to aid employees with medical, emotional, or behavioral problems. Some of these problems include alcohol and drug abuse, and marital, family, gambling, legal, financial, and psychological difficulties.

Section 2. GENERAL COVERAGE. Employee effectiveness can deteriorate for many reasons. Often it is personal or family problems that affect job performance. The Company's EAP is designed to help employees with these problems, including referral to appropriate professional services. Employees or their family members who are suffering from any type of personal problem are encouraged to voluntarily seek diagnostic counseling and treatment services available under the EAP.

employers must determine if there is sufficient reason for testing. The individual's privacy interests must be balanced against the public's interest in seeing that employee performance is not impaired. Random testing is not justified absent a reasonable suspicion of an employee alcohol or drug problem.[27]

Various federal and state fair employment practice statutes may effect drug testing in the workplace.[28] In some cases, testing may be disallowed if it has a disproportionate adverse effect on minorities or certain national origin groups.[29] Employers who administer drug tests may be subject to liability under various litigation theories, including invasion of privacy, defamation, and false imprisonment. Before conducting a search for drugs in the workplace, an employer should limit employees' privacy expectations by giving prior notice that searches can occur. If the employer creates a privacy expectation through a handbook or employment policy it may be required to follow that policy. Disclosing a drug test's results to those who do not need to know the information may impose liability.[30]

Statutory obligations may require public or private employers to provide rehabilitation programs to employees who abuse alcohol or drugs.[31] Moreover, courts have found that employers are obligated to offer rehabilitation to employees with alcohol or drug problems before termination can occur.[32] Statutes may also require employers to expunge records detailing work problems and disciplinary action related to alcohol and drug use upon an employee's retirement.[33] Under the Vocational Rehabilitation Act of 1973,[34] expungement may be required if these records are inaccurate;[35] acquired by fatally flawed procedures that do not protect employees' rights; or prejudicial without serving any governmental purpose.

B. Procedural Considerations

Employers contemplating the adoption of an alcohol and drug testing program must seriously consider its scope, purpose, and effect regarding these issues:

1. Necessity of drug testing

2. Employee group to be tested

3. Notification of all employees to be tested

4. Employees' consent to being tested, obtained at hiring or prior to testing

5. Restriction of alcohol or drug testing to situations where employees' on-the-job impairment is evident

6. Documentation by supervisors of employees' behavior that suggests alcohol or drug impairment

7. Documentation of the facts and circumstances that created a reasonable suspicion of substance use if testing is performed based on this suspicion

8. Interviews with employees about illnesses or prescription drugs that may adversely affect their job performance

9. Selection of a reputable laboratory to analyze employees' test samples

10. Employer's response to employees who have a positive test result or who refuse to take a test

11. Arrangements for a second test to confirm positive results

12. Protection of confidentiality of test results

13. Employees' authorization for employer to disclose test results under specified circumstances, obtained at hiring or prior to testing

14. Strengthening of current restrictions on the use or possession of alcohol or drugs on employer property

15. Union participation in establishing a testing program through bargaining over the changes in work rules or practices resulting from adopting a testing program under a collective bargaining agreement

1. Minimizing Liability

To minimize liability for violating the privacy rights of employees as a result of alcohol and drug testing, the employer should:

1. Obtain a signed consent form. Before an applicant or employee is tested for alcohol or drugs, he or she should sign a consent form. The consent form should solicit information regarding the individual's use of prescription or nonprescription medication to eliminate false positive test results. For example, therapeutic cold medicines such as Contac and Sudafed can create a false positive result indicating amphetamine use. By showing the employee's willingness to be tested, the consent form may help protect the employer against claims for invasion of privacy, defamation, false imprisonment, and assault and battery.

2. Perform a follow-up test. An initial screening test indicating a positive result for an individual should be verified by a confirmation test given to all applicants or employees. Employers may wish to perform confirmation tests for applicants where:

   a. there are few applicants and therefore additional test costs will be minimized;

   b. the initial test is positive regarding an otherwise highly qualified applicant; and

   c. the applicant desires confirmation in contesting an adverse employment decision.

3. Safeguard the specimen. The individual should witness his or her name being marked on the specimen. A documented chain of custody must be maintained to ensure that the specimen is attributed to the correct individual.

4. Restrict test disclosure. Test results should not be publicized, even if the tests are considered accurate and there is no risk of publication of a false fact.

5. Use split samples. Initially, the laboratory should split the specimen into two samples. Every sample should be preserved for a reasonable time period (for example, 60 to 90 calendar days). During this period, the applicant or employee who provided the sample should be permitted to have the sample evaluated independently at his or her expense. An employee who has the opportunity to confirm the test results independently may be less likely to challenge those results. If an applicant is not permitted to independently confirm his or her test results because he was not given the information, a separate sample should be retained in case the applicant challenges an adverse employment decision.

C. Alcohol and Drug Use Policies

In introducing an alcohol and drug policy to employees, the employer should use a letter to stress the importance of the policy and to summarize its main points.

Letter of Introduction of Policy

Dear *(Employee's Name)*:

We are all aware that alcohol and drug use are major problems throughout our society. As you know, the Company has made a commitment for a work environment free from alcohol and drug substances. The Company's primary objectives are the health and safety of all employees, the fulfillment of obligations to customers and the public, the protection of private and public property, and the preservation of the confidence placed in the Company by the community.

The Company has carefully considered how best to fulfill these responsibilities. As a result, the Company has prepared an Alcohol and Drug Use Policy. The Company's purpose is to discourage alcohol and drug use so all employees can benefit from a healthy and safe workplace. Here are some highlights of the Alcohol and

Drug Use Policy that will become effective on *(Date)*:

1. *Voluntary assistance*. Employees who voluntarily seek assistance on a timely basis through the Employee Assistance Program (EAP) or the Company's Medical Department for any problem, including alcohol or drug use, may do so without jeopardizing employment status, provided that prescribed treatment is followed and work performance is acceptable. In some cases temporary reassignment may be necessary.

2. *Alcoholic beverages*. Employees will not consume alcoholic beverages during regular or overtime working hours, during paid or unpaid meal periods when the employee will be returning to work following the meal period, or during work hours when the employee is representing the Company away from Company facilities. Also, employees will not report to work under the influence of alcoholic beverages or possess alcoholic beverages on Company property.

3. *Other substances which alter mental or physical capacity*. Use, possession, sale, or purchase of other substances that may alter mental or physical capacity while on the job or on Company property is prohibited. Employees will not report to work under the influence of these substances.

4. *Searches*. To help ensure a work environment free of alcohol and drugs, the Company may search employees work areas and employees' personal effects located on Company property.

5. *Physical/clinical tests*. Employees may be physically examined and/or clinically tested:

    a. if there are reasonable grounds for believing an employee is either under the influence of or is improperly using alcohol or drugs in violation of the policy;

    b. as part of Company-required physical examinations;

   c. as a follow-up to a rehabilitation program; or

   d. on a random, announced basis when deemed necessary
     for health and safety reasons.

6. *Prescribed treatment.* Employees undergoing prescribed medical treatment with a substance that may alter physical or
mental capacity must report this to the Medical Department.

7. *Reporting violations.* Employees who observe or have knowledge of a violation of the Alcohol and Drug Use Policy by
employee or other in the workplace are obligated to
promptly report the violation to their immediate supervisor
and/or the Human Resources Department. Any supervisor
who receives a report or who observes a violation must
report the information to the responsible supervisor and/
or the Human Resources Department.

8. *Imminent Threat to Safety.* In any instance where there exists
an imminent threat to the safety of persons or property as
a result of an employee's apparent unfitness for duty, the
observing employee will immediately contact his or her supervisor and the Human Resources Department.

9. *Disciplinary action.* Unlawful involvement with alcohol and
drugs on or off the job is a serious breach of conduct. Violations of the Alcohol and Drug Use Policy will result in disciplinary action up to and including termination.

10. *Law enforcement notification.* Appropriate law enforcement
agencies will be notified if criminal violations are involved
or suspected.

11. *Applicability.* The Alcohol and Drug Use Policy applies to all
Company employees regardless of position or work location.

Each of us has a responsibility for diligent, professional performance and conduct that reflects the trust of the public and our
fellow employees. To protect this trust, please cooperate with the

Company in implementing this policy and help us provide a healthy and safe workplace.

Alcoholism and drug use are important topics, and I am sure each of us can understand the need to strictly adhere to the requirements outlined herein. If you have any questions concerning this matter, please contact your supervisor promptly.

Thank you for your continued cooperation.

Very truly yours,

_____

President

Alcohol and Drug Use: Basic Policy

Alcoholic beverages are not permitted on the Company's premises, at Company-sponsored functions, or in Company-owned vehicles. Illegal controlled substances are not permitted on the Company's premises, at Company-sponsored functions, or in Company-owned vehicles. This policy applies to any prescription drugs that may have an adverse impact on an employee's ability to work safely while using these drugs. It is the employee's responsibility to obtain the permission of his or her physician to work while using the prescription medicine and to inform the Company of this so it can properly evaluate the situation.

Alcohol and Drug Use: Comprehensive Policy

Section 1. PURPOSE. The Company is committed to protecting the health and safety of the public and its employees. This policy supports that commitment by maintaining an alcohol- and drug-free workplace.

Section 2. APPLICABILITY. This policy has Company-wide applicability.

Section 3. DEFINITIONS.

a. *Alcohol.* Any beverage that may be consumed and that has an alcohol content.

b. *Disciplinary Action.* Action taken against an employee whom the Company has found in violation of Company policies.

c. *Drug.* Any physical or mind altering substance or any "controlled substance" or "controlled dangerous substance." These include but are not limited to any nonprescribed drug, narcotic, heroin, cocaine, or marijuana or a prescribed drug which is abused or not used as directed by a physician.

d. *Employee.* All employees regardless of position or work location.

e. *Responsible Supervisor.* The supervisor to whom the employee directly reports.

Section 4. REQUIREMENTS. Employees will not consume alcoholic beverages during regular or overtime working hours, during paid or unpaid meal periods if returning to work following the meal period, or during working hours when representing the Company away from Company facilities. Additionally, employees will not report to work under the influence of alcoholic beverages or possess alcoholic beverages on Company property.

The use, possession, sale, or purchase of other substances which may alter mental or physical capacity while on the job or on Company property is prohibited. Employees will not report to work under the influence of these substances. For a list of these substances, see Section 3c of this Policy.

The unlawful involvement with alcohol or drugs on or off the job is a serious breach of conduct. Each employee has an obligation to advise the Company of any known violations of this policy. Failure to report known violations will result in disciplinary action up to and including termination.

To protect the intent of this Policy to maintain a safe work environment free of alcohol and drugs, the Company applies this Policy to all contractors, business invitees, visitors, and guests to Company property.

Section 5. DRUG AND ALCOHOL TESTING.   To help ensure an alcohol-and drug-free workplace, the Company may search employees' work areas and employees' personal effects located on Company property. The Company also may require physical examinations and/or clinical tests of employees for the presence of alcohol or drugs during working hours:

    a. if there are reasonable grounds for believing an employee is either under the influence of alcohol or drugs;

    b. as part of any Company-required medical examination;

    c. as a follow-up to a rehabilitation program; and

    d. on a random basis where health and safety requirements so necessitate.

If the alcohol or drug test reveals positive results, the employee will be suspended pending joint evaluation by the affected supervisor, Human Resources Department, and Medical Department. Employees whose physical examinations and/or test results are positive are subject to disciplinary action up to and including termination. If the test results are negative, the matter will be closed.

All Company employees and all applicants whose assignment will make them employees will be physically examined and/or chemically tested for the presence of alcohol and drugs. The hiring process will be terminated for all applicants whose examinations and/or test results are positive. Employees who test positive will be terminated unless they seek voluntary assistance.

Section 6. VOLUNTARY ASSISTANCE.   Employees who voluntarily seek assistance on a timely basis through the Employee Assistance Program or the Company's Medical Department for an alcohol- or drug-related problem, prior to the Company identifying the problem, may do so without jeopardizing their employment status provided that prescribed treatment is followed and work performance is acceptable. In some cases temporary reassignment may be necessary.

Section 7. PRESCRIBED TREATMENT. Employees who are undergoing prescribed medical treatment with a substance that may alter physical or mental capacity must report this to the Medical Department.

Section 8. REPORTING VIOLATIONS. Any supervisor who observes a violation or receives a violation report must, as soon as practicable, report the information to the Human Resources Department.

Employees who observe or have knowledge of a violation by an employee or another in the workplace have an obligation to promptly report this to their supervisor and/or the Human Resources Department.

Section 9. IMMINENT THREAT TO SAFETY. In any instance where employees feel there exists an imminent threat to safety of persons or property, they must immediately contact the responsible supervisor and/or the Human Resources Department.

Section 10. RESPONSIBLE SUPERVISOR ACTION. Supervisors must ensure that all employees are familiar with and comply with this policy. They must notify the Human Resources Department of any known or suspected violation. When a responsible supervisor observes or receives a report of a possible violation, he or she will:

    a. confirm that the Human Resources Department has been advised;

    b. follow further directions of the Human Resources Department, which may include conducting an initial evaluation;

    c. report to the Human Resources Department the results of any initial evaluation he or she is asked to conduct. If no apparent violation has occurred, the matter will be closed;

    d. determine in conjunction with the Human Resources Department whether it is advisable or necessary to suspend an employee with or without pay or to reassign him or her pending completion of the investigation; and

e. recommend any proposed disciplinary action and ensure that the recommendation is reviewed, approved, and implemented by the Human Resources Department.

When a supervisor observes or receives a report of a possible violation by an outside party, including contractors, business invitees, visitors or guests, he or she will:

a. advise the individual's responsible supervisor if that individual is a contractor. If the individual is a business invitee, visitor, or guest, the supervisor will advise the sponsor of the individual's access to the facility;

b. advise the Human Resources Department; and

c. provide further assistance or cooperation as may be requested.

Section 11. HUMAN RESOURCES. It is the responsibility of the Human Resources Department to:

a. ensure that appropriate procedures and policies are communicated to all employees;

b. review recommended disciplinary actions and ensure the actions are in accordance and consistent with Company procedure;

c. ensure that appropriate Divisions/Departments are notified of and participate in the recommendations resulting from investigations; and

d. assemble a complete, comprehensive, and coherent file on incidents in which personnel action is taken.

Section 12. OTHER RESPONSIBILITIES. The following are other responsibilities for administration of this policy and are not intended to supersede other requirements.

a. All employees shall:

1. become informed of and comply with the policy;

2. cooperate with investigations;

3. report any known policy violation; and

4. respond immediately to any threat to the safety of person or property caused by another individual's impairment.

b. Department managers shall:

1. ensure that all subordinates are conversant with and comply with the policy and

2. review investigative reports and disciplinary action recommendations.

c. Human Resources Department shall:

1. communicate policy to all employees, including new hires;

2. arrange for alcohol and drug testing; and

3. review investigative reports and recommend disciplinary action.

d. Medical Department shall:

1. supervise physical examinations and testing for presence of alcohol or drugs and

2. apprise the Human Resources Department and the responsible supervisor of the results of any examinations or tests.

Applicant/Employee Consent Form 1

I, (Name), understand that the physical examination I am about to receive includes:

( ) A blood test to detect the presence of alcohol or drugs in my system

( ) A urine test to detect the presence of alcohol or drugs in my system

I understand that if I decline to sign this consent and decline to take the test, the physical examination will not be completed. The Human Resources Department will be notified and my application for employment will be rejected or my employment will be terminated. I understand that the test results and other medical information will be released only to authorized Company personnel. I have ingested the following specified drugs or alcoholic beverages within the last 96 hours:

( ) Sleeping pills _____

( ) Diet pills _____

( ) Pain relief pills _____

( ) Cold tablets _____

( ) Anti-malarial drugs _____

( ) Prescription drugs _____

( ) Any other medication or substance _____

( ) Alcoholic beverages _____

I hereby ( ) consent
          ( ) refuse to consent

to the physical examination including the test(s) to detect the presence of alcohol or drugs in my system.

Date_____ Signature _____

Date_____ Witness _____

Applicant/Employee Consent Form 2

I hereby voluntarily consent to the collection of urine and blood specimens from me for testing by the Company for alcohol, drugs, and controlled substances. Furthermore, I give my consent for the release of the test results to the Human Resources Department. I understand that any positive result may preclude my employment.

_____   _____

Date   Signature

Agreement for Employee Reinstatement
Following Alcohol or Drug Use

It is hereby agreed as follows:

1. *(Employee's Name)* recognizes that the Company will conditionally reinstate *(him or her)* after successful completion of a rehabilitation program at *(Name and Location of Rehabilitation Program)*, provided the following conditions are met:

*(List conditions)*_____

_____

_____

2. If within the next *(Time Period)*, *(Employee's Name)* is unable to perform job duties due to alcohol or drug use, discontinues an alcohol or drug rehabilitation program, or fails to meet the conditions set forth above, discipline up to and including termination may result.

(Employee's Name) agrees to cooperate in any additional alcohol or drug testing that the Company in its discretion deems appropriate during the *(Time Period)* immediately following reinstatement. If there is a failure to cooperate, discipline up to and including termination may result.

Date _____

(Employee) _____

(Union Representative) _____

(Employer) _____

VI. Acquired Immunodeficiency Syndrome (AIDS)

A. AIDS Privacy Principles

Acquired Immunodeficiency Syndrome (AIDS) is a disease that affects the body's immune system and renders it vulnerable to infections and viruses. This disease quickly has become a significant workplace privacy issue and has raised questions regarding AIDS testing, confidentiality of diagnosis, and the hiring and termination of infected individuals.

Constitutional protections of employees' privacy interests regarding alcohol and drug testing are applicable to AIDS testing as well. Mandatory AIDS testing is illegal because it infringes on employees' privacy interests by requiring employees to provide personal information that is unrelated to the job.[36] Significant psychological trauma might accompany an erroneous diagnosis resulting from a test. The employee's most intimate personal relationships could be affected by a positive test. A positive reading might be construed falsely to perceive an employee as a homosexual or a drug user.[37]

Testing for AIDS may be permissible if it is only one of many medical tests and procedures an employer uses to determine whether an applicant or employee can perform job-related duties.[38] Safety-sensitive positions may also permit AIDS testing. For example, a hospital has the right to require HIV testing to fulfill its obligations to employees, patients, and the public concerning infection control, health, and safety.[39] If the employer determines AIDS testing is necessary, the reason for the test must be related to job duties. The employer must also take steps to safeguard the privacy of those tested.

Federal and state fair employment practice statutes[40] may recognize AIDS as a protected disability. While these statutes differ in some aspects, their underlying intent is similar. Employees capable of working without endangering themselves or others should be allowed to do so regardless of a physical or medical condition which is or is perceived to be disabling.[41]

B. Preliminary Issues

Much of the general public is not yet fully educated regarding the causes of AIDS, how it is transmitted, and the effects on its victims. Because of this, the presence of AIDS in the workplace must be approached with sensitivity and tolerance on the part of employers. Before implementing an AIDS policy, employers should consider the following preliminary issues:

1. Develop a Plan for dealing with AIDS before being faced with an infected employee.

2. Do not feel compelled to announce an AIDS policy absent genuine workplace concerns because:

   a. premature adoption of an AIDS policy may lead employees to believe that the employer knows of an AIDS risk at the workplace and may cause unnecessary concern;

b. it is difficult for the employer to commit to any particular course of action without knowing the circumstances of how the AIDS issue will arise; and

c. the best policy is a case-by-case approach unless some special risk of transmission exists, for example, the possibility of needle-stick injuries.

3. Designate a small group of senior managers to deal with the AIDS issue. The group should include people knowledgeable about the medical, human resources, and legal issues of AIDS.

4. Educate employees on AIDS as a first step in any policy. Advise employees that the consensus of medical evidence shows no risk of AIDS being contracted in a normal work environment.

5. Realize that, given current technology, screening applicants or employees for AIDS may not be effective because the most common blood serum AIDS antibody tests provide almost no useful, job-related information and in some states this testing is unlawful.[42]

6. Determine if any federal, state, or local regulations would prohibit employees with infectious diseases from working in or near certain areas.

7. Require all employees who are diagnosed with AIDS or any other infectious or communicable disease to provide:

a. a physician's certificate outlining any specific restrictions under which the employee should work and

b. a statement explaining if the employee's exposure to common viruses carried by other workers might pose an imminent and substantial risk to his or her health.

8. Make efforts to reasonably accommodate the AIDS-infected employee if the physician requires that work or exposure to others be restricted. Accommodation can be made through:

   a. a redefinition of the employee's job;

   b. transfer to a position in a less threatening environment; and/or

   c. consultation with the physician attending a pregnant, AIDS-infected employee.

9. Permit the employee with AIDS to continue working in his or her job if the physician imposes no restrictions and there are no other health or safety restrictions imposed by law.

10. Utilize one of several options when faced with an employee who refuses to work with an AIDS-afflicted co-worker:

    a. counsel the employee;

    b. discipline the employee in accordance with progressive discipline procedures;

    c. inform the employee of employer policies regarding insubordination and harassment of employees who are members of a protected class; or

    d. seek the conciliation and remedial powers of a fair employment practice agency to resolve the situation.

11. Treat AIDS victims, whether they continue to work or are no longer able to work, in the same manner as employees with long-term, debilitating diseases.

12. Respect the privacy rights and statutory rights to confidentiality of medical information of AIDS-infected employees. Disclosure to anyone other than those individuals with a need to know that an employee has AIDS can lead to:

    a. costly litigation and/or

    b. increased anxiety among co-employees.

C. AIDS Policy

AIDS Policy

Section 1. PURPOSE. The Company will deal with acquired immunodeficiency syndrome (AIDS) in a humanitarian and non-discriminatory manner while assuring the safety and health of all employees. The Company will educate all employees in the facts of this disease.

Section 2. NONDISCRIMINATION. The Company is committed to a responsible policy of nondiscrimination regarding AIDS. An employee infected with AIDS will be accorded the same treatment as an employee suffering from a long-term disability.

Section 3. CONFIDENTIALITY. The Company will respect all employees infected with AIDS by maintaining the confidentiality of this information.

Section 4. EMPLOYMENT. The Company will hire or continue to employ individuals who have AIDS or are suspected of having AIDS as long as these persons remain qualified to perform their jobs. (The physical demands of certain positions may necessitate deviations from this policy.) The Company will employ AIDS-infected individuals and at the same time preserve the safety and morale of all employees. According to the best medical evidence available to date, casual contact in the workplace with employees who have AIDS or who have been exposed to the AIDS virus will not result in the transmission of AIDS.

Section 5. POLICY UPDATES. The Company will remain informed of the latest medical knowledge pertaining to this disease. Should it subsequently appear that the presence of AIDS may present a danger to employees, the Company will make appropriate policy revisions.

Endnotes

1   *See* Conveyor Co., 38 Lab. Arb. (BNA) 1141 (1962) (Roberts, Arb.) (employer's good-faith right to require physical examination).

2   *See, e.g.,* Pittsburgh Plate Glass Co., 52 Lab. Arb. (BNA) 985 (1969) (Duff, Arb.) (employer has a right to require physical examination after an employee returns from sick leave).

3   *See, e.g.,* Chris-Craft Corp., 27 Lab. Arb. (BNA) 404 (1956) (Bothwell, Arb.) (employer could require physical examination of employees who were recalled).

4   Conchemco, Inc., 55 Lab. Arb. (BNA) 54, 97 (1970) (Ray, Arb.).

5   *See* Appendix A sections III.F and IV.H for a list of other federal and state fair employment practice statutes.

6   *See, e.g.,* Lapham v. Commonwealth Unemployment Compensation Bd., 103 Pa. Commw. 144, 519 A.2d 1101 (1987) (employer's failure to curtail workplace smoking constituted compelling and necessitous reason for employee to leave employment and entitled him to unemployment compensation).

7   *See, e.g.,* Schober v. Mountain Bell Tel., 96 N.M. 376, 630 P.2d 1231 (1980).

8   *See, e.g.,* Fuentes v. Workmen's Compensation Appeals Bd., 16 Cal. 3d 1, 547 P.2d 449, 128 Cal. Rptr. 673 (1976).

9   *See, e.g.,* H-N Advertising & Display Co., 88 Lab. Arb. (BNA) 329 (1986) (Heekin, Arb.) (employer's failure to convene joint safety committee to review plant conditions and make recommendations regarding employer's smoking policy violated collective bargaining agreement).

10   Town of Rocky Hill & AFSCME, Local 1303-112, Council No. 4, Pub. Bargaining Cas. (CCH) ¶ 44,547 (Conn. St. Bd. of Lab. Rel. 1986) (service policy on computer conditioned on smoke-free environment).

11   *See* Appendix A sections III.F and IV.H for a list of federal and state fair employment practice statutes.

12   *See* Appendix A sections III.F and IV.H for federal and state fair employment practice statutes.

13   29 U.S.C. §§ 701-796 (1988).

14   Vickers v. Veterans Admin., 549 F. Supp. 85 (W.D. Wash. 1982).

15 *See, e.g.,* Grusendorf v. City of Okla., 816 F.2d 539 (10th Cir. 1987) (public employer did not infringe on a firefighter trainee's constitutional rights by terminating him for smoking a cigarette in violation of rule barring trainees from smoking); Kensell v. Oklahoma, 716 F.2d 1350 (10th Cir. 1983) (Constitution does not empower federal judiciary to impose no-smoking rules in workplace); *see also* Gasper v. Louisiana Stadium & Exposition Distribution. 418 F. Supp. 716 (E.D. La. 1976), *aff'd,* 577 F.2d 897 (5th Cir. 1989), *review denied,* 439 U.S. 1073 (1979) (right to breathe air free of tobacco smoke is not a fundamental right protected by the Constitution).

16 *See* Schober v. Mountain Bell Tel., 96 N.M. 376, 630 P.2d 1231 (1980); Fuentes v. Workmen's Compensation Appeals Bd., 16 Cal. 3d 1, 547 P.2d 449, 128 Cal. Rptr. 673 (1976).

17 *See also* Rossie v. State of Wis., 133 Wis. 2d 341, 395 N.W.2d 801 (1986).

18 Smith v. Western Elec., 643 S.W.2d 10 (Mo. Ct. App. 1982). It was stated that:

> [T]he tobacco smoke of co-workers smoking in the work area is hazardous to the health of employees in general and plaintiff in particular. The allegations also show that defendant (employer) knows the tobacco smoke is harmful to the plaintiff's health and that defendant has the authority, ability, and reasonable means to control smoking in areas requiring a smoke-free environment. Thereby, by failing to exercise its control and assume its responsibility to eliminate the hazardous condition caused by tobacco smoke, defendant has breached and is breaching its duty to provide a reasonably safe workplace....

Id. at 13.
     See also Carroll v. Tennessee Valley Auth., 697 F. Supp. 508 (D.D.C. 1988) (employee claiming injury from passive smoke entitled to sue employer for intentional infliction of emotional distress).

19 *See* Appendix A section IV.W.

20 *See, e.g.,* Brotherhood of Maintenance v. Burlington N., 802 F.2d 1016 (8th Cir. 1986) (stressing the importance of EAP confidentiality).

21 Employee Assistance Professional Association, Code of Ethics (1992).

22 *See, e.g.,* 42 U.S.C. §§ 290dd-3, 290ee-3 (1988) (confidentiality of alcohol and drug patient records); Mass. Gen. Laws Ann. ch. 119, § 41A (West 1982) (reporting of child abuse).

23 *See* Davis v. Monsanto Co., 627 F. Supp. 418 (S.D. W. Va. 1986) (communication to employer by an EAP provider of employee's suicidal

feelings and homicidal feelings toward his wife and others were privileged because employer had statutory duty to maintain safe workplace); *see also* Tarasoff v. Regents of Univ. of Cal., 17 Cal. 3d 425, 551 P.2d 334, 131 Cal. Rptr. 14 (1976) (when therapist determines or, pursuant to professional standards of care should have determined that patient presents serious danger of violence to another, therapist incurs obligation to use reasonable care to protect intended victim against this danger; this may require therapist to take certain action, including warning intended victim or others likely to apprise victim of danger).

24   U.S. Const. amend. IV.

25   *See, e.g.,* Cal. Const. art. 1.

26   Patchogue-Medford Congress of Teachers v. Board of Educ., 70 N.Y.2d 57, 510 N.E.2d 325, 517 N.Y.S.2d 456 (1987).

27   *See* Copeland v. Philadelphia Police Dep't, 840 F.2d 1139 (3d Cir. 1988), *cert. denied*, 490 U.S. 1004 (1989) (random testing of police officers permitted where reasonable suspicion of alcohol or drug problem is present); Transport Workers Local 24 v. SEPTA, 884 F.2d 709 (3d Cir. 1989) (random testing of employees holding safety-sensitive positions within public transportation authority permitted, since drug use by operating employees involved in accidents causing injury presents a significant safety hazard to the public).

28   *See* Appendix A sections III.F and IV.H for a list of federal and state fair employment practices statutes.

29   *See* Chanet v. Southern Ry., 847 F.2d 718 (11th Cir. 1988) (requirement to validate drug test, which employer used to confirm its belief that a terminated employee had used marijuana while on duty, regarding substantial adverse impact on blacks).

30   *See, e.g.,* Bratt v. International Business Machs. Corp., 785 F.2d 352 (1st Cir. 1986) (employer liable for invasion of privacy for disclosing private medical information about an employee). *But see* Ellenwood v. Exxon Shipping Co., 6 I.E.R. Cas. (BNA) 1628 (D. Me. 1991) (employer did not invade privacy of employee who alleged that his employer told co-workers that employee had undergone treatment for alcoholism; publicity argument requires wide public disclosure of private facts, and employee could show that employer informed only small group of individuals).

31   *See, e.g.,* Cal. Lab. Code §§ 1025-1028 (West Supp. 1992) (California statute requiring employer-sponsored alcohol and drug rehabilitation programs); *see also* Kelley v. Schlumberger Technology Corp., 849 F.2d 41

(1st Cir. 1988) (employer negligently inflicted emotional distress on an employee terminated for failing a drug test that involved direct observation of the urination act); Sharpless Coal Corp., 91 Lab. Arb. (BNA) 1065 (1988) (Stoltenberg, Arb.) (alcohol and drug control program was unreasonable by permitting observation of urination for testing purposes).

32   *See* McElrath v. Kemp, 714 F. Supp. 23 (D.D.C. 1989) (requiring employer to allow an alcoholic employee the option of taking leave without pay to participate in a rehabilitation program); Fergenson v. United States Dep't of Commerce, 680 F. Supp. 1514 (M.D. Fla. 1988) (employer should have known employee was an alcoholic through chronic, excessive absenteeism, and was required to provide disabled employee with rehabilitative assistance prior to initiating disciplinary proceedings).

33   *See* Callicotte v. Carlucci, 731 F. Supp. 1119 (D.D.C. 1990).

34   29 U.S.C. § 794a (1988).

35   *See* Chastain v. Kelley, 510 F.2d 1232, 1236 (D.C. Cir. 1975) (court has a right to order expungement of inaccurate records).

36   *See, e.g.,* Glover v. Eastern Neb. Community Office of Retardation, 686 F. Supp. 243 (D. Neb. 1988), *aff'd,* 867 F.2d 461 (8th Cir.), *cert. denied,* 493 U.S. 932 (1989) (mandatory AIDS testing at a facility for mentally retarded patients is a constitutionally impermissible search and seizure).

37   *See, e.g.,* Little v. Bryce, 733 S.W.2d 937 (Tex. Ct. App. 1987) (employer's hasty termination of employee falsely believed to have AIDS constituted defamation).

38   *See* Anonymous Fireman v. City of Willoughby, 770 F. Supp. 402 (N.D. Ohio 1991) (mandatory AIDS testing as part of annual physical examination of firefighter and paramedic is reasonable search under Fourth Amendment. Even though city had no reason to suspect that employee has AIDS, when employee had high risk of contracting or transmitting AIDS and universal precautions and voluntary testing would not prevent spread of AIDS, testing is necessary to protect other employees and public from risk of exposure and to provide safe workplace); Local 1812, AFGE v. Department of State, 662 F. Supp. 50 (D.D.C. 1987) (AIDS testing not enjoined for State Department Foreign Service employees who are stationed worldwide); *but see* Glover v. Eastern Neb. Community Office of Retardation, 686 F. Supp. 243 (D. Neb. 1988), *aff'd,* 867 F.2d 461 (8th Cir.), *cert. denied,* 493 U.S. 932 (1989) (mandatory AIDS testing at a facility for mentally retarded patients is a constitutionally impermissible search and seizure).

39   *See* Leckelt v. Board of Comm'rs, 909 F.2d 820 (5th Cir. 1990) (hospital properly terminated licensed practical nurse for insubordination after he refused to disclose his HIV status in response to an inquiry prompted by employee's high risk potential).

40   *See* Appendix A sections III.F and IV.H for federal and state fair employment practice statutes.

41   Cain v. Hyatt, 734 F. Supp. 671 (E.D. Pa. 1990) (AIDS is protected disability and, therefore, termination of an attorney merely because he had a heightened risk of future job disability as a result of the disease is prohibited); Raytheon Co. v. Fair Employment & Hous. Comm'n, 212 Cal. App. 3d 1242, 261 Cal. Rptr. 197 (1989) (AIDS is physical disability for which employee cannot be excluded from the workplace, even though morale of other employees may be injured); M.A.E. v. Doe & Roe, 388 Pa. Super. 589, 566 A.2d 285 (1989) (AIDS is a disability unrelated to the job under Pennsylvania Human Relations Act); Benjamin R. v. Orkin Exterminating Co., 390 S.E.2d 814 (W. Va. 1990) (AIDS is classified as a disability in West Virginia Human Rights Act). *But see* Burgess v. Your House, 326 N.C. 205, 388 S.E.2d 134 (1990) (employee who tested positive for HIV infection but otherwise showed no AIDS symptoms was not disabled because disease did not limit any major life activities at this time).

42   *See* Appendix A section IV.A.

Workplace Information Collection and Distribution

I. Introduction

The employer continues to collect and distribute employment information after an applicant is hired. Generally, this involves updating, maintaining, and using information that already has been obtained, or procuring new information to satisfy business or operational requirements. For example, collection of new information may be required for performance evaluations, promotions, and disciplinary actions.

At times employers may use surreptitious methods, both legal and illegal, to collect workplace information. In addition, employees, outside third parties, and unions may seek to solicit or distribute information at the workplace. Depending on the employer, various restrictions may be placed on these activities. This chapter reviews procedures for the collection and distribution of information in the workplace regarding searches, monitoring, and surveillance. This chapter also examines procedures for literature solicitation and distribution.

II. Searches

A. Search Privacy Principles

Employer security problems have broadened from concerns over property and information theft to methods of safeguarding the workplace from alcohol and drug use. Searches can create significant workplace privacy problems for employers by uncovering information that employees have not voluntarily revealed and that may not be job-related. Employees who are wrongfully stopped and searched may assert several claims against employers, including invasion of privacy,[1] defamation, false imprisonment, false arrest, malicious prosecution, intentional infliction of emotional distress, constitutional right infringement, and violations of federal and state fair employment practice statutes.[2]

False imprisonment arises when an employer detains employees, however briefly, to search their bags, cases, purses, or persons through a total restraint on the freedom to move that is against the employees' will.[3] Generally, employees must be aware of the restraint and the restraint must be perceived as total—merely stopping an employee is not a total restraint. The restraint, however, need not be lengthy or physically confining. An employee, for example, need not be locked in a room to be considered restrained. Advising an employee not to leave a certain area of the workplace may be a sufficient restraint.[4] However, if an employee remains free to leave despite being asked questions or being accompanied to or from work during an investigation, false imprisonment has not occurred.[5]

Employer liability can be incurred through a false arrest for theft brought about by direct employer action where insufficient evidence is present.[6] Generally, not until the employer causes an arrest does it incur potential false-arrest liability.

The employer does not initiate a false arrest by providing truthful information to law enforcement authorities and allowing them to make a determination.[7] However, if the employer gives information to the police and, knowing it to be untrue insists on arrest anyway, it may be liable for causing false arrest.[8] An employer can defend itself against claims of initiating false arrest or imprisonment if it can show probable cause for the arrest or detention.[9] "Probable cause" means having more evidence for the arrest than against it. The employer must have a good-faith, reasonable belief in the validity of the arrest and detention. A signed, uncoerced statement by the employee admitting responsibility may protect an employer from liability.[10]

To establish the tort of malicious prosecution, an employee generally must show that the employer made a false accusation, with knowledge of its falseness or with a reckless disregard for its truth, that caused arrest, confinement, or other damages to him or her. This may arise in search situations when theft is alleged and the employer goes beyond disciplining the employee by causing a meritless criminal prosecution to be instituted.[11]

Defamation consists of libel or slander. Libel involves a written communication while slander relates to an oral communication. In the employment context, defamation requires the employee to show that the employer's accusation of a crime or some other act brought disrepute to him or her. The accusation must have been made falsely or with reckless disregard for its truth and communicated to others orally or in writing. An employer's liability for defamation may arise out of a workplace search if the employer wrongly accuses an employee of theft and communicates the accusation to others not entitled to this information.[12] Should the employer's search lead to an erroneous accusation causing the employee emotional upset with serious physical manifestations, a claim for intentional infliction of emotional distress may also be made.[13]

Searching employee property that is brought onto the employer's premises may infringe on employees' constitutionally protected privacy interests. Here the privacy interest of the employee must be balanced against the employer's interest in continued operations. The employer must determine if honoring the employee's privacy right will adversely impact legitimate employer interests in a healthy and productive workforce or the integrity of its premises. The employer's right to such a search depends on the employee's privacy expectation in the particular workplace setting and circumstances. For example, an employee may have a greater privacy right in personal effects brought into the workplace than in employer property that is given to the employee (such as a locker). This right also may depend on whether a private or public sector employee is involved and if a federal or state constitutional interest is present.[14]

The Fourth Amendment to the United States Constitution protects each citizen against unreasonable searches and seizures by government agents where the individual maintains a reasonable privacy expectation from governmental intrusion; for example, police must have a valid search warrant to examine an employee's locker. In some situations, the police may require the assistance of an employer in an investigation. Searches at the request of the police may deem a private sector employer as the agent of the police where federal constitutional protections would apply.[15] The employer must have a valid search warrant when it is acting in this capacity.[16] A warrantless search at the request of the police would violate the employee's Fourth Amendment rights, and evidence obtained through an improper search could be excluded from a criminal proceeding.[17] The employee could bring action for damages against the employer for a violation of the employee's constitutional rights. Waiver of Fourth Amendment rights could occur, however, by the employee consenting without coercion to the search.[18]

Formal notice should be provided to employees that lockers, desks, and vehicles may be searched by the employer without employee consent or awareness.[19] The employer is advised to state this policy in writing; an unwritten but established employer practice of searching lockers and trucks may not be adequate. For example, one employer had a 12-year record of inspecting lockers that included three or four inspections for cleanliness and at least one inspection for the purpose of finding an illegal weapon. Even though the history of inspection was longstanding, it was not sufficient to counter a public employee's reasonable expectation of privacy regarding his locker.[20]

Search of employees' purses, lunchboxes, and pockets should be undertaken only after the employer has provided clear notice of its intention. In addition to notification, the employer should obtain employee consent prior to conducting these searches. Violations of the privacy expectations in employees' personal items are a substantial intrusion into the employees' affairs. It is important that an employee's knowledge of a workplace policy and assent to a search be established prior to any disciplinary action to counter future claims by the employee that consent was coerced and, therefore, the search was invalid.

The search criteria developed by arbitrators under collective bargaining agreements may offer additional guidance in evaluating employees' privacy rights pertaining to searches in the workplace. According to these criteria, employers may impose reasonable rules regarding searches where the searches are made a condition of employment.

Although many searches are intended to discover evidence pertaining to specific employee misconduct, some inspections are preventive rather than accusatory. Often employers conduct regular examinations of employees as they enter and leave to prevent the theft of employer property or the introduction of contraband onto the employer's premises. Similarly, employers have the right to conduct reasonable searches of employees' persons and belongings as they enter or leave the workplace, particularly where there are *bona fide* reasons involving theft or workplace drinking.[21]

Generally, the security procedure must be clearly established, fairly administered, and understood by all employees. Where an arbitrator determines that an inspection rule has not been consistently applied or has been promulgated without sufficient notice to employees regarding their obligations, any disciplinary action may be modified.

As long as employees are informed of their obligations under search policies, an employer may prescribe compliance with the rules as a condition of employment. In one case, the arbitrator sustained an employee's termination for refusing a pocketbook search because the employer had in place a carefully defined policy which required employees to permit inspections of large purses brought onto the employer's premises.[22] In addition, certain employee privileges may be made contingent on the employer's right to conduct searches. For example, providing locker space to employees can be conditioned on the employer's right to inspect locker contents at any time.[23]

Policies requiring employees to submit themselves and their personal property to security examinations as an employment condition should be unambiguous and narrowly constructed to avoid unnecessary and unanticipated privacy intrusions.[24] Before conducting a search of an employee or his or her personal effects, an employer should always try to obtain permission.[25] Employers should exercise caution in examining an employee's belongings that are not situated in an employer container such as a locker. The employer should have probable cause to believe that a search will uncover relevant evidence of suspected misconduct.[26]

Arbitrators generally support discipline resulting from searches for drugs if the employer has a well established and clear work rule prohibiting drug use or possession at the workplace.[27] In one case, two civilian employees of the United States Air Force parked their cars on the military reservation where they worked. The employer determined that searches of the cars were necessary when security dogs trained to detect the presence of drugs alerted an accompanying security officer. The searches were conducted either with employee consent or under a search warrant, and marijuana and drug related paraphernalia were seized from the employees' cars. Both employees received written reprimands that were sustained.[28]

In another case, lockers used by guards stationed at a nuclear power plant were searched for marijuana. Although the guards as a group were not notified of the search, the union acknowledged the employer's right to search guards' lockers as part of the employer's efforts to maintain discipline and safety, and the search was found to be proper.[29]

Employers may conduct searches within their property for business-related purposes, even though the search may be intrusive, as long as clearly defined rules govern the procedures and the investigative activity does not violate workers' rights. Employer disciplinary action in response to employee misconduct will be sustained provided that it resulted from lawful, good-faith security techniques undertaken by an employer. When the circumstances surrounding a search suggest duress or deception of an employee, problems may arise over the enforceability of the search, and this creates potential employer liability.

B. Search Procedures

In developing procedures for searches in the workplace, the employer should consider the following guidelines:

1. Applications should provide that employees agree to employer searches.

2. The search procedure and policy should be communicated and explained to all employees.

3. Employees should not be selected for searches randomly, arbitrarily, capriciously, or discriminatorily.

1. Theft Investigations by Human Resources Staff

In investigating alleged workplace thefts, the human resources staff should:

1. Notify and consult with legal counsel immediately upon learning of theft allegations, and determine if legal counsel should participate in the investigation.

2. Evaluate the need for special expertise in theft situations involving:

   a. time mischarging, purchasing fraud, travel pay fraud, and other financial misconduct where an accountant may need to be involved or

    b. theft of computer services where a computer expert may be necessary.

3. Establish the essentials of the alleged theft regarding:

    a. who performed the alleged theft;

    b. against whom the act was perpetrated;

    c. other persons involved;

    d. nature of the improper act; and

    e. when the act occurred.

4. Determine whether to inform the suspected employee of the investigation and suspend him or her pending the outcome or to leave the employee at the workplace so the employer can obtain additional evidence of any wrongdoing.

5. Investigate by using established procedures.

    a. Examine all pertinent records and documents.

    b. Obtain signed statements from witnesses who may later take a position adverse to the employer.

    c. Interview all potential witnesses, including employees and outside parties.

        1. Avoid group interviews.

        2. Be impartial and avoid conveying a prosecutorial image.

        3. Take thorough, detailed, and exact notes by:

            a. using the language of the witnesses;

            b. including proper names, job titles, salary grades, and reporting relationships for all persons interviewed and mentioned; and

            c. reviewing notes with the person interviewed to fill gaps or make necessary corrections.

        4. Exhaust all pertinent lines of inquiry.[30]

C. Search Policy

Search Policy [31]

The Company reserves the right to question any person entering and leaving its property and to inspect any person, locker, vehicle, package, purse, handbag, briefcase, lunchbox, or other possession carried to and from its property. This policy encompasses all Company employees.

III. Monitoring

A. Monitoring Privacy Principles

Monitoring involves using mechanical or electronic devices in a surreptitious manner to obtain information on workplace activities. The most common devices used involve computer, telephone, and video technology. The extent of workplace monitoring is unknown because it is done without employee awareness. Monitoring potential exists anytime computers or telephones are used in the workplace. Federal and state statutes regulate certain workplace monitoring by the employer.[32] An employer may subject itself to workplace privacy claims when it knowingly uses monitoring devices to obtain non-job-related information that may reveal employees' speech, belief, and association interests. Invasion of privacy,[33] defamation,[34] or public policy[35] violations could be alleged.

Title III of the federal Omnibus Control and Safe Streets Act of 1968 (Title III)[36] prohibits all private individuals and organizations, including employers, from intercepting wire or oral communications of others. Similar prohibitions exist under state intercept statutes.[37] However, these prohibitions have been narrowed in the employment context by the federal statute's *extension phone exemption*. This permits employers to intercept certain employee telephone conversations, and obviously impacts workplace privacy rights.

The statute allows employers to monitor employee telephone conversations by listening on an extension of the employer's telephone system, if this is done as part of the employer's business. Courts have permitted monitoring of an employee based on the employer's suspicion that business matters with a competitor might be discussed.[38] Employees handling telephone transactions with the public may be monitored, and personal calls also may be intercepted. Title III does not prohibit photographic surveillance of employee performance.

Employers affect workplace privacy through use of various monitoring devices including:

1. Wiretaps

2. Beepers

3. Pen registers and touch tone decoders

4. Diodes

5. Voiceprint identification

6. Cordless telephones

7. Spotters

Wiretaps are federally governed by Title III.[39] Placement of wiretaps must be based on probable cause, which includes establishing that normal investigatory techniques have not been or will not be successful. Court authorization and approval by the United States or state Attorney General or Assistant Attorney General is required. Wiretaps can be authorized for a limited time period not to exceed thirty days and are restricted to certain crimes such as drug trafficking, counterfeiting, and bribery. States have similar prohibitions on wiretapping.[40]

The placement of wiretaps on an employer's premises probably would arise through the request of a law enforcement agency. When this occurs, "state action" requirements would be present and certain constitutional protections would apply to safeguard the employee's privacy rights.

Beepers are devices which transmit a traceable signal. They are generally placed in a vehicle or airplane to monitor its location. Law enforcement agencies sometimes use beepers as a surveillance aid. Beepers are not regulated by Title III because they cannot transmit speech and do not intercept oral communications. However, use of a beeper to locate an individual has been held to constitute a search under the Fourth Amendment requiring a prior court order of law enforcement authorities.[41]

Beepers could be used by employers to locate employees with their vehicles who are suspected of deviating from scheduled delivery routes or spending time at home and not on the employer's business. Depending on how they are used by an employer, beepers may create the potential for a constitutional violation as an illegal search.

Pen registers and touch tone decoders record outgoing telephone calls by electronically noting the number dialed and the date, time, and length of the call. They may be used to trace nontoll employee calls. Title III generally does not prevent use of touch tone decoders because, as with beepers, no interception of oral communication is involved. Title III does not regulate pen registers, but Fourth Amendment considerations require a court order by law enforcement authorities prior to their use.[42]

Diodes prevent disconnection of a call and are useful in tracing local telephone calls. Diodes are not prohibited by Title III because they do not record a conversation, but merely locate the source of a call.

Voiceprint identification involves analysis of recorded speech through a graphic representation of the voice to identify the speaker. It is prohibited by Title III only when obtained by improper means; for example, a wiretap. A similar method, voice spectrogram analysis, has reached the standard of scientific acceptance and reliability necessary for admissibility as evidence in a courtroom.[43]

Cordless telephones operate similarly to a radio. Conversations over cordless telephones frequently can be overheard by others over their telephones or AM or FM radio receivers. Whether these unintended interceptions violate Federal Communication Commission (FCC) regulations, Title III, or state statutes has not yet been determined. However, the eavesdropping prohibition contained in FCC regulations provides that no person, directly or indirectly, may use a radio frequency device for the purpose of overhearing or recording private conversations of others unless all parties of the conversation consent.[44]

Employers also are subject to state statutes that regulate the use of human agents—"spotters" posing as customers to monitor employees.[45] These statutes generally prohibit employee discipline or termination based on a spotter's report, unless the report is provided to the employee or the spotter is employed exclusively by that employer to conduct the entire investigation.

Through these and other methods an employer may monitor employee job performance or other activities. For example, employers who are concerned about employees' personal telephone calls may use certain electronic devices for verification. Use of any of these methods raises significant concerns over privacy rights similar to those created when these methods are used for law enforcement activities. Because of this, the same standards and protections for their use should apply in both situations, preventing their arbitrary or discriminatory use. For each use of a monitoring device, the employer should show a legitimate business need based directly on a concern regarding workplace health, safety, or preservation of production.

B. Preliminary Procedures

Before undertaking monitoring in the workplace, the employer should:

1. Review the applicability of any federal or state statutes regulating the proposed monitoring.

2. Ensure that the monitoring is job-related.

3. Clearly notify employees that job performance may be subject to monitoring.

4. Obtain the employee's written consent to performance monitoring as a condition of employment.

5. Disclose to employees what mechanical or electronic devices may be used for monitoring job performance.

6. Disclose to employees when, where, and how these mechanical or electronic devices may be used for monitoring job performance.[46]

C. Acceptable Uses

Workplace monitoring may be used to measure and document employee transactions involving:

1. planning and scheduling of personnel and equipment;

2. evaluation of employee performance and personnel decisions such as promotion, retraining, or termination;

3. increase in productivity by providing feedback on speed, work pacing, and other measurable skills;

4. provision of security for employer property, including intellectual property and personnel records;

5. investigation of incidents of misconduct, crime, or human error; and

6. increase of employer control through discouraging union-organizing activities or identifying dissidents.

D. Monitoring Policies

Work Performance Monitoring Policy

The Company may periodically monitor or review employee work performance through the use of mechanical or electronic devices. Among the mechanical or electronic devices that the Company may use are telephone monitoring, beepers, pen registers, touch tone decoders, and diodes. These may be used to limit personal calls at the workplace, to review driver routes, or to investigate workplace problems including but not limited to theft and use of illegal drugs.

Work Performance Monitoring: Employee Authorization

I understand that as a condition of employment the Company may periodically monitor or review my work performance by using mechanical or electronic devices. Among the devices that the Company may use are telephone monitoring, beepers, pen registers, touch tone decoders, and diodes. I expressly consent to this work performance monitoring.

_____   _____
Date   Employee Signature

IV. Surveillance

A. Surveillance Privacy Principles

Unlike monitoring, surveillance generally involves physical scrutiny of employees without their knowledge. Surveillance may be done through observation, extraction, or reproduction. Observational surveillance involves viewing the employee at the workplace, although the employee may be unaware of this monitoring. Surveillance by extraction generally involves collection of employee information through questionable testing; for example, a polygraph examination[47] or honesty testing.[48] Reproduction surveillance comprises the collection of employee information through photographic, recording, or similar devices.

Employers use surveillance for various reasons which may or may not be legal, depending on the circumstances and the scope of the surveillance. Employers may make many uses of surveillance including determining the extent of union organization activity,[49] surveilling the workplace for job performance evaluations,[50] manipulating employees to agree with the employer's position on certain matters affecting employment conditions,[51] photographing employees,[52] and electronically monitoring employees.[53]

B. Surveillance Methods

1. Union Meeting Surveillance

The right to engage in union activity is a workplace privacy right that is protected by federal and state labor relations statutes,[54] and involves preservation of individuals' rights to freely associate. Employers may violate employees' privacy rights through the illegal attendance or observation of union meetings by the employer or the employer's representative. The uninvited attendance of an employer's representative at a union meeting is generally unlawful because it interferes with employee rights under federal and state labor relations statutes. Under the National Labor Relations Act (NLRA),[55] an employer did not engage in unlawful surveillance when its supervisor openly attended a union meeting and left when asked.[56] However, a school board member's insistence on being present at union membership meetings in the school's auditorium, without union permission, was unlawful despite a law requiring public meetings to be open to the public.[57]

In another case, a supervisor's arrival at a union meeting prompted a union official to inform the membership that the supervisor could be asked to leave. When the membership said nothing, the union official invited the supervisor to stay because the meeting was not secret and he knew the supervisor would carry any desired information to the employer. Through this invitation, the surveillance was lawful.[58]

Illegal surveillance may occur if the employer's representative is near or in close proximity to a union's meeting place. A sheriff and a county correctional officer did not attend a union meeting;

however, they unlawfully surveilled union activities by remaining in a parked car outside a union meeting.[59] Driving a car slowly near a union's meeting place so that a supervisor could observe employees entering and leaving was found unlawful.[60] An employer sitting in a parked car near a union hall's entrance was found to have acted improperly because there was no legitimate purpose to his presence.[61]

However, if presence at a meeting place is accidental, no unlawful action has occurred. For example, a public university's representative did not unlawfully observe a union meeting by walking past the meeting room's open door because a legitimate reason existed for passing by the room—he was on his way to prepare another room for inspection by a university benefactor.[62] Likewise, a private sector supervisor's chance presence at a restaurant during a union meeting was lawful;[63] and a company president did not unlawfully view a union meeting by arriving at the union's parking-lot meeting while delivering rent for the parking lot to its owner.[64]

2. Workplace Surveillance

Mere observations of employees by an employer is not in itself a violation of employees' privacy rights. However, when an employer's surveillance becomes overzealous, it may become actionable. Employers sometimes avoid the NLRA proscription against surveilling union activities by observing employees at the workplace. One employer used a one-way mirror to watch a union card solicitor during working hours and followed the card solicitor around the workplace. These actions were not a violation of the NLRA because all employees were being similarly observed.[65]

Placing a supervisor's desk in a certain location may be a legitimate method to ensure that employees are working. One employer was permitted to move his desk next to two known union adherents to ensure the employees were working and not spending work time on union or other outside activities.[66] In a similar case, a plant superintendent's use of a desk in an employee work area while the superintendent was on crutches was lawful. This was not in response to union organizational activity but was the result of the supervisor's physical infirmity.[67] Furthermore, even though a known union activist had been watched, a supervisor's elevated office was also lawful because from the elevated office the supervisor could observe all employees during working hours.[68]

Instructing a supervisor to remain at the workplace near union meetings may be lawful if the action is a result of past theft, fire, or employee disciplinary problems.[69] However, possible employee sabotage cannot be used as a pretext for unlawful surveillance—there must be a legitimate suspicion of sabotage to justify it.[70]

Publicly observing union activities may not be unlawful. For example, no violation occurred where supervisors stood behind the employer's glass door entrances and watched the union distribute literature to employees leaving work because the union's literature dissemination was conducted in full public view.[71] Observing employees signing union authorization cards in the employer's parking lot in full public view also was lawful.[72] Even where a plant superintendent observed union card solicitation on a public road from the employer's parking lot, no violation occurred. The superintendent was in the parking lot on his way to work (a lawful purpose) and did not take notes or hide his presence.[73]

Workplace surveillance has been attempted by retaining certain information in employee personnel files. Retention of material in an employee's file naming the employee as a union officer was unlawful.[74] Designating on an employee performance evaluation whether or not the employee elected dues checkoff constituted unlawful surveillance. This served no legitimate purpose and was a violation because the surveillance was secret and unknown to the employees.[75]

3. Employee Manipulation

Employee manipulation involves an employer's attempts to circumvent employees' rights under federal and state labor relations statutes to engage in protected union activity.[76] Manipulation occurs where the employer attempts to convince the employee that its position should be followed. For example, the employer may manipulate employees to refrain from exercising their legal rights to join, assist, or form a union. The legality of the employer's activity is evaluated by considering:

1. the background against which it occurs;
2. the nature of the information sought;
3. the position of the employer's questioners;
4. the location of the activity; and
5. the interrogation method used.

Generally, an employer cannot ask employees to report union attempts to obtain signed authorization cards or to report names of union organizers. In one case, a supervisor unlawfully told employees to report union harassment to sign authorization cards.[77] However, an employer lawfully invited employees to report if they were threatened during a union campaign.[78] The employer maintained the right to assure that its workforce was free from physical threats. The same employer, however, was found to have acted unlawfully for requesting a newly hired employee to report union harassment. The request was so vague as to invite employees generally to inform on fellow workers who were engaged in union activity.[79]

A supervisor's request for an employee to report "anything going on" was not unlawful. The supervisor was referring to sabotage or wanton negligence suspected of causing defective products. No reasonable basis existed for believing that the supervisor was referring to a union organizational campaign.[80]

4. Camera Surveillance

The most revealing surveillance device is the camera. Observation by camera may occur through film or videotape. Camera surveillance of lawful union picketing can constitute unlawful interference under federal labor legislation[81] even though the surveillance is not used to retaliate against the picketing employees.

Such observation may intimidate employees. Even though employer surveillance films are not developed into photographs, a violation can occur.[82]

The completed act of taking a photograph is not necessary for violation to occur. It is not even necessary to take photographs. Illegal surveillance was found where an employer approached pickets with a camera. Raising the camera and focusing was found to be sufficient to coerce and restrain the striking employees.[83] Similarly, displaying a camera and appearing to take pictures of union hand-billing activities was unlawful.[84]

Camera surveillance by a union may not be unlawful. A representation election was upheld even though a union business agent photographed employees.[85]

Where litigation potential exists, an employer may take photographs for court proceedings. Photographing strikers on the picket line was lawful where photographs were taken to assure strikers' compliance with a court consent decree limiting the number of picketers at the employer's premises.[86]

Photographs are proper if the employer seeks evidence of work rule violations. A department store lawfully photographed union organizers talking with employees during store hours. The store had the right to prevent union solicitation on the selling floor.[87]

5. Electronic Surveillance

Related to camera surveillance is surveillance by electronic or mechanical means, usually involving the use of tape recorders or computers. Like a camera, electronic surveillance records employee activities. It makes a record of an employee's speech and writings. Employers can be liable for electronic surveillance of employees by an employer's middle-management executives. An employee may also be disciplined for using a concealed tape recorder at meetings with his employer.[88]

C. Surveillance Guidelines

Before undertaking surveillance of employees, the employer should:

1. review applicable federal or state statutes regulating the proposed surveillance;

2. ensure that the surveillance is job-related;

3. clearly notify employees that they may be subject to surveillance;

4. obtain employees' written consent to surveillance as a condition of employment;

5. disclose to employees what mechanical, electronic, or other devices may be used for surveillance;

6. disclose to employees when, where, and how these mechanical, electronic, or other devices may be used for surveillance.

D. Work Performance Surveillance Policies

Work Performance Surveillance Policy

The Company may periodically monitor, surveil, or review employee work performance through the use of mechanical, electronic, or other methods which may include photographing, recording, observing, telephone monitoring, and using beepers, touch tone decoders, or diodes.

Work Performance Surveillance: Employee Authorization

I understand that, as a condition of employment, the Company may periodically surveil, monitor, or review my work performance by using mechanical, electronic, or other methods. I expressly consent to this work performance surveillance.

_____   _____

Date   Employee Signature

V. Literature Solicitation and Distribution

A. Privacy Principles

Employees' privacy is affected through the employer's regulation of the literature that is solicited and distributed at the workplace. This regulation or restriction curtails certain aspects of the employees' constitutional rights of free speech, freedom to associate, and the right to information.[89] Additionally, regulation may cause employees to refrain from exercising union organizational rights under federal and state labor relations statutes.[90]

These workplace privacy interests normally arise when literature is brought into or distributed at the workplace by employees or third parties. Some workplace activities which an employer may attempt to regulate include the reading of "adult" literature or the soliciting of donations for a charitable organization during lunch periods.

Solicitation should be distinguished from conversation. Simple discussion of a subject, even if that subject is the union, may not warrant the application of an employer's no-solicitation rule. Distributing union authorization cards to be signed and returned to a union organizer is considered solicitation. All other literature dissemination is considered distribution. Although literature distribution may be prohibited in work areas,[91] the employer may prohibit employee literature distribution during nonwork time[92] in nonwork areas only where a necessity to maintain discipline or production exists.[93] Nonwork areas are those locations where employees eat, clean up, and use restroom facilities.

Employer rules may be found invalid where they discriminate against union organizing activities by allowing more permissive solicitation and distribution for other activities. Employer policies that attempt to control solicitation and distribution should restrict all such activities to nonwork areas during nonwork times equally, regardless of the material's content. Should employers retaliate against employees for engaging in literature solicitation and distribution where invalid rules or no rules exist, the discipline may be overturned and reinstatement and back pay orders may result.

B. Acceptable Prohibitions

Federal and state labor relations boards have set certain presumptions regarding employer rules regulating the union's right to solicit employees and distribute literature.[94] Employer rules regarding literature solicitation and distribution are generally valid absent a showing of the employer's anti-union animus or discrimination. It is presumptively valid for an employer to promulgate a rule prohibiting:

1. union solicitation by employees in work areas during working time;[95]

2. solicitation by employees during nonworking time, even if on employer property;[96]

3. literature distribution by employees in work areas at any time;[97] and

4. literature distribution by employees in nonwork areas during nonwork time on the employer's premises.[98]

C. Literature Solicitation and Distribution Policies

Literature Solicitation and Distribution Policy: Form 1

Solicitation, distribution of literature, and trespassing by non-employees on these premises are prohibited.

Literature Solicitation and Distribution Policy: Form 2

Distribution of advertising material, handbills, or other literature in working areas of this plant is prohibited at any time.

Literature Solicitation and Distribution Policy: Form 3

Solicitation by an employee of another employee is prohibited while either the person doing the soliciting or the person being solicited is on working time. Working time is the period when an employee is required to performs his or her job duties.

Endnotes

1   *See, e.g.*, Love v. Southern Bell Tel., 263 So. 2d 460 (La. Ct. App. 1972) (using a locksmith to force entry into trailer home of employee who failed to report to work).

2   *See* Appendix A sections III.F and IV.H for a list of federal and state statutes affecting searches.

3   *See, e.g.*, Tocker v. Great Atl. & Pac. Tea Co., 190 A.2d 822 (D.C. Ct. of App. 1963) (denying employee right to leave).

4   *See* Schanafelt v. Seaboard Fin. Co., 108 Cal. App. 2d 420, 239 P.2d 42 (1951) (employer words that employee not depart sufficient to constitute false imprisonment); Black v. Kroger Co., 527 SW.2d 794 (Tex. Ct. App. 1975) (words of threat by employer sufficient for false imprisonment).

5   *See* Faniel v. Chesapeake & Potomac Tel. Co., 404 A.2d 147 (D.C. Ct. of App. 1979) (duration of employee's detention insufficient to support false imprisonment by employer); Delan v. CBS, Inc., 111 Misc. 2d 928, 445 N.Y.S.2d 898 (1981) (employer intent to confine not sufficient to support false imprisonment).

6   *See* Turner v. Mellon, 257 F.2d 15 (1953) (employer must actively bring about employee's arrest to incur liability; merely giving information to police in good faith will not impose liability).

7   *Id.*

8   *See* Ramsden v. Western Union, 71 Cal. App. 3d 873, 138 Cal. Rptr. 426 (1977) (employer liability for false arrest may result where information disclosed to police is known to be incorrect).

9   *See* Veras v. Truth Verification Corp., 87 A.D.2d 381, 451 N.Y.S.2d 761 (1982), *aff'd*, 457 N.Y.S.2d 241, 57 N.Y.2d 947, 443 N.E.2d 489 (1982) (employer's good-faith belief in employee's guilt constituted probable cause for arrest); Oabrou v. May Dep't Stores Co., 462 A.2d 1102 (D.C. 1983) (good-faith, reasonable belief constituted probable cause).

10   *See* Jacques v. Firestone Tire & Rubber Co., 183 Cal. App. 2d 632, 6 Cal. Rptr. 878 (1960).

11   *See, e.g.*, Wainauskis v. Howard Johnson Co., 339 Pa. Super. 266, 488 A.2d 1117 (1985) (malicious prosecution sustained for alleged theft).

12   *See, e.g.*, Holloway v. K-mart Corp., 113 Wis. 2d 143, 334 N.W.2d 570 (1983) (falsely accusing employee of stealing).

13   *See, e.g.,* Hall v. Macy Dep't. Stores, 242 Or. 131, 637 P.2d 126 (1981) (security investigator's false statements during female clerk's interview regarding cash shortages and threatening prosecution).

14   *See, e.g.,* O'Connor v. Ortega, 480 U.S. 709 (1987) (unauthorized search of public employee's desk). *See* Appendix A sections I and II for federal and state constitutions affecting privacy.

15   *See* Lucas v. United States, 411 A.2d 360 (D.C. 1989), *reh'g. denied,* 414 A.2d 830 (1980).

16   *See* State v. Pohle, 160 N.J. 576, 390 A.2d 692 (1989), *rev'd on other grounds,* 166 N.J. Super. 504, 400 A.2d 109 (1979).

17   *Id.*

18   United States v. Bunkers, 521 F.2d 1217 (9th Cir. 1975), *cert. denied,* 423 U.S. 489 (1979).

19   *See* O'Connor v. Ortega, 480 U.S. 709 (1987).

20   United States v. Speights, 557 F.2d 362 (3d Cir. 1977).

21   *See* Dow Chem. Co., 65 Lab. Arb. (BNA) 1295 (1976) (Lipson, Arb.).

22   Aldens Inc., 51 Lab. Arb. (BNA) 469 (1968) (Kelliher, Arb.).

23   *See* Thrifty Drug Stores Co., 64 Lab. Arb. (BNA) 997 (1975) (Fellman, Arb.)

24   *See* Scott Paper Co., 52 Lab. Arb. (BNA) 57, 58-59 (1969) (Williams, Arb.) (limited permissible searches to those specifically covered by express company rules).

25   *See* Ross-Meehan Foundries, 55 Lab. Arb. (BNA) 1078, 1080 (1970) (King, Arb.).

26   *See* Kawneer Co., Inc. 86 Lab. Arb. (BNA) 297 (1985) (Alexander, Arb.) (reasonable evidence existed for employer to search employee's toolbox).

27   American Meat Packing, 79 Lab. Arb. (BNA) 1327 (1982) (Malinowski, Arb.) (the burden of proof on the employer in drug-related cases is substantial, if not tantamount to a standard imposing guilt "beyond a reasonable doubt").

28   U.S. Air Force Logistics Command, 78 Lab. Arb. (BNA) 1092 (1982) (Feldman, Arb.).

29   Burns Int'l Sec. Serv., 78 Lab. Arb. (BNA) 1104 (1982) (Traynor, Arb.).

30   *See* Thomas Murphy, *Investigating, Handling, and Protecting Against Employee Theft and Dishonesty, in* JEROME KAUFF, EMPLOYMENT PROBLEMS IN THE WORKPLACE 22, 23-24 (1986).

31   *See* KENNETH McCULLOCH, TERMINATION OF EMPLOYMENT ¶ 41,107 (1984). This policy may also be included as a notice on the application or as a separate form to obtain the employee's written consent to the workplace search.

32   *See* Appendix A sections III.N and IV.M for federal and state statutes affecting monitoring.

33   *See, e.g.,* Vernars v. Young, 539 F.2d 766 (3d Cir. 1976) (reading employee's mail).

34   *See, e.g.,* Sias v. General Motors Corp., 372 Mich. 542, 127 N.W.2d 357 (1964) (informing employees not entitled to information regarding reasons for termination).

35   *See, e.g.,* Novosel v. Nationwide Ins. Co., 721 F.2d 894 (3d Cir. 1983) (possibility of asserting a Fourth Amendment constitutional infringement as a public policy breach).

36   Omnibus Crime and Control Act, 18 U.S.C. §§ 2510-2520 (1988).

37   *See* Appendix A section IV.M for state statutes affecting monitoring.

38   *See* Briggs v. American Air Filter Co., Inc., 630 F.2d 414 (5th Cir. 1980).

39   18 U.S.C. §§ 2510-2520 (1988).

40   *See* Appendix A section IV.M.

41   *See* United States v. Holmes, 521 F.2d 859 (5th Cir. 1975).

42   *See* United States v. Giordano, 416 U.S. 505 (1974).

43   *See* People v. Rogers, 86 Misc. 2d 868, 385 N.Y.S.2d 228 (1976).

44   47 C.F.R. § 15.11 (1992).

45   *See* Appendix A section IV.M for state statutes applicable to monitoring.

46   OFFICE OF TECHNOLOGY ASSESSMENT, THE ELECTRONIC SUPERVISOR: NEW TECHNOLOGY, NEW TENSIONS 38 (1987).

47   *See, e.g.,* Southwire Co., 282 N.L.R.B. 117 (1987).

48   *See, e.g.,* Minnesota v. Century Camera, Inc., 309 N.W.2d 735 (Minn. 1981).

49   *See, e.g.,* Custom Coating & Laminating Corp., 249 N.L.R.B. No. 765 (1980).

50   *See, e.g.,* Nader v. General Motors Corp., 25 N.Y.2d 560, 307 N.Y.S.2d 647 (1970) (employee's privacy invaded only if the information sought is of a confidential nature and the surveillance was unreasonably intrusive).

51   *See, e.g.,* Rossmore House, 269 N.L.R.B. 1176 (1984), *enforced as* Hotel & Restaurant Employees, Local 11 v. NLRB, 760 F.2d 1006 (9th Cir. 1985) (employee interrogation to convince employee that union was unnecessary).

52   *See, e.g.,* School Board of Escambia County v. Public Employee Relations Comm'n, 350 So. 2d 819 (Fla. Dist. Ct. App. 1977) (employer's photographing of picketing employees found to be coercive).

53   *See, e.g.,* NLRB v. J.P. Stevens & Co., 563 F.2d 8 (2d Cir. 1977) (union organizer's motel room illegally placed under electronic surveillance by employer).

54   *See* Appendix A sections III.L and IV.O.

55   29 U.S.C. §§ 151-168 (1988).

56   Litton Educ. Publication, Inc., Am. Book Div., 214 N.L.R.B. No. 413 (1974).

57   Whiteboro Cent. Sch. Dist., Pub. Bargaining Cas. (CCH) ¶ 41,642 (N.Y.L.R.B. 1980).

58   NLRB v. Computed Time Corp., 587 F.2d 790 (5th Cir. 1979).

59   Plymouth County House of Correction & Jail, Pub. Bargaining Cas. (CCH) ¶ 40,107 (Mass. L.R.B. 1977).

60   Filler Prods., Inc. v. NLRB, 376 F.2d 369 (4th Cir. 1967).

61   Custom Coating & Laminating Corp., 249 N.L.R.B. 765 (1980).

62   University of Maine, Pub. Bargaining Cas. (CCH) ¶ 41,346 (Me. L.R.B. 1979).

63   C & M Sportswear Mfg. Corp., 183 N.L.R.B. 230 (1970).

64   Aircraft Plating, Inc., 213 N.L.R.B. 664 (1974).

65   J.C. Penney Co., Inc., 209 N.L.R.B. 313 (1974).

66   East Side Shopper, Inc. 204 N.L.R.B. 841 (1973).

67   United States Indus., Inc. Durango Boot Div., 247 N.L.R.B. 361 (1980).

68 Tartan Marine Co., 247 N.L.R.B. 646 (1980).

69 Peerless of Am., Inc., 198 N.L.R.B. 982 (1972).

70 Alexander Dawson, Inc., 228 N.L.R.B. 165, *enforced on other grounds*, 586 F.2d 1300 (9th Cir. 1978).

71 J.H. Block & Co., Inc., 247 N.L.R.B. 262 (1980).

72 Chemtronics, Inc., 236 N.L.R.B. 178 (1978).

73 Phillips Indus. Components, Inc., Subsidiary of Phillips Indus. Inc., 216 N.L.R.B. 885 (1975).

74 State of Illinois, Dep't of Personnel & Children & Family Serv., Pub. Bargaining Cas. (CCH) ¶ 40,214 (Ill. Ofc. of Collective Bargaining 1977).

75 Illinois Bureau of Employment Sec., Pub. Bargaining Cas. (CCH) ¶ 41,229 (Ill. Ofc. of Collective Bargaining 1979).

76 *See* Appendix A sections III.L and IV.O for federal and state labor relations statutes.

77 Poloran Products of Miss., Inc., 217 N.L.R.B. 704 (1975).

78 Massey Stores, Inc., 245 N.L.R.B. 1077 (1979).

79 *Id.*

80 Randall's, 157 N.L.R.B. 86 (1966).

81 *See* 29 U.S.C. §§ 151-168 (1988).

82 Faulhaber, Co., 129 N.L.R.B. 561 (1960).

83 Electri-Flex Co., 238 N.L.R.B. 713 (1979).

84 Fluid Chem. Co., Inc., 203 N.L.R.B. 244 (1973).

85 AFSCME, Local 1584 v. Manatee County, Pub. Bargaining Cas. (CCH) ¶ 41,111 (Fla. L.R.B. 1979).

86 Pittsburgh & New Eng. Trucking Co., 238 N.L.R.B. 1706 (1978).

87 Franklin Stores Corp., 199 N.L.R.B. 52 (1972).

88 Yoder v. Commonwealth, Dep't of Labor & Indus., 92 Pa. Commw. 177, 498 A.2d 491 (1985).

89 *See* Appendix A sections I and II for federal and state constitutional protections.

90 *See* Appendix A sections III.L and IV.O.

91   *See* Eastex, Inc., 215 N.L.R.B. 271 (1974), *enforced,* 550 F.2d 198 (5th Cir. 1977), *petition for reh'g denied,* 556 F.2d 1280 (5th Cir. 1977), *aff'd,* 437 U.S. 1045 (1978) (the term "working areas" is that portion of a facility where production is actually performed).

92   *See* Essex Int'l, Inc., 211 N.L.R.B. 749, 750 (1974).

93   Eastex, Inc. v. NLRB, 437 U.S. 556 (1978).

94   *See generally* JOHN FEERICK, HENRY BAER, AND JONATHAN ARFA, NATIONAL LABOR RELATIONS BOARD REPRESENTATION ELECTIONS—LAW, PRACTICE & PROCEDURE § 3.3 (2d ed. 1985).

95   *See* Veeder-Root Co., 192 N.L.R.B. 973 (1971).

96   *See* Peyton Packing Co., 49 N.L.R.B. 828 (1943), *enforced,* 142 F.2d 1009 (5th Cir. 1944); *but see* House of Mosaics, Inc., 215 N.L.R.B. 704 (1974) (a rule barring solicitation in the building at all times was lawful, since evidence that the rule was nondiscriminatory and promulgated for disciplinary reasons overcame the invalidity presumption).

97   *See* Rockingham Sleepwear, Inc., 188 N.L.R.B. 698 (1971), *enforced,* 80 L.R.R.M. (BNA) 180 (4th Cir. 1972).

98   *See* Republic Aviation Corp. v. NLRB, 324 U.S. 793 (1945); Stoddard-Quirk Mfg. Co., 138 N.L.R.B. No. 615 (1962).

7

Personal Privacy in the Workplace

I. Introduction

Employees' personal concerns generally involve employees exercising certain duties, choices, or rights. Workplace privacy interests are affected when employers attempt to limit, restrict, or prohibit accommodation of these interests. This chapter reviews workplace privacy issues that may arise out of employees' personal concerns including jury or witness duty, voting time, whistle-blowing, dress and grooming codes, spousal policies, nepotism, third party representation, performance evaluations, religious accommodation, privacy misconduct, sexual harassment, sexual orientation, and restrictive covenants.

II. Jury and Witness Duty

A. Jury and Witness Duty Privacy Principles

A strong public policy implicit in decisional law[1] and federal and state constitutions and statutes[2] encourages jury service. The employee's responsibility to fulfill jury or witness duty requirements is a societal obligation with which an employer cannot interfere.

Statutory protections of this obligation generally entitle employees to take time off for jury duty or for a court appearance as a witness when reasonable notice is given to the employer.[3] The employer is prohibited from terminating or discriminating against an employee for taking time off for either purpose.

Employees serving as jurors or witnesses are not required to work at their jobs while fulfilling these social responsibilities. For example, an employer violated a federal statute protecting jurors' employment status by threatening an employee with loss of job security for serving on a jury. The employer further violated the statute by requiring the employee to make up work hours lost through jury service by working evenings and Sundays.[4] This and other similar statutes were designed to permit citizens to serve as jurors and witnesses with minds and bodies free from worry or stress and to devote full and undivided attention to the effective administration of the judicial system. Employers are prohibited from distracting employees from serving as effective jurors or witnesses by requiring part-time employment in conjunction with full-time jury duty.[5] For their part, employees must cooperate with the employer by promptly disclosing the times and dates of the jury or witness service.[6]

B. Developing Procedures

In developing jury and witness duty procedures, the employer should:

1. review federal and state statutes for any established requirements, including time off for or payment of employees serving jury or witness duty;

2. require employees to present proof of jury or witness duty; and

3. require employees to give adequate notice of the dates and times of the jury or witness duty.

C. Jury and Witness Duty Policy

Jury and Witness Duty Policy

Upon receiving a summons to report for jury or witness duty, an employee will present the summons to his or her immediate superior on his or her next working day. The employee will be excused from employment for the day or days required in serving as a juror or witness in any court created by the United States or the State of *(State's Name)*. This will be considered an excused absence. Full-time employees will be entitled to their usual compensation less any compensation received for serving as jurors or witnesses upon written presentation to the Company indicating that they have served as a juror or witness.

III. Voting Time

A. Voting Time Privacy Principles

Voting is another general right which involves the personal privacy interests of employees. The act of voting reflects individuals' political choices and how these choices are exercised. At the workplace, employees' privacy in speech, beliefs, and association may be affected by any employer actions which inadvertently or intentionally interfere with the voting process.

As with jury or witness duty, strong public policy implicit in decisional law[7] and federal and state constitutions and statutes[8] encourages voting. Some states require that an employee be given time off to vote.[9] In other states, time off for voting is strictly an employer decision. Regardless of whether voting time is required or voluntarily granted, employers must ensure that this time is given absent any discrimination toward employees that use the time to vote. Also, employers may not attempt to coerce employees into casting their votes in a particular manner.[10]

B. Procedural Considerations

In developing voting time procedures, the employer should consider the following guidelines:

1. Review applicable federal and state statutes for any requirements regarding time off for voting or compensation of employees who take time.

2. Do not direct or attempt to influence how employees vote.

3. Require employees to submit requests for voting time in advance of the election date to avoid unnecessary interference with employer schedules and production.

4. Require employees to provide written proof that time off was used for voting.

5. Verify that employees are eligible to vote by having employees sign an Authorization to Vote form which indicates:

    a. that the employee is a registered voter for the subject election and

    b. that falsification of eligibility may result in employee discipline up to and including termination.

C. Voting Time Policy

Time Off for Voting

Section 1. TIME OFF. Company employees are entitled to vote at general, primary, or presidential primary elections. When registered voter-employees do not have sufficient time outside of regular working hours to vote, they may take off as much working time as will enable them to vote, when this time is added to their available voting time outside their working hours. Employees will be allowed time off for voting only at the beginning or end of their regular working shifts, whichever allows them the most free time for voting and the least time off from their regular working shift, unless otherwise mutually agreed upon by the employer and employee. Employees who are election officers may absent themselves from their work schedule on election day without being subject to demotion, suspension, or termination.

Section 2. COMPENSATION. Employees may take off as much time as will enable them to vote, however, they will be compensated for no more than two hours.

Section 3. TIME OFF NOTICE. If employees know or have reason to believe that time off is needed to vote, they must notify the Company at least five (5) working days in advance of the voting date.

IV. Whistle-blowing

A. Whistle-blowing Privacy Principles

Whistle-blowing consists of three possible employee actions. The first involves the employee's reporting of the unlawful and/or improper conduct of fellow employees to the employer. The second action involves the employee reporting to government authorities the unlawful and/or improper conduct of the employer. And finally, the employee may report to government agencies the employer's asking or requiring the employee to participate in unlawful actions.[11] An employees's privacy interests in speech, belief, and association interests are affected by the employer's reaction to the whistle-blowing incident, especially if the reaction is discipline or termination of the employee. Often, the whistle-blowing employee is disciplined or terminated by the employer either prior to or after the employee's action. When confronted with employee complaints, employers should investigate the allegations before instituting discipline.

Federal and state statutes are offering increasing protection for whistle-blowing actions of employees.[12] For example, an employer acted improperly by terminating the in-service training director of a nursing home who threatened to report patient abuse to a state enforcement agency.[13] In a similar case, an apartment manager was improperly terminated for refusing his employer's orders to enter apartments and search private papers.[14] The court based its decision on a well recognized common-law right for tenant privacy.

B. Developing Procedures

In developing procedures to properly evaluate whistle-blowing incidents, the employer should:

1. review applicable federal and state statutes protecting whistle-blowers;

2. establish internal complaint procedures for resolving whistle-blowing incidents; and

3. offer protection from retaliation for employees with legitimate whistle-blowing complaints.

C. Whistle-blowing Policy

Whistle-blowing Protection

Section 1. PURPOSE. It is the Company's policy to follow and enforce all federal, state, and local laws applicable to it and to require its employees to do likewise. Every employee has the responsibility to assist in implementing this policy.

Section 2. REPORTING COMPANY VIOLATIONS. A violation of this policy should be reported to an employee's immediate supervisor through a written report which is signed by the employee. However, if reporting a violation to the immediate supervisor is not practical, a written, signed, and dated statement should be submitted by the employee to the Director of Human Resources so that an investigation may be undertaken.

Section 3. NO RETALIATION FOR FILING COMPLAINTS. There will be no retaliation by the Company or any of its employees against any employee who makes a good-faith report pursuant to this policy, even if investigation shows that no violation has occurred.

Section 4. CORRECTIVE ACTION. It is the responsibility of the Company to correct or prevent violations of federal, state, and local laws applicable to it. This is a legal obligation. A violation can subject the Company and its employees to publicity leading the public, customers, and the government to hold an adverse image of the Company.

Section 5. VIOLATION OF THIS POLICY. The procedures outlined herein must be followed before an employee reports alleged violations to any news medium, government agency, or other outlet. The Company should have the opportunity to conduct an investigation before outside agencies are involved, and each employee should ensure that the Company can undertake this internal investigation. Employee complaints that do not follow this procedure will constitute a policy violation. Adhering to the reporting requirements of this policy is a condition of employment.

V. Dress and Grooming Codes

A. Dress and Grooming Code Privacy Principles

Employees' expression of their personal style may be one of the more significant privacy interests that employers may seek to affect or regulate at the workplace. Dress and grooming rules inherently inhibit or restrict the employee's freedom of personal expression at the workplace. Through these rules the employer may designate the clothing type, uniform, or hair style that must be worn by employees or that are prohibited from being worn at the workplace. In effect, the employer is determining the image that its employees project, and this has a direct impact on employees' privacy interests.

Dress and grooming standards may be legally imposed by the employer as part of health and safety requirements, customer relations, image, or business type.[15] Standards also may arise informally through employee peer pressure. The workplace norm among employees becomes a dress and grooming standard that they have established over a given time period, and oftentimes new employees must conform or be ostracized even though the employer has no formal written policy.

An employer's dress and grooming policies may violate federal and state fair employment practice statutes.[16] For example, where a bank required its managers to wear what the employer considered a "bank career ensemble," it violated the Civil Rights Act of 1964 (Title VII).[17]

B. Developing an Acceptable Code

In establishing acceptable parameters of a dress and grooming code, employers must consider:

1. health and safety requirements that require specific clothing so that employees are not injured;

2. customer relations where a professional image needs to be projected; and

3. business type that may require uniforms.

C. Dress and Grooming Code

Dress and Grooming Code

The Company acknowledges that the employee has a right to dress and groom as he or she chooses while at the workplace, unless the employee's dress or grooming has an adverse effect on the Company's business or the employee's health and safety.

VI. Hiring of Spouses

A. Spousal Hiring Privacy Principles

Spousal policies may restrict or deny employment with the same employer because two individuals are or become husband and wife. As a workplace privacy issue, spousal policies affect employees' interests in choosing their associates free of employer interference. Spousal policies restrain or penalize employees for taking part in life's basic relationship of husband and wife. Likewise, it discriminates against employees who become romantically involved or live together absent a formal marriage.

Marriage or subsequent marriage may legally result in a refusal to hire, transfer to another department, demotion, or termination. Spousal policies generally have been permitted as a reasonable employer method of eliminating possible employee conflicts or favoritism that may originate in or grow out of the husband and wife relationship. Spousal policies are regulated by federal and state fair employment practice statutes;[18] however, in some cases constitutional[19] and other claims relating to conflict of interest or contractual relationships also may be asserted.[20]

B. Procedural Considerations

In developing procedures to handle spousal relationships in the workplace, employers should:

1. review applicable federal and state fair employment practice statutes;

2. ensure equal application to both sexes and a neutral effect on both spouses; and

3. establish job-relatedness by evaluating:

   a. how spouses may support one another;

   b. if the marital relationship may generate emotional problems detrimental to job performance;

c. if favoritism may exist between spouses; and

d. if a spouse in a supervisory position over the other spouse may be less inclined to recognize or deal with unsatisfactory job performance.

C. Spousal Hiring Policy

Employment of Spouses

Each employee is entitled, if otherwise qualified, to work with his or her spouse. The Company does not discriminate against an applicant or employee regarding working conditions, workplace assignment, or other employment privileges because the spouse of that applicant or employee is also a Company employee. However, this does not apply to employment of the spouse of an employee who has the responsibility to hire, discipline, terminate, or conduct performance evaluations of the position involved. That spouse may not be hired or, if already in such a position, may be transferred or terminated.

VII. Nepotism

A. Nepotism Privacy Principles

Nepotism is the practice of favoring employees' relatives over others in employment opportunities. As a workplace privacy interest, nepotism affects association considerations by encouraging working relationships with relatives. Courts generally have permitted nepotism policies,[21] finding, for example, that any difference attributable to nepotism usually disappears in an integrated workforce where the employer engages in extensive outreach efforts.[22] Moreover, an employer prohibition on nepotism is a reasonable method of minimizing employee conflict or favoritism arising out of family relations. Policies that encourage nepotism usually are challenged under federal and state fair employment practice statutes.[23]

B. Preparing Procedures

In developing nepotism procedures, employers should:

1. review applicable federal and state statutes and

2. seek to maintain a neutral effect on all minority groups to ensure that they are given an equal opportunity for position openings.

C. Nepotism Policy

Nepotism Policy

Section 1. FAMILY MEMBER EMPLOYMENT.   Regarding a family member of a current or former employee, the Company will not:

a. refuse to hire that individual;

b. terminate that individual from current employment; or

c. discriminate against that individual in compensation or in terms, conditions, or privileges of employment.

Section 2. CONFLICT OF INTEREST.   The Company is not required to hire or continue in employment an individual if the employment would:

a. place the individual in a position of supervisory, appointment, or grievance adjustment authority over a member of the individual's family or in a position of being subject to the authority exercised by a member of the individual's family; or

b. cause the Company to disregard a *bona fide* occupational requirement reasonably necessary to the normal operation of the Company's business.

Section 3. MEMBERS OF AN INDIVIDUAL'S FAMILY.   Members of an individual's family include: wife, husband, son, daughter, mother, father, brother, sister, brother-in-law, sister-in-law, son-in-law, daughter-in-law, mother-in-law, father-in-law, aunt, uncle, niece, nephew, stepparent, and stepchild.

VIII. Third Party Representation

A. Third Party Representation Privacy Principles

When employees are confronted by an employer over a privacy claim or wish to assert their own privacy claims at the workplace, it is important that they not do this alone. For the employee, it may be important to have another person present as a witness when privacy matters arise with the employer. Third party representation through a union steward or another employee may assist an employee in confronting employer claims against the employee or in the employee's assertion of a claim.

Investigatory interviews involve situations in which the employer confronts an employee with possible discipline or termination as a result of employee misconduct. The right to representation at investigatory interviews is an important workplace issue. Representation allows an employee the opportunity to safeguard certain workplace privacy interests when discipline or termination arises or is threatened. These privacy interests include those present in speech, beliefs, information, association, and lifestyle.

Private[24] and public[25] sector employees have a qualified right to union representation during employer-initiated investigatory interviews. The right arises when the employee reasonably believes the investigation will result in disciplinary action, but only if the employee specifically requests union representation. When an employee demands union representation, the employer has two alternatives. First, the investigation may be pursued without an interview. Second, union representation may be allowed, but the participation of the representative may be restricted. There is no obligation to bargain with the union at the interview and the employer may insist on hearing only the employee's version. A similar right has been suggested for non-union private sector employees.[26]

B. Procedural Guidelines

In dealing with third party representation rights, the employer should consider these guidelines:

1. An investigatory interview is a meeting in which the employee is asked questions about employee misconduct, and the employee reasonably believes that this interview will result in disciplinary action.

2. The employee must affirmatively request representation to invoke his or her rights.

3. The employee's request for representation can be made before the interview or at any time during the interview.

4. There is no obligation that the employer advise the employee of his or her right to request representation.

5. Upon the employee's timely request, the employer should disclose the subject matter to the employee prior to the investigatory interview and permit the employee to consult privately with a representative if he or she so requests.

6. The employer can insist that the representative remain silent until the employee gives his or her own account of the incident, but the employer cannot insist that the representative be silent for the entire investigatory interview.

7. The representative can assist the employee and clarify any misconceptions that may arise, but the employer can insist in hearing only the employee's account.

8. The representative does not have to be brought in if the employee is disciplined without any interrogation or questioning; however, if the employer wants to question the employee in the meeting after imposing the discipline, the employee can request the presence of the representative.

9. If an employee requests a representative, the employer may legally decide not to have any interview whatsoever and simply proceed with the investigation through other means.

C. Third Party Representation Policies

Third Party Representation: Union Employer

Prior to any discipline of an employee, the Union will be given an opportunity to discuss the matter with the Company. If an employee suspects discipline, he or she may request and will be permitted to speak privately with one union representative before being interviewed by the Company.

A member of the union bargaining unit who is requested to meet with a manager or supervisor for the imposition of disciplinary action will be entitled to be accompanied by a union representative. The employee will receive reasonable prior notice of the topics to be discussed.

Third Party Representation: Non-Union Employer

Any employee who is requested to meet with a manager or supervisor for the imposition of disciplinary action will be entitled to be accompanied by another employee of his or her choosing. The employee will receive reasonable prior notice of the topics to be discussed.

IX. Performance Evaluations

A. Performance Evaluation Privacy Principles

Performance evaluation is the process of establishing written standards of performance criteria, and telling employees about those standards, and frequently informing them how they are performing in relations to the standards. Personnel actions such as transfers, assignments, promotions, and pay increases often may be based on performance evaluations.

Employees' privacy interests raised during performance evaluations require that evaluations be undertaken and information collected, used, maintained, and disclosed with the utmost care.

Evaluations affect speech, belief, and association interests because these records influence employee advancement, compensation, and assignment. Because of the sensitivity of this information, confidentiality must be preserved by the employer. Improper use of this information may limit the employee's opportunities for advancement. For example, unfairly building a termination case against an employee through negative performance evaluations subjected an employer to liability.[27] Performance evaluations also must be accurately completed to ensure that a correct evaluation occurs.[28]

Failure to preserve the confidentiality of a performance evaluation may result in employer liability for wrongful information disclosure or maintenance of inaccurate information arising out of invasion of privacy, defamation,[29] intentional infliction of emotional distress if conduct is outrageous,[30] negligent maintenance or disclosure of employment records,[31] or public policy violations. Contractual breaches also may arise where employment handbooks[32] and collective bargaining agreements[33] create certain expectations on the part of employees.

B. Performance Evaluation Procedures

It is important that the employer accurately and regularly evaluate employee job performance. The following characteristics are the earmarks of an effective performance evaluation:

1. Performance evaluations should be conducted annually.

2. Performance evaluations should review:

   a. Job knowledge

   b. Work quality

   c. Work quantity

   d. Initiative

   e. Adaptability

   f. Dependability

    g. Cooperation

    h. Areas needing improvement

    i. Punctuality

    j. Attendance

3. Performance evaluations should allow the employer to identify areas in which employees are performing adequately and areas in which improvement is necessary.

4. Performance evaluations may be used in employment decisions including promotion, layoff, or termination.

1. Performance Evaluation Interview

A performance evaluation interview should be conducted in a comfortable setting and should place the employee at ease. It should not be confused with a disciplinary interview. Prior to the interview, the following steps should be undertaken:

1. Schedule the meeting in advance to allow all parties sufficient time to prepare.

2. Arrange a location that provides privacy and freedom from interruptions.

3. Inform the employee of the meeting.

4. Compile the employee's last performance evaluation and job description and the employer's current salary guidelines.

5. Allow sufficient time for the interview.

6. Choose an appropriate time that allows an opportunity for follow-up with the employee before the day is over.

7. Become familiar with the employee's personality and how he or she is likely to react to the interview.

During the interview:

1. Discuss the employee's typical performance and do not over-emphasize recent or isolated events.

2. Discuss all factors evaluated rather than scrutinizing one or two in particular.

3. Maintain consistency and objectivity.

4. Do not be overly influenced by previous performance evaluations.

5. Discuss with the employee plans for future development.

6. Identify methods for improving in deficient areas and for gaining additional skills.

Take these steps after the interview:

1. Have the employee acknowledge the review by signing it and providing any written comments.

2. Follow up the review on a regular basis prior to the next performance evaluation to intermittently gauge the employee's progress.

2. Uses of Evaluations

Performance evaluations are used by employers to:

1. enable an employee to better understand his or her job and the areas of satisfactory and unsatisfactory performance;

2. provide a supervisor with a formal mechanism by which to review each employee's performance and discuss it with the employee;

3. permit the supervisor to increase the employee's morale by complementing positive aspects of performance, while enabling the employee to become more efficient through discussion of weaknesses in performance; and

4. minimize wrongful termination claims over job performance in that:

   a. a terminated employee who has been counselled and made aware of his or her negative performance will have a more positive perception of employer fairness and

b. the employee will know that the employer's case is documented.

3. Training Evaluators

A performance evaluation is only as good as those who conduct it. With training, managers and supervisors will be able to accurately and objectively evaluate employees. Training should point out problem areas that evaluators should avoid, such as:

1. a personal tendency toward leniency or harshness on the part of the evaluator which may produce an inaccurate measure of the employee's abilities;

2. the "halo effect," rating someone highly simply because the particular employee is well-liked, or rating someone poorly because the individual is disliked;

3. the "central tendency," or the inclination to rate all employees as average;

4. the "similar-to-me effect," or giving high evaluations to those who are most like the rater and poor evaluations to those who are dissimilar;

5. the "most-recent-error effect," or considering only the employee's most recent performance while disregarding the employee's typical and overall performance; and

6. the stereotyping or rating of an employee based on the evaluator's personal opinion of or dislike for that employee's dress style, hair length, race, religion, national origin, disability, or other personal trait.

4. Guidelines for Supervisors

The following guidelines should be considered in conjunction with the potential problem areas discussed in the "Training Evaluators" section of this chapter. These guidelines should be reviewed by a supervisor in completing a performance evaluation to ensure that the supervisor gives an unbiased employee evaluation

1. Consider the employee's typical performance during the entire evaluation period.

2. Do not be wrongly influenced by a prior performance evaluation.

3. Use accurate data obtained from careful observation.

4. Compare the performance of the employee being reviewed with performance of other individuals in the same position.

5. Consider each performance factor independently of the others.

6. Do not permit salary level attained or length of service to affect the performance evaluation.

7. Do not let personal feelings bias the performance evaluation.

C. Performance Evaluation Documents

Performance Evaluation Policy

Section 1. PURPOSE. Frequent communication with employees concerning performance is essential. Ongoing, positive communications can motivate and reinforce outstanding performance, which is the ultimate goal of the Company's performance evaluation system. Also, communications may focus attention on performance which needs improvement. Timely discussion of an unsatisfactory situation will help prevent it from becoming a major problem at a review which may come several weeks or months later. An effective performance evaluation will:

a. guide the employee into action necessary for maximum growth;

b. help the supervisor to determine the type of management guidance and development needed by the employee;

c. provide direction to assure that the employee's efforts are channeled toward specified objectives;

d. provide each supervisor with the means to analyze employee performance; and

e. result in more effective work, since employees tend to work better if they know what is expected of them and they can measure their progress.

Section 2. REQUIREMENTS. All supervisors are required to conduct performance evaluations in accordance with the following schedule:

a. For newly hired, newly transferred, and promoted employees:

   1. the first performance evaluation will occur three (3) months after the starting date in the new position;

   2. the second performance evaluation will follow three (3) months after the first; and

   3. the third and subsequent performance reviews will occur at least annually thereafter.

b. All other employees will be evaluated on an annual basis.

c. Performance appraisals in addition to these may be initiated by the supervisor if a significant deterioration or improvement in performance warrants deviation from the normal schedule.

Section 3. PROCEDURE. The following procedure will be used to conduct performance evaluations:

a. The Human Resources Department will notify the supervisor approximately one (1) month in advance of the review date by forwarding a performance evaluation form.

b. The employee's job description is the basis for the performance evaluation. Before completing the performance evaluation, the supervisor will ensure that the job description is current. If necessary, the description will be revised to reflect any significant changes in job content.

c. In completing the performance evaluation, the supervisor will review performance of employees as set forth in the job description. Consideration will also be given to employee growth and development and performance improvements that have occurred since the last performance evaluation. This can be done readily by comparing actual accomplishments against plans made at the previous review.

d. Objective, quantifiable measures will be used whenever possible to evaluate performance, and specific examples of employee behavior which illustrate performance ratings will be noted on the performance evaluation.

e. Once the performance evaluation is completed, the supervisor must secure approval of the next management level.

f. After the appropriate approvals have been obtained, the original evaluation form should be sent to the Human Resources Department, who will verify that the form has been completely and correctly filled out.

g. When the original performance evaluation form is returned from the Human Resources Department to the supervisor, an appointment will be made with the employee to discuss the review. Reasonable advance notice will be given and the time scheduled will be adequate to allow for a full discussion. The interview itself will be conducted in privacy and without interruptions.

h. During the interview, the supervisor will explain each rating individually, using examples to illustrate why the performance rating was chosen.

i. After completing the review of past performance, the supervisor and the employee will jointly determine development plans and performance goals for the next rating period. Development plans identify specific ways the employee will try to improve deficient areas or gain additional skills. Performance goals are objective, work-oriented targets the two agree are reasonable and realistic given the employee's current performance level, expected improvement, and external factors which may affect accomplishment. The supervisor will guide, rather than dominate, this phase of the review and will encourage employee participation. Achievement of these plans and goals requires the full acceptance and support of both parties.

j. Once the interview is completed, the supervisor must secure the employee's written acknowledgment of the review and his or her written approval of the development plans and performance goals.

k. The supervisor will give the employee a photocopy of the development and goals sections of the performance evaluation form and will keep a photocopy of the sections for his or her own records. The original performance evaluation including the development and goals sections should then be sent to the Human Resources Department.

Section 4. DEFINITIONS. The following definitions will be used by the supervisor in evaluating employee performance of individual factors and on an overall basis:

a. *Marginal*. Performance of a fully trained employee does not meet acceptable level and requires improvement. An overall rating of Marginal that does not prompt improved performance could result in termination or demotion and should never result in a salary increase.

b. *Provisional*. Performance does not meet acceptable levels in all areas, but the employee is steadily improving and exhibits the potential to become proficient with continued training. A Provisional rating is often given to inexperienced new employees.

c. *Proficient/Effective:* Performance fully meets standards set for the position on a consistent basis. This should be the expected level in a position. An employee operating at this level is doing a good job.

d. *Superior.* Performance consistently exceeds standards set for the position.

e. *Outstanding.* Performance so exceeds standards for the position that the excellence of the individual's work is clearly recognized by all. This level of performance is far above the Proficient/Effective level and is normally achieved by only a small percentage of employees.

Section 5. CONFIDENTIALITY. All documents obtained as part of the performance evaluation process, including the performance evaluation, will be kept confidential and may be disclosed only to the employee or to those persons who may require the information in the course of their job-related duties.

Performance Evaluation Form

Name_____   Date_____

Position/Title_____   Location_____

Department_____

PART I—Major Position Responsibilities

List the significant duties as described on the job description.

_____

_____

_____

PART II—Performance of Objectives

Summarize below three to five of the most important objectives undertaken since the last performance evaluation and comment on the results achieved.

Objectives　　　　　　　　　　　　Results Achieved

_____　　　　　　_____

_____　　　　　　_____

_____　　　　　　_____

_____　　　　　　_____

_____　　　　　　_____

_____　　　　　　_____

PART III—Other Comments on Performance

Identify any difficulties encountered in achieving results, quality and quantity of work produced, and like factors.

_____

_____

_____

PART IV—Knowledge and Skills

Identify and comment on the two or three skill areas in which performance over the evaluation period indicates high competence or need for improvement.

Demonstrated skills which lead to a high level of performance:

_____

_____

_____

Skills which need improvement (Be specific in illustrating how greater skill in these areas could have improved past performance):

_____

_____

_____

PART V—Performance Rating

Considering all aspects of demonstrated job performance, rate the employee's overall performance rating by indicating a position in the scale.

Marginal   _____

Provisional   _____

Proficient/Effective   _____

Superior   _____

Outstanding   _____

PART VI—Action Plans for Improving Performance in Present Job

1. What on-the-job actions will be taken before the next performance evaluation to help the employee improve performance?

Actions to be taken by the employee:

_____

_____

_____

Actions to be taken by the supervisor:

_____

_____

_____

2. Specific training program recommendations:

_____

_____

_____

3. Improvements expected:

_____

_____

_____

PART VII—Other Comments

Record significant points arising from the discussion of the performance evaluation.

_____

_____

_____

_____

PART VIII

Evaluation Prepared By:_____

Supervisor's Signature_____

Title_____Date_____

Check Appropriate Block:

[ ] I have discussed the contents of this performance evaluation with my supervisor and I concur with it.

[ ] I have reviewed the content of this performance evaluation with my supervisor and I do not concur with it. My comments:

   [ ] Are attached

   [ ] Are not attached

   [ ] Will be submitted later

Employee signature_____

Date_____

X. Religious Accommodation

A. Religious Accommodation Privacy Principles

The religion an employee practices and how he or she expresses religious beliefs are personal choices unrelated to the individual's job performance. The employer is affected only if an employee's adherence to his or her religion conflicts with workplace policies or rules. For example, a workplace policy might require all employees to join an industry union; however, an employee's religion may prohibit union membership.[34] Other potential conflicts involve dress and grooming codes,[35] hours of work requirements,[36] and bans on work during sabbath celebrations required by an individual's religious beliefs.[37] It is the employee's responsibility to communicate to the employer any workplace problem created by his or her religious beliefs.

Generally federal and state fair employment practice statutes require employers to attempt accommodation of certain religious practices.[38] For example, under the federal Civil Rights Act of 1964 (Title VII), an employer is obligated to offer an accommodation to an employee's religious practice, and this accommodation must be a reasonable solution to the conflict.[39] Reasonable accommodation is not required, however, if it would result in undue hardship to the employer's business.

B. Procedural Considerations

Employee requests for religious accommodation must be evaluated on a case-by-case basis to determine the extent of accommodation necessary and its effect on the employer. Before reacting to a request, the employer should:

1. evaluate the possible effect on the safety of all employees affected by the accommodation;
2. contact the union if a religious accommodation would affect the terms of an existing collective bargaining agreement; and
3. determine if the accommodation would impose undue hardship on the employer.

C. Religious Accommodation Policy

Religious Accommodation Policy

The Company and its employees will not discriminate against an employee on the basis of the employee's religious beliefs. It is the responsibility of the affected employee to inform the Company of any religious accommodation that is sought. The Company will use its best efforts to accommodate the employee's religious practice provided that no undue hardship is created for the Company or its employees and the accommodation does not affect the safety or health of other employees in the workplace.

XI. Privacy Misconduct by Employees

A. Misconduct Privacy Principles

Employers are not the only potential source of privacy misconduct at the workplace. Employees' privacy interests may be affected by the actions of other employees. Co-workers may abridge workplace privacy interests present in speech, beliefs, associations, information, and lifestyles in a variety of workplace situations. When such infringement occurs, the employer necessarily becomes involved as the general overseer of all activity in the workplace. It may be obligated by law to mediate the situation and to take disciplinary action.[40]

In one case, an employee brought a pornographic movie to work and played several minutes of it during training session breaks. This alleged joke could have had serious implications in terms of sexual harassment and infringement of others' privacy rights, and the court deemed as warranted the employer's written reprimand of the offending employee.[41] Theft of other employees' property is also an example of privacy misconduct which may warrant employer action. For example, an employer's termination of a 27-year exemplary employee who admitted to 10 incidents of petty theft from co-workers was found to be a reasonable disciplinary action.[42] Likewise, a supervisor was found liable for intentionally interfering with the relations of a female employee where she refused his romantic advances and was verbally and physically harassed at the workplace.[43]

Privacy misconduct also may be alleged if an employee asserts his freedom of speech interests in a manner that affects other employees. For example, an employee's poetry critical of management was found to be protected speech, because the employer could not prove that the employee influenced co-workers by distributing the writings.[44] However, an employee's writing falls outside the freedom of speech protection, and therefore warrants employer action, if there is evidence of intent to disrupt or undermine morale of the workforce and publication or posting of the writing by the employee.[45]

Employees' misconduct also may affect the privacy interests of the employer and others outside of the employer's workforce. This misconduct may involve the misuse of information in the possession of the employer and may result in discipline or termination. For example, a police officer was terminated for misusing a computerized law enforcement information system to disclose criminal justice information to a gas station owner regarding a recently hired attendant, whom the owner then terminated. The officer was terminated for misusing employer information and this termination was sustained.[46]

Furthermore, employees whose duties take them off the employer's premises can affect the privacy interests of nonemployees. For example, a telephone installer was justifiably terminated for voyeuristic "peeping Tom" activities.[47]

B. Developing Misconduct Procedures

In developing privacy misconduct procedures, the employer should consider:

1. An employee's physical privacy of his or her person;
2. An employee's privacy interests in the collection, maintenance, use, and disclosure of information; and
3. Applicable federal and state statutes where employer liability may result from sexual harassment, disclosure of employment records, and other employer actions.

C. Privacy Misconduct Policy

Privacy Misconduct Policy

The Company considers employee privacy to be paramount. The Company and its employees must ensure this. Physical intrusions of another employee's personal privacy will not be tolerated. Information will be collected, maintained, used, and disclosed with employee privacy interests protected. Only when a job-related use, Company business justification, or governmental- or court-required disclosure exists will employee privacy interests be compromised. Failure to follow this policy may result in disciplinary action up to and including termination.

XII. Sexual Harassment

A. Sexual Harassment Privacy Principles

As a workplace privacy interest, sexual harassment is prohibited by federal and state fair employment practice statutes[48] and is unlawful whether or not the employee suffers an economic or tangible loss.[49] Even absent such loss, employees can assert a sexual harassment claim if the harassment is severe and pervasive enough to create a "hostile working environment."[50] Conduct that creates a "hostile working environment" may consist of:

1. unwelcome sexual advances;

2. requests for sexual favors;

3. visual harassment in the forms of cartoons or drawings;

4. physical interference with normal work or movement in blocking or following an employee; or

5. verbal harassment through jokes, slurs, and derogatory comments.

Unlawful harassment also exists if employment or receipt of employment benefits is conditioned on the employee's submission to sexual advances or if rejection of these advances is used as the basis for employment decisions. These two situations are known as "quid pro quo" harassment.

Employees of either sex may be victims of sexual harassment,[51] as may employees of any sexual preference. Although discrimination on the basis of sexual preference is not unlawful under either federal or state fair employment practice statutes, sexual harassment of a homosexual by another homosexual is unlawful.[52] Additionally, conduct need not be sexual in nature to be considered evidence of harassment. For example, hostility toward women because of their gender can be manifested through incidents other than explicit sexual advances.

Employer liability for sexual harassment by its employees is consistent with the principle that an employer is liable for torts committed by one employee against another where the employer could have prevented the occurrence through reasonable care in hiring, supervising, or disciplining its workers.[53] A duty is imposed upon an employer to prevent reasonably anticipated sexual harassment.

Generally, employers are strictly liable in quid pro quo cases, regardless of whether the offending supervisor's conduct is known to the employer. This conclusion is based on the theory that the supervisor relies on his or her employer-given authority to hire, fire, or promote employees in attempting to control employment conditions.[54] This employer liability is taken a step further by statutes which may hold the employer responsible even for the acts of nonemployees who sexually harass employees if the employer knew or should have known of the conduct and failed to take immediate and appropriate corrective action.[55]

Sexual harassment also may form the basis of unemployment compensation claims. For example, unemployment compensation benefits were awarded to an employee who left her position because of a co-worker's sexual harassment.[56] The evidence was sufficient to establish a compelling and necessitous reason for employment separation.

Employers can minimize their liability for sexual harassment by investigating promptly upon learning of the problem and by taking remedial steps.[57] Remedial action may consist of reiterating to the workforce the employer's sexual harassment policy, along with promptly initiating investigations for sexual harassment and disciplining those who violate the policy. Privacy interests also may need to be considered in sexual harassment investigations. For example, names and addresses of other individuals who may have been harassed are required to be protected from release.[58] However, remedial action may not comprise retaliation against an employee who holds and acts on a good-faith belief that sexual harassment is occurring.[59]

B. Sexual Harassment Procedures

There are several actions an employer can take to prevent sexual harassment in the workplace and to respond to any incidents which occur.

1. Develop a policy that:

   a. defines sexual harassment;

   b. prohibits sexual harassment;

   c. contains a complaint or grievance procedure that does not require the employee to initially raise the sexual harassment concern with the harasser; and

   d. imposes discipline up to and including termination for those guilty of sexual harassment.

2. Discuss sexual harassment concerns at training and supervisor meetings.

3. Investigate all sexual harassment complaints.

1. Investigation of Incidents

The following procedure should be used to investigate employee sexual harassment claims:

1. Upon receiving a sexual harassment complaint, the Human Resources Department staff should:

   a. discuss it with the employee who filed the complaint;

   b. advise the employee that because of the sensitive nature of sexual harassment the complaint should not be discussed with co-workers or others;

   c. interview the alleged harasser;

   d. interview other persons with pertinent information, for example, witnesses or persons who also have had problems with the alleged harasser;

   e. inform or reiterate the sexual harassment policy to the alleged harasser;

   f. advise any involved supervisor that retaliation against the complaining employee is prohibited;

   g. hold a meeting of the entire workforce to discuss the problem if the identity of the alleged harasser is unknown; and

   h. maintain the confidentiality of the complaint, the identities of all persons involved, and the information collected during investigation.

2. Appropriate discipline up to and including termination should be imposed if it is determined that sexual harassment occurred.

3. Upon concluding its investigation, the human resources staff should contact the complainant to:

   a. explain what action has been taken;

   b. request the complainant to report other sexual harass-
      ment occurrences; and

   c. reiterate that the employer forbids sexual harassment.

C. Sexual Harassment Policies

Sexual Harassment Policy

Section 1. PURPOSE.   It is the purpose of this policy to ensure a work environment free of all forms of sexual harassment or intimidation.

Section 2. POLICY.   It is the Company's policy to regard sexual harassment as a very serious matter and to prohibit it in the workplace by any person and in any form.

Section 3. PROCEDURE.

a. Each supervisor has an affirmative duty to maintain his or her workplace free of sexual harassment.

b. Each supervisor will discuss this policy with all employees and assure them that they are not required to endure insulting, degrading, or exploitative sexual harassment.

c. No supervisor will threaten or insinuate, either explicitly or implicitly, that an employee's refusal to submit to sexual advances will adversely affect the employee's employment, evaluation, wages, advancement, assigned duties, shifts, career development, and other conditions of employment.

d. Other sexually harassing conduct in the workplace, whether committed by supervisors or nonsupervisory personnel, is prohibited. Such acts include but are not limited to:

   1. unwelcome sexual flirtations, advances, or propositions;

   2. verbal or written abuse of a sexual nature;

   3. graphic verbal comments about an individual's body;

    4. sexually degrading words used to describe an individual; and

    5. the display in the workplace of sexually suggestive objects or pictures.

e. Any employee who believes he or she has been sexually harassed should report the alleged act immediately to the Human Resources Department. *If the complaint involves someone in the employee's direct line of supervision, the employee should inform another manager of the complaint.* The complaint will be investigated by the Human Resources Department and the employee will be advised of the findings and conclusion.

f. There will be no discrimination or retaliation against any employee for making a sexual harassment complaint.

g. All actions taken to resolve sexual harassment complaints through internal investigations will be conducted confidentially.

h. Any supervisor, agent, or employee who is found after appropriate investigation to be guilty of sexual harassment will be subject to appropriate disciplinary action up to and including termination.

Sexual Harassment: Confidentiality

Section 1. COMPLAINTS. All employees are responsible for assuring that the workplace is free of sexual harassment. Any employee who has a sexual harassment complaint against anyone in the workplace, including supervisors, co-workers, or visitors, must bring the problem to the Company's attention. *If the complaint involves someone in the employee's direct line of supervision, then the employee should inform another manager of the complaint.*

Section 2. COMPLAINT CONFIDENTIALITY. All complaints will be handled promptly and special privacy safeguards will be applied in handling sexual harassment complaints. All employees should be aware that the identities of the complaining party and the person accused of sexual harassment will be kept confidential. The Company will retain as confidential all documentation of allegations and investigations.

Sexual Harassment Complaint Form

Name_____

Position_____

Department_____

Shift_____

Immediate Supervisor_____

1. Describe the sexual harassment incident(s)._____

_____

_____

_____

_____

_____

_____

_____

_____

2. Who was responsible for the sexual harassment incident(s)?_____

_____

_____

_____

_____

_____

_____

3. Identify any witnesses to the sexual harassment incident(s)._____

_____

4. Where did the sexual harassment incident(s) take place?_____

_____

_____

_____

5. List the date(s) and time(s) that the sexual harassment incident(s) occurred.___

Date

Employee Signature

XIII. Sexual Orientation

A. Sexual Orientation Privacy Principles

Of increasing concern to employers is the liability that may arise out of adverse employment actions based on an employee's sexual orientation. At present, homosexual men and women do not have a constitutionally protected right under the due process clause of the Fourteenth Amendment to challenge sodomy statutes prohibiting consensual homosexual acts, even in the privacy of their own homes. However, this subject is unclear and employers should proceed cautiously. They should not base employment decisions on sexual orientation.[60]

Federal fair employment practice statutes do not protect employees from discrimination based on their sexual orientation.[61] Some states, however, have adopted fair employment practice statutes specifically prohibiting this type of discrimination.[62] Employees' sexual orientation has no bearing on job performance and, therefore, is personal information that is extraneous and unrelated to the employment relationship. To minimize their vulnerability to litigation, employers should refrain from inquiring into the sexual

orientation of applicants or employees and should avoid employment decisions based on this orientation.

B. Procedural Guidelines

The employer should consider the following guidelines in dealing with sexual orientation at the workplace:

1. Review applicable federal and state fair employment practice statutes.

2. Prohibit all adverse actions by employees and managers
   against another employee based on his or her sexual orientation.

3. Safeguard as confidential information regarding an employee's sexual orientation.

C. Sexual Orientation Policy

Sexual Orientation Policy

The Company will not discriminate in hiring, promotion, discipline, or termination on the basis of an employee's sexual orientation.

XIV. Restrictive Covenants

A. Restrictive Covenant Privacy Principles

Restrictive covenants generally involve certain affirmative employee responsibilities toward their employer during employment
and after employment separation. They are often included as part
of written employment contracts. Subject matters covered by restrictive covenants include the employee's commitment not to compete with the former employer for a specified time within a certain
geographical territory; disclosure of customer lists, information
and data; disclosure of trade secrets learned during the course of

employment; and grants to the employer of sole rights to inventions, products, and information developed during employment.

These covenants impact employees' privacy interests by limiting opportunities and curtailing use of inventions, products, information, formulas, processes, techniques, and knowledge that were developed, learned, or obtained by the employee at the workplace. They may affect employees' opportunities to associate with certain individuals or companies and interfere with employees' pursuit of future employment opportunities.

Restrictive covenants are enforceable if they are reasonable and consistent with the public interest. To be enforceable, a postemployment restraint must:

1. reasonably protect a legitimate employer interest;
2. be limited in duration and geographic area; and
3. be reasonable in terms of the activities prohibited.[63]

The courts determine reasonableness of the covenant by reviewing the interest the employer seeks to protect. Generally, the employer's need for protection is balanced against the hardship imposed on the employee.

B. Procedural Safeguards

Restrictive covenants are so varied and complex that no set of procedures can completely protect employers from nondisclosure of confidential information or trade secrets. However, employers can minimize unfair competition by present and former employees by following these guidelines:

1. Review the advisability of requiring employees to sign a restrictive covenant by:

   a. avoiding use of an overbroad covenant on all employees without distinction. Restrictive covenants are not appropriate for every employee and extremely broad covenants may be held unenforceable as an improper restraint of trade; and

    b. tailoring a narrow covenant to key employees. This may deter the threat of trade secret misappropriation by reminding these employees of their nondisclosure obligation.

2. Establish a written policy of confidentiality that:

    a. includes a statement on the confidential nature of certain business information;

    b. avoids broad statements such as "All business information is confidential"; and

    c. tailors the policy to meet the needs of the business.

3. Preserve the confidentiality of critical business information by:

    a. stamping sensitive documents "confidential" and keeping them in a secure place;

    b. restricting the circulation of confidential information on a need-to-know basis;

    c. preventing suppliers or customers from having unlimited access to trade secrets;

    d. using written agreements protecting the business from unauthorized disclosure by an outsider where access is unavoidable;

    e. restricting access to areas of the facility where confidential trade information is kept; and

    f. using sign-in and -out logs and name badges for access to the employer's premises.

4. Realize that protection of confidential information depends on:

    a. knowledge of this type of information outside the employer's business;

b. employees' knowledge of information;

c. value of the information to the employer and its competi-
tors;

d. effort and money expended by the employer in developing information; and

e. difficulty for others to acquire or duplicate the information.

C. Restrictive Covenant Policies[64]

Confidential Information Policy

From time to time an employee may have access to confidential
information involving Company affairs, customers' advertising,
news stories prior to their release dates, and other privileged information. Unauthorized disclosure of this information is detrimental
to the Company. At no time should an employee knowingly discuss
the contents of this information or remove it from the Company's
premises. Confidential information must be *kept* confidential. An
employee's failure to maintain confidential information may result
in discipline up to and including termination.

Disclosure or Use of Trade Secrets Policy

While employed with the Company, employees will have access to and become acquainted with information of a confidential
or proprietary nature. This information is or may be applicable to
or related to the Company's present or future business, research,
development, or investigation, or the business of any Company
customer. Trade secret information includes but is not limited to
devices, secret inventions, processes, compilations of information,
records, specifications, and information concerning customers or
vendors. Employees will not disclose any Company trade secrets
directly or indirectly, or use them in any way, either during the
term of their employment or any time thereafter, except as required
in the course of Company employment.

Solicitation of Customers Policy

As an employment condition, all Company customers that employees service during their employment and all prospective customers from whom employees have solicited business while in the Company's employ shall be solely the Company's customers. For a period of one year immediately following employment termination, employees will neither directly nor indirectly solicit business regarding products or services competitive with those of the Company from any of the Company's customers with whom employees had contact in the one year prior to their termination.

Solicitation of Employees Policy

As a condition of employment, employees agree that the Company has invested substantial time and effort in assembling its present workforce. For a period of one year after employment termination, employees will neither directly nor indirectly induce or solicit any of the Company's employees to leave Company employment.

Disclosure and Assignment of Inventions Policy

As a condition of employment, employees agree to disclose to the Company any and all inventions, discoveries, improvements, trade secrets, formulas, techniques, processes, and know-how, whether or not patentable and whether or not made or conceived by them either solely or in conjunction with others during their employment, which relate to or result from the actual or anticipated business, work, or research in development of the Company, and which result, to any extent, from use of the Company's premises or property, or are suggested by any task assigned to them or any work performed by them for or on the Company's behalf. Employees acknowledge and agree that all of these inventions will be the sole property of the Company and employees hereby assign to the Company their entire rights and interests in any inventions.

Endnotes

1   *See, e.g.*, Nees v. Hocks, 272 Or. 210, 536 P.2d 512 (1975) (employee wrongfully terminated for expressing desire to serve on a jury).

2   *See* Appendix A sections I, II, III.J, and IV.N for a list of constitutional and statutory jury duty protections.

3   *See, e.g.*, Cal. Lab. Code § 230(c) (West 1971) (California statute prohibiting termination for taking time off for jury service).

4   United States ex rel. Madonia v. Coral Springs, 731 F. Supp. 1054 (S.D. Fla. 1990).

5   *See* Lever Bros. Co., 65 Lab. Arb. (BNA) 867 (1975) (D'Angelo, Arb.).

6   *See* Ferrar v. Columbia Univ., 695 F. Supp. 1544 (S.D. N.Y. 1990) (arbitration award determined that employee was terminated for just cause and termination did not violate state's public policy favoring jury service since employee refused to divulge jury hours, failed to report to work when directed, and stated he would do as he wished regardless of employer's requests).

7   *See, e.g.*, Bell v. Faulkner, 75 S.W.2d 612 (Mo. Ct. App. 1984) (refusing to vote as employer wished).

8   *See* Appendix A sections I, II, and IV.Y for statutes regulating employee voting time.

9   *See, e.g.*, Cal. Elec. Code § 14350 (West 1977) (California statute requiring employers to allow employees time off for voting).

10   Bell v. Faulkner, 75 S.W.2d 612 (Mo. Ct. App. 1984).

11   *See, e.g.*, Tameny v. Atlantic Richfield Co., 27 Cal. 3d 167, 610 P.2d 1330, 164 Cal. Rptr. 839 (1980) (termination for refusal to participate in employer price-fixing plan).

12   *See* Appendix A sections III.Q and IV.Z for federal and state whistle-blowing statutes.

13   McQuasy v. Bel Air Convalescent Home, Inc., 69 Or. App. 107, 684 P.2d 21 (1985).

14   Kessler v. Equity Management, Inc., 82 Md. App. 577, 572 A.2d 1144 (1990).

15   *See* Baker v. California Land Title Co., 349 F. Supp. 235, 238-39 (C.D. Cal. 1972), *aff'd*, 507 F.2d 895 (9th Cir. 1972), *cert. denied*, 422 U.S. 1046 (1975) (male employees hair length).

16   *See* Appendix A sections III.F and IV.H for federal and state fair employment practice statutes.

17   Caroll v. Talman Fed. Sav. & Loan Ass'n, 605 F.2d 1028 (7th Cir. 1979), *cert. denied,* 445 U.S. 929 (1980).

18   *See* Appendix A sections III.F and IV.H for federal and state fair employment practice statutes.

19   *See, e.g.,* Cutts v. Fowler, 692 F.2d 138 (D.C. Cir. 1982) (constitutionality of federal civil service spousal policy).

20   *See* Miller v. Fairfield Communities, Inc., 299 S.C. 23, 382 S.E.2d 16 (1989) (golf professional whose continued employment with resort community was conditioned on wife's resignation from position with competing real estate firm failed to establish that his constructive termination violated public policy or interfered with contractual relationships).

21   *See* Theiss v. John Fabick Tractor Co., 532 F. Supp. 453 (E.D. Mo. 1982) (promotion given to daughter of employer's president not a violation of fair employment practice statute).

22   *See* Holder v. City of Raleigh, 867 F.2d 823 (4th Cir. 1989) (employer's preference for hiring friends and relatives may be relevant evidence but is not conclusive to establish discrimination).

23   *See* Appendix A sections III.F and IV.H for federal and state fair employment practice statutes.

24   *See* NLRB v. J. Weingarten, Inc., 420 U.S. 251 (1975) (acknowledged employee's right to union representation at investigation interviews for private sector employees).

25   *See, e.g.,* Beaver County Community College, 17 P.P.E.R. ¶ 17035 (Pa. L.R.B. 1986) (acknowledged employee's right to union representation at investigatory interviews for Pennsylvania's public sector employees).

26   *See* Slaughter v. NLRB, 794 F.2d 120 (3d Cir. 1986) (it is at least permissible to interpret the National Labor Relations Act as guaranteeing unorganized employees the right to representation at investigatory interviews). *But see* E.I. DuPont de Nemouri & Co., 289 N.L.R.B. No. 81 (1988), *petition for review denied,* 876 F.2d 11 (3d Cir. 1989) (representation right does not apply to non-union employees under NLRA; however, employees may request presence of a fellow employee at a disciplinary interview).

27   McKnight v. General Motors Corp., 705 F. Supp. 464 (E.D. Wis. 1989) ($100,000 in compensatory damages and $500,000 in punitive damages).

28   *See, e.g.,* Chamberlain v. Bissell, Inc., 547 F. Supp. 1067 (W.D. Mich. 1982) (employer negligence in conducting performance evaluations).

29   *See* Wendler, Jr. v. DePaul, 346 Pa. Super. 479; 499 A.2d 1101 (1985) (negative employee performance evaluation).

30   Beeman v. Safeway Stores, 724 F. Supp. 674 (W.D. Mo. 1989) (employee not given adequate time to correct performance where conditions imposed by employer were onerous).

31   *See, e.g.,* Bulkin v. Western Kraft E., Inc., 422 F. Supp. 437 (E.D. Pa. 1976) (employee suffered embarrassment and an adverse credit rating because the employer disclosed inaccurate information contained in the employee's personnel file).

32   *See* Diggs v. Pepsi Cola, 861 F.2d 914 (6th Cir. 1988) (promise of continued employment as long as employee performs satisfactorily may create implied contract when tied to performance evaluation system).

33   *See, e.g.,* Pa. Dep't of Agric., 18 P.P.E.R. ¶ 18003 (Pa. L.R.B. 1986) (union entitled to review performance evaluations of employees who are in the same job classification as the grievants).

34   McDaniel v. Essex Int'l, Inc., 696 F.2d 34 (6th Cir. 1982) (religious belief prohibiting membership in unions must be reasonably accommodated by employer).

35   *See* Bhatia v. Chevron U.S.A., Inc., 734 F.2d 1382 (9th Cir. 1984) (employer requiring employee of Sikh religion to remove facial hair for respirator wearing).

36   Trans World Airlines, Inc. v. Hardison, 432 U.S. 63 (1977) (employer not required to bear more than a *de minimis* cost in giving employee time off for sabbath celebration).

37   *Id.*

38   *See* Appendix A sections III.F and IV.H for federal and state fair employment practices statutes.

39   Ansonia Bd. of Educ. v. Philbrook, 479 U.S. 60 (1986) (school board made a reasonable accommodation through its leave policy offering time off to a teacher whose religion required him to refrain from secular work on holy days).

40   *See, e.g.,* Island Creek Coal Co., 87 Lab. Arb. (BNA) 844 (1986) (Stoltenberg, Arb.) (employees peering into female dressing room).

41   Washoe County, 1988 Pub. Empl. Bargaining Cas. (CCH) ¶ 49,201 (1988) (Staudohar, Arb.); *see also* Kraft, Inc., 89 Lab. Arb. (BNA) 27 (1987) (Goldstein, Arb.) (employee properly suspended after showing other employees sexual and racial slurs he had written on pictures in in-house magazine, where this activity could create an offensive work environment). *But see* RMS Technologies, Inc., 94 Lab. Arb. (BNA) 297 (1990) (Nicholas, Jr., Arb.) (termination for bringing adult humor magazine to work was too severe).

42   City of Palo Alto, 90 Lab. Arb. (BNA) 361 (1988) (Koven, Arb.).

43   Lewis v. Oregon Beauty Supply Co., 302 Or. 616, 733 P.2d 430 (1987).

44   Sam Shainberg Co., 54 Lab. Arb. (BNA) 135 (1970) (Caraway, Arb.).

45   *Id.*

46   City of Sterling Heights, 89 Lab. Arb. (BNA) 723 (1987) (Keefe, Arb.). *But see* Press Democrat Publishing Co., 93 Lab. Arb. (BNA) 969 (1990) (McKay, Arb.) (suspension for examining contents of supervisor's computer basket was excessive).

47   General Tel. Co., 90 Lab. Arb. (BNA) 689 (1988) (Goldstein, Arb.).

48   *See* Appendix A sections III.F and IV.H for federal and state fair employment practice statutes.

49   Meritor Sav. Bank v. Vinson, 477 U.S. 57 (1986).

50   *See e.g.,* Rabidue v. Osceola Refining Co., 805 F.2d 611 (6th Cir. 1986) (court, relying on decision in Meritor Savings Bank v. Vinson, held that plaintiff must "demonstrate respondeat superior liability in a hostile environment case by proving that the employer, through its agents or supervisory personnel, knew or should have known of the charged sexual harassment and failed to implement prompt and corrective action"; here, employee claimed that a co-employee created a hostile environment through vulgar language and sexually oriented posters); Waltman v. International Paper Co., 875 F.2d 468 (5th Cir. 1989) (harassment coupled with sexual graffiti throughout employer's premises sufficient to create continuously hostile environment).

51   *See* Showalter v. Allison Reed Group, Inc., 767 F. Supp. 1205 (D.R.I. 1991) (males forced to have sex with supervisor's female secretary were sexually harassed).

52   *See, e.g.,* Wright v. Methodist Youth Servs., Inc., 511 F. Supp. 307 (N.D. Ill. 1981) (male supervisor's overt homosexual advances toward

male employee while at work is prohibited, as it is equivalent to heterosexual harassment).

53   Hall v. Gus Constr. Co., 842 F.2d 1010 (8th Cir. 1988) (employer had actual knowledge of the harassment because foreman, its agent, had observed many incidents of abuse).

54   *See* Hensen v. City of Dundee, 682 F.2d 897 (11th Cir. 1982) (employer found strictly liable for harassment of a female police dispatcher where police chief denied the dispatcher's request to attend police academy after she refused the chief's sexual advances).

55   29 C.F.R. § 1604.11(e) (1992).

56   United States Banknote v. Unemployment Compensation Bd., 133 Pa. Commw. 317, 575 A.2d 673 (1990).

57   *See* Swentek v. USAIR, Inc., 830 F.2d 552 (4th Cir. 1987).

58   *See* Cook v. Yellow Freight Sys., 132 F.R.D. 548 (E.D. Cal. 1990).

59   *See* Jenkins v. Orkin Exterminating Co., Inc., 646 F. Supp. 1274 (E.D. Tex. 1986).

60   *See* Bowers v. Hardwick, 478 U.S. 186 (1986).

61   *See, e.g.,* 42 U.S.C. §§ 2000e-1 through 2002-17 (1988) Civil Rights Act of 1964 (Title VII); Smith v. Liberty Mut. Ins. Co., 569 F.2d 325 (5th Cir. 1978).

62   *See, e.g.,* Wis. Stat. §§ 111.31-111.36 (1983); *see also* Doe v. Boeing Co., 823 P.2d 1159 (Wash. 1992).

63   *See, e.g.,* Boldt Mach. & Tools, Inc. v. Wallace, 469 Pa. 504, 366 A.2d 902 (1976) (restrictive covenant was overbroad because it was of an unreasonable length of time and extended to employer's entire sales area while employee's assigned territory comprised only a portion of it).

64   The forms contained in this section are not intended to constitute an employment contract. Relevant contract and employment matters must be evaluated before restrictive covenants should be used. It may be necessary to provide additional consideration if current, rather than new employees, are requested to enter into restrictive covenants to make these documents enforceable. Likewise, without adequate disclaimers, a restrictive covenant might be construed to offer a continued employment term modifying an intended at-will employment relationship.

8

Privacy Outside the Workplace

I. Introduction

Even though workplace commitments are finished for the day, the employee may still be subject to employer privacy intrusions outside the workplace. Depending on the employer's business and the employee's position, an employer may attempt to regulate and hold the employee accountable for certain actions.

The employer may attempt to influence, interfere with, restrict, or prohibit a variety of employee activities and actions that occur during nonworking hours. Such employer limitations may affect employees' community involvement, social commitments, financial arrangements, other employment opportunities, living arrangements, romantic involvements, recreational pursuits, and associations in general. Employer limitations may be directly stated in policies or imposed through indirect constraints brought about by peer pressure or the employer's social structure.

Privacy concerns arise over whether activities outside the workplace are strictly a personal employee matter subject only to criminal and civil laws and statutory and constitutional regulation. Generally, employers are permitted to hold employees accountable for and limit their outside pursuits that are directly related to the employees' jobs and that pose a direct financial threat or loss to the employer; for example, if an employee engages in a business which competes with the primary employer. However, employers may improperly affect employees' privacy interests by attempting to regulate or influence activities and pursuits that are not job-related; for example, employees' choices of friends, romantic relations, and political affiliations. Unfortunately, it is not always clear when an employer may legitimately regulate or be concerned with employee activities outside the workplace.

At times, employer interests regarding loyalty, conflict of interest, activities outside of work, and so forth may be interrelated. Each may arise under factual circumstances that involve one or more employer interests, yet each has its own distinct characteristics. For example, an employee who holds a second job may evoke the employer interests of loyalty and conflict of interest. Although several interests may overlap in one situation, this chapter reviews as separate topics the areas outside the workplace most frequently subject to legitimate employer regulation and influence to more clearly explain the distinct features of each area. The chapter will discuss policies and procedures relating to outside employment, employee loyalty, conflicts of interest, noncriminal misconduct, criminal misconduct, and residency requirements.

II. Outside Employment

A. Outside Employment Privacy Principles

The number of employees who hold jobs in addition to their primary positions is increasing at virtually all workforce levels. Outside employment may be sought for a variety of reasons, most commonly to supplement income or to prepare for a future job opportunity. Holding another job while working for an employer, or moonlighting, is not in itself subject to employer regulation or prohibition. The secondary job may be legitimately regulated or prohibited only if it interferes with performance or work attendance or affects the employer economically. Employer regulation or prohibition affects the employee's association and lifestyle privacy interests by influencing the economic opportunities the employee can or cannot pursue outside the workplace.

In any moonlighting situation, the primary employer's concerns are whether employees will continue to devote appropriate efforts to their work and whether the secondary job presents a breach of employee loyalty, conflict of interest, or threat to the primary employer's business interest. At the same time, the employee is attempting to improve his or her skills or economic condition. These competing interests must be balanced. The most effective way to achieve this balance is to decide each instance of outside employment on its own facts.

Holding another job while working for an employer is not in itself improper. However, an employee's outside interests can be legitimately questioned when they closely resemble the employer's business or services. For example, termination of a cigarette salesman was upheld because he operated his own vending machine company that supplied cigarettes.[1] However, termination in these instances is not absolute. Consider the case of a city plumber who was terminated for doing plumbing work on his own time without a required license. Despite established work rules prohibiting outside employment, the arbitrator ordered that the employee be reinstated because he had not been warned of possible discipline and other employees who had violated the employer's outside employment rules were reinstated after a suspension and continued in both jobs.[2]

The employer may also take action when an employee's secondary employment interferes with performance or attendance at the primary job. The employer may be justified in requiring the employee to resign from the secondary job in these circumstances.[3] Again, however, this is not an absolute employer right.[4] The facts of each situation must be examined before the employer acts against the employee and his or her outside employment.

B. Preliminary Considerations

Employers reasonably expect employees to devote their strongest work efforts to the primary employer's business. A written policy which states the employer's limitations on outside employment will safeguard this expectation. Before implementing a restrictive policy, however, the employer should consider whether:

1. the employer can limit legitimate business opportunities of employees;

2. the employee's outside business interests will subject the employer to unfavorable publicity or cause the employer to lose business;

3. the employee's outside business interests are inconsistent with the employer's interests; and

4. the employee's outside business interests will have an adverse affect on the employee's job performance because he or she must devote time and effort to an additional job.

C. Outside Employment Policies

Outside Employment Prohibited

The Company will not knowingly hire or retain any person who is otherwise employed. While employed with the Company no employee will be permitted to hold outside employment.

Outside Employment Conflict of Interest

Employees may engage in outside employment provided it does not interfere with their job performance and that it is not with an employer who competes with the Company. Employees will not use their positions with the Company to exploit outside employment interests. Employees engaged in outside employment must immediately inform their supervisor.

Outside Employment Interfering with Performance

Company employment will be considered the employee's primary employment. Prior to engaging in compensated outside employment, the employee must notify the Company and obtain written approval. Compensated outside employment will be limited to avoid impairment of employees' job performance. Should there be a conflict in employment, the supervisor and the Human Resources Department will review the situation. If the dispute cannot be resolved, the employee may be required to discontinue outside employment or be subject to employment separation.

Outside Employment Disclosure

Employees may engage in outside employment as long as this employment is disclosed to the Company and is determined by the Company not to interfere with the employee's primary job performance. Each employee must disclose in writing all outside employment. Failure to disclose outside employment or a misrepresentation of outside employment may result in disciplinary action up to and including termination.

Outside Employment Approval

Employees desiring to engage in or who currently are engaged in outside employment must provide written notification to the Company's Human Resources Department. Outside employment may not be continued or entered into without written authorization by the Company.

III. Loyalty

A. Loyalty Privacy Principles

Loyalty affects the employee's daily nonadverse relationship with the employer. Upon accepting an employment offer, the new employee makes an implied promise to serve the employer faithfully and honestly in the performance of duties and other actions in the workplace. Each employee, from the rank-and-file worker to an officer or director, is expected to exhibit loyalty toward the employer.[5] If the employee fails in this, the employer may have reason to discipline or terminate the employee.

A significant privacy issue is raised, however, by employers who demand the loyalty of employees outside the workplace even if employees' activities do not conflict with employer interests. This employer regulation may hinder the employees' development of association, lifestyle, and economic opportunities. For example, it would be unreasonable for an employer to attempt to limit the work activities of an employee's family members.

Employers may properly discipline or terminate employees if their outside activities breach the expectation of loyalty by affecting the employer's business operations. For example, an employee may be terminated for engaging in outside business activities that result in less work for the employer or for attempting to interfere with the employer's business or customers.[6] Loyalty problems also may arise if an employee attempts to appropriate the employer's business opportunities[7] or to encourage other employees to terminate employment.[8] Planning to begin another business while still an employee[9] or carrying out preparations for other employment on the current employer's working time[10] also are breaches of loyalty and subject to employer action.

B. Procedural Determinations

To determine if employees' actions outside the workplace constitute a breach of loyalty, the employer should evaluate whether the following possible results of the actions have occurred or might take place:

1. Deprivation of legitimate business opportunities for the employer

2. Derogatory effect on the business operations of the employer

3. Inconsistency with the employer's interests

4. Devotion of time and effort to the outside activities to the extent that performance would be adversely affected

C. Loyalty Policy

Loyalty Policy

Employees will not engage directly or indirectly in any outside relationship or activity that defers or adversely affects their primary responsibilities, interests, duties, or loyalties in actively furthering the Company's business.

IV. Conflict of Interest

A. Conflict of Interest Privacy Principles

At times, an employee's actions may be at odds with his or her employer's business concerns. The employee has a duty to avoid such conflicts of interest and to inform his or her employer upon discovery of any actual or potential conflicts. Often it is not the conflict itself that results in problems but the employee's failure to disclose the conflict to the employer or to divest of the conflict after warning by the employer.[11] In some cases, termination may be a proper employer response to an employee's deliberate failure to disclose a conflict.[12] Conflicts of interest also may comprise other employer concerns, such as employee loyalty[13] and outside employment restrictions or prohibitions.[14]

In one case, a conflict of interest was raised by a newspaper's sportswriter whose duties included picking favorites to win horse races. During the employment relationship, the sportswriter became part-owner of a horse. Although the employee refrained from picking favorites when his horse was racing, he continued to choose winners of races involving other horses of the same stable. The employee's ownership of a horse raised a conflict of interest because it gave the sportswriter an appearance of impropriety.[15]

Another employee action which may be a conflict of interest is the publication of negative oral or written information about the employer.[16] In the case of a public utility company, an employee wrote a letter opposing nuclear power and containing substantial falsehoods to a local newspaper. The written reprimand given to the employee was sustained because the letter was created as part of the employment relationship and not out of the employee's status as a private citizen.[17]

Marital and family relationships also may create conflicts of interest in the workplace. Generally, an employer may publish and institute a rule prohibiting employment of a married couple or a current employee's sibling or close family member. Problems arise when an employer who has no published rule terminates the spouse of an employee or gives one spouse the opportunity to resign.[18] Termination in this case is based on the employer's belief that an inherent conflict of interest exists when family members work closely together. Employers argue that conflicts between family loyalty and obligations to the employer are increased when family members are also co-workers and that these conflicts negatively affect the employment relationship, leaving the employer with unsatisfactory employee performance. This problem may be solved by prohibiting the employment of closely related family members or by not permitting family members to supervise relatives.

Employers also may claim that certain romantic relationships conflict with the employer's effective operation. For example, an employer properly terminated an employee who attended a company outing accompanied by a woman who was not his wife, but who the employee presented as his wife.[19] Although freedom of association is an important social right that ordinarily should not dictate employment decisions, the right to associate with a nonspouse at an employer's outing without fear of termination is not a social right. However, employers may not implement a blanket policy prohibiting certain relationships outside the workplace. For example, one employer cited conflict of interest to justify the termination of an employee for dating a sales representative from a competing company. The employer previously had expressed a policy of not interfering in the employee's personal affairs unless a detrimental effect on the employee's work performance resulted.

This policy accorded the employees a privacy expectation to hold a job with the employer even though off-duty conduct might not be approved by the employer. In this case, the employer could present no evidence of an actual conflict of interest; the employee did not have access to sensitive information that could have been used by the competitor and the employee's job performance was unaltered. The termination was overturned.[20]

B. Procedural Considerations

The employer should consider the following factors when deciding if an employee's actions constitute a conflict of interest:

1. Deprivation of legitimate business opportunities for the employer

2. Inconsistency with the employer's interests

3. Derogatory effect on the employer's business operations or public image

C. Conflict of Interest Policy

Conflict of Interest Policy

Section 1. ADVERSE PECUNIARY INTEREST. No employee will:

a. engage directly or indirectly in any business transactions or private arrangement for profit that accrues from or is based on his or her position or authority with the Company or

b. participate in the negotiation of or decision to award contracts, the settlement of any claims or charges in any contracts, the making of loans, rate fixing, guarantees, or other things of value with or for any entity in which he or she has a financial or personal interest.

Section 2. MISUSE OF INFORMATION. No employee may use, for his or her own personal gain or for the gain of others, any information obtained as a result of employment and not generally available to the public, nor may he or she disclose this information.

Section 3. MISUSE OF COMPANY FACILITIES AND EQUIP-MENT.   No employee may use Company equipment, supplies, or properties for personal gain for purposes other than those designated and authorized by the Company.

Section 4. OUTSIDE EMPLOYMENT.   No employee may engage in or accept outside employment or render services for another unless this outside employment or service is approved in advance and in writing by the Company.

Section 5. VIOLATION.   Employees who refuse or fail to comply with the policies set forth herein may be subject to disciplinary action including but not limited to reprimands, suspensions, and termination.

V. Noncriminal Misconduct

A. Noncriminal Misconduct Privacy Principles

Noncriminal misconduct involves wrongdoing by an employee outside the workplace that does not result in the employee being charged with a crime. Employee misconduct may affect the employment relationship. even if it occurs during nonworking hours and somewhere other than the employer's premises. When the misconduct directly relates to or has some impact on the employment relationship, the employer may be justified in taking adverse action against the employee.[21] Furthermore, the employee's actions may bring the employer into disrepute, a circumstance which also may warrant employer discipline. However, even though the employer may properly discipline or terminate the employee guilty of misconduct, the difficulty arises in determining when an employer's legitimate business interests supersede the employee's privacy interests in maintaining a life that is separate from the workplace and employer control.

To justify actions stemming from employee misconduct outside the workplace, employers generally must prove that the employee's adverse actions have caused actual business loss, have injured the employer's reputation, or have affected the employer's ability to maintain order in the workplace. For example, a bus operator was terminated when he was publicly identified as an acting grand dragon of the Ku Klux Klan. The arbitrator ruled the termination proper because a danger of physical violence existed along with a threatened employee wildcat strike and public economic boycott against the employer if the driver was not terminated.[22] It must be noted, however, that it was the employee's actions that were at issue, not his beliefs.

Another instance of employee misconduct in which employers may legitimately involve themselves is physical fighting. Normally, fights outside the workplace over personal matters would not be subject to employer regulation; however, if the fight pertains to the employment relationship and affects the work environment, the employer's concern may be justified. For example, an employer may take adverse action against an employee whose misconduct outside the workplace involves physical assault on his or her supervisor.[23] Similarly, misconduct at employer-sponsored events outside the workplace and off the employer's premises may result in disciplinary action; for example, if an employee threatens co-workers while attending such an event.[24]

The potential for adverse publicity also has caused employers to attempt to regulate employee business interests outside the workplace. For example, police officers who had part-ownership interest in a video rental store could not be prohibited through departmental regulations from renting or selling sexually explicit videotapes. The distribution of sexually explicit films was found to be protected speech under the First Amendment, and this protection outweighed the city's fear of an erosion of respect for and confidence in the police department.[25] Similarly, an employee was permitted to maintain an action against the employer who had terminated her because she was told by a supervisor that she would not be terminated for appearing in a Playboy magazine layout. These oral assurances by the supervisor altered her at-will employment status by creating an enforceable oral contract and negating her termination.[26]

B. Procedural Evaluations

To determine if an employee's noncriminal misconduct outside the workplace warrants an adverse employment action, the employer should consider:

1. the type of misconduct;

2. the employee's position;

3. injurious effect upon the employer's reputation; and

4. the source and degree of adverse publicity.

C. Noncriminal Misconduct Policy

Off-Duty Noncriminal Misconduct Policy

Section 1. OFF-DUTY NONCRIMINAL MISCONDUCT. Employee misconduct that does not result in criminal charges and that occurs outside the workplace may result in disciplinary action up to and including termination, depending on the nature of the conduct and its adverse impact on the Company's business.

Section 2. DETERMINATION. Among other factors, the following will be considered in making any disciplinary determination for incidents involving off-duty noncriminal misconduct:

a. the nature of the misconduct;

b. the employee's explanation, if available;

c. the extent to which allowing the employee to continue in his or her position would be detrimental to the physical well-being of the employee, co-workers, or other persons;

d. the nature of the employee's job duties, including responsibility and the discretion that must be exercised as part of those duties;

e. the extent to which the employee must deal directly with the public; and

f. any undue hardship to the employee which would result from his or her temporary reassignment.

VI. Criminal Misconduct

A. Criminal Misconduct Privacy Principles

Employees' off-duty misconduct which involve arrest or conviction may result in disciplinary action by the employer. When an employee's arrest or conviction has an adverse impact on the employer's business, disciplinary action or termination is generally considered appropriate.[27] Criminal misconduct outside the workplace may particularly affect the public sector employer. The sensitive nature of certain public sector positions and the likelihood and effect of negative publicity make it probable that criminal activities by public employees outside the workplace may have an indirect but damaging impact on the employer's business.[28]

An employee's arrest, indictment, or conviction for misconduct outside the workplace may warrant disciplinary action if the misconduct adversely affects the job performance of the employee or fellow employees or is directly or indirectly detrimental to the employer's business. For example, a dairy driver-salesman was one of ten people arrested in a raid on a night club and charged with Sunday liquor purchase, prostitution, pandering, and conducting obscene exhibitions involving men and women. The employee's suspension was sustained, pending the outcome of the trial, because of possible damage to the employer's image and goodwill.[29] The driver-salesman's duties necessitated a close personal relationship with customers and the seriousness of the charges increased the potential harm to the employer's business.

Even if the courts find an employee guilty of criminal misconduct, employer action is not justified absent a negative effect on the employer. Criminal convictions did not justify a teacher's termination for actions the employer considered immoral. The teacher was convicted of public intoxication, driving while intoxicated, and driving without a valid license. Newspaper articles on the incident were not widely circulated, no notoriety resulted, and no evidence was presented that the teacher was ever intoxicated on school property or in the classroom. Because the teacher's actions did not impair his job performance or harm the employer's operation, the employer was ordered to reinstate the teacher.[30]

Assault by an off-duty police officer of an on-duty police officer who had placed the off-duty officer under arrest was just cause for termination, even though the off-duty police officer was acquitted of all criminal charges and was granted unemployment compensation benefits after his termination.[31] Assaulting another police officer constituted conduct unbecoming an officer, providing just cause for the termination. The employee's actions reflected poorly on the police department by affecting its morale and destroying public respect and confidence in its operations.

If an employee's arrest does not result in conviction, the employer may have to reverse any adverse employment action based on the arrest. In one case, an employee was suspended by her employer pending resolution of an indictment for conspiracy to transport cocaine from Mexico to Georgia. A court order indicated that her case had been placed on its nonactive case docket, but the employer nevertheless terminated her. A trial court later dismissed the criminal indictment. The employer was not required to reinstate the employee when her case was placed on the nonactive docket but, once the indictment was dismissed, the employer was required to prove that she committed a criminal offense because the employee's discipline was linked with the criminal charge. The employer had the right to review the evidence in the trials of the employee's alleged co-conspirators, but the evidence did not support a finding that the employee was guilty of the offenses charged or of any lesser charge for which she could be terminated; therefore, reinstatement was appropriate.[32]

B. Determining Employer Action

The employer should use the following factors to determine if adverse action is justified by an employee's criminal misconduct outside the workplace:

1. Nature of the employee's misconduct

2. Result of the criminal misconduct (arrest, indictment, or conviction)

3. The employee's explanation, if available

4. Effect on job performance of the employee or fellow employees

5. Detriment to the employer's business

6. Negative oral or written publicity

C. Criminal Misconduct Policy

Criminal Misconduct Policy

Section 1. CRIMINAL MISCONDUCT CONSTITUTING A FELONY OR RELATED TO EMPLOYMENT. As soon as practicable after an employee has been formally charged with criminal misconduct which constitutes a felony under the laws of this state or is related to his or her employment, the employee will be suspended without pay. If the charge results in a conviction in a court of law, the employee may be terminated.

Section 2. CRIMINAL MISCONDUCT OTHER THAN A FELONY OR NOT RELATED TO EMPLOYMENT. As soon as practicable after an employee is formally charged with criminal misconduct other than a felony or that is not related to his or her employment, the Human Resources Department will conduct an inquiry and make a preliminary determination regarding whether or not the employee should continue to perform his or her duties pending the outcome and final determination of the investigation.

(See Section 3 (INVESTIGATION) and Section 4 (FINAL DETERMI-NATION) of this policy.) The preliminary investigation will be conducted under the following guidelines:

a. *Purpose.* The purpose of the preliminary determination is to minimize the effect which the accusation of a crime by an employee may have upon the Company's ability to function, pending an investigation and final determination regarding the existence of sufficient reason for employee disciplinary action.

b. *Factors to be Considered in Making the Preliminary Determination.* In making the preliminary determination, the Human Resources Department will consider, among other factors:

1. The nature, weight, and source of the accusations against the employee

2. The employee's explanation, if available

3. The nature of the employee's duties, including the discretion exercised as part of those duties

4. The relationship of the accusation to the employee's duties

5. The extent to which allowing the employee to continue in his or her position would be detrimental to the physical well-being of the employee, co-workers, or other persons

6. The extent to which the employee must deal directly with the public

7. Any undue hardship to the employee that would result from a temporary reassignment of the employee

c. *Preliminary Determination.* The preliminary determination will consist of one of the following alternatives to be implemented by the Human Resources Department:

1. Allow the employee to continue to perform duties pending the outcome and final determination of the investigation.

2. Reassign the employee to less sensitive duties within the Company pending the outcome and final determination of the investigation.

3. Suspend the employee without pay pending the outcome and final determination of the investigation.

d. *Contact with Law Enforcement Agency.* In considering the nature, weight, and source of the accusations against an employee, the Company will contact the law enforcement agency involved in the accusations to verify the charge and to obtain all available information.

e. *Employee Status.* After the preliminary determination is made, the employee will remain in the status selected by the Human Resources Department pending the outcome and final determination of the investigation as outlined in Section 3 (INVESTIGATION) and Section 4 (FINAL DETERMINATION) of this policy. This status will be temporary and will have no bearing on the final determination.

Section 3. INVESTIGATION. Any employee formally charged with criminal misconduct will be subject to an immediate investigation conducted by the Human Resources Department:

a. *Purpose.* The purpose of the investigation will be to determine if sufficient reason exists for disciplinary action including but not limited to suspension, demotion, or termination.

b. *Conduct of Investigation.* In the investigation, all relevant facts will be promptly gathered and considered. The investigation will be completed within twelve (12) working days. The following contacts may be a part of the investigation:

1. *Law Enforcement Agencies.* The Human Resources Department may request the assistance of any law enforcement

agency involved in the matter; however, this will not relieve the Department of the responsibility to make an independent evaluation.

2. *Employee.* The Human Resources Department will afford the employee an opportunity to respond to the accusations, to have representation during meetings relating to the investigation if representation is requested, and to submit additional information.

Section 4. FINAL DETERMINATION. After completion of the investigation, the Human Resources Department will have five (5) working days to make a final determination regarding whether the investigation's results establish sufficient reason for disciplinary action. The Company's President will review this decision and ratify the Human Resources Department's decision absent an abuse of discretion by the Department. In determining whether sufficient reason for disciplinary action exists, the Human Resources Department will consider, among other factors:

a. The nature, weight, and source of the accusations against the employee

b. The employee's explanation, if available

c. The nature of the employee's duties, including the amount of discretion exercised as part of those duties

d. The relationship of the accusation to the employee's duties

e. The extent to which allowing the employee to continue in his or her position would be detrimental to the physical well-being of the employee, co-workers, or other persons

f. The extent to which the employee must deal with the public

Where sufficient reason for disciplinary action exists, the Human Resources Department will immediately take the appropriate disciplinary action including but not limited to suspension, demotion, or termination. If, based on information available at the time of investigation, a finding of sufficient reason is not made, the employee will be notified of the disposition and will retain or be retroactively reinstated to his or her position.

VII. Residency Requirements

A. Residency Privacy Principles

Generally, a person's residence is the structure in which he or she lives on a daily basis and where he or she intends to stay. Physical presence for a long time period, however, is not dispositive of residence. Other factors may include: (1) voting place; (2) mailing address; (3) driver's license address; (4) where one keeps clothing; (5) location of property owned; and (6) where rent is paid.

Employer regulation of its employees' residency directly affects employees' privacy interests in association and lifestyle. Employers who implement residency requirements are, in effect, choosing where their employees live and, consequently, the amount of their mortgage or rental payment. Employers may also curtail access to other employment opportunities by imposing geographical limits on employees.

Residency requirements are valid when such requirements are necessary to serve legitimate employer interests. Frequently, public employment positions involving teachers, police, and fire fighters are subject to residency requirements. Public employers in these cases may be mandated by a local law or a collective bargaining agreement to impose such requirements. However, even if a law or collective bargaining agreement recognizes the employer's right to establish rules and regulations for the safe and efficient conduct of its business, a residency requirement must be reasonable and justifiable. One public employer, for example, required all employees to live within three miles of the workplace. Even though a collective bargaining agreement allowed some employer regulation, an arbitrator overturned the rule because the three-mile limit was too restrictive and was without valid reason.[33]

Residency requirements imposed on applicants may be found suspect under fair employment practice statutes when they have a disparate impact on minorities, unless the employer can show substantial justification for the practices. Although employment practices may appear fair and neutral, if they are found to have a disparate impact on a protected group they will be invalidated unless they are shown to have a "manifest relationship to the employment in question."[34] Policies designed to "help our own" and to foster pride in the community by hiring only local residents will not justify employment practices that have a disparate impact on protected groups.[35]

B. Procedural Considerations

Procedures restricting employees' areas of residence should:

1. have a practical justification if rules require employees to live within a convenient distance from; for example, to facilitate call-backs to the premises in emergencies;

2. be based upon the employer's legitimate job-related desire to have employees involved in the community's affairs; and

3. require employees to meet the residency requirement within a certain time limit.

C. Residency Policy

Residency Policy

Section 1. RESIDENCE. Residence is the place or locality in which an employee lives and manifests an intent to continue to live. Factors providing evidence of intent to maintain residency include:

a. Rent, lease, or purchase of a property that the employee has made his or her home

b. Payment of state and local taxes

    c. Registration within *(State's Name)* of personal property including bank accounts, stocks, bonds, and automobiles

    d. Possession of a current *(State's Name)* motor vehicle operator's license

    e. Current registration to vote in *(State's Name)*

Section 2. APPLICATION. Residency requirements will be as follows:

    a. Persons hired will be legal residents of this state, unless residence has been waived by the Human Resources Department because of unique job requirements, and will reside within *(Describe Area)*.

    b. The Director of Human Resources, upon submission of satisfactory justification, may limit hiring to individuals who are residents of this state residing within *(Describe Area)*.

Section 3. WAIVER. The Director of Human Resources may waive the residency requirement if there appears to be an inadequate supply of well qualified residents within *(Describe Area)* available for a particular position.

Endnotes

1   Phillips Bros., Inc., 63 Lab. Arb. (BNA) 328 (1974) (Stern, Arb.).

2   City of Rockville, 76 Lab. Arb. (BNA) 140 (1981) (Levitan, Arb.).

3   *See, e.g.,* Climate Control, 89 Lab. Arb. (BNA) 1062 (1987) (Cromwell, Arb.) (termination reduced to suspension provided that employee resigned from second job which caused frequent absences from primary job).

4   Mercoid Corp., 63 Lab. Arb. (BNA) 941 (1974) (Kossoff, Arb.) (employee was reinstated after being terminated for working a second job while on sick leave from his primary employment because he had worked this job for several years with the primary employer's approval).

5   *See, e.g.,* Arnold's Ice Cream Co. v. Carlson, 330 F. Supp. 1185 (E.D.N.Y. 1971) (employees prohibited from forming competing business).

6   *See, e.g.,* Westwood Chem. Co. v. Kulick, 570 F. Supp. 1032 (S.D.N.Y. 1983) (breach of employee's good faith and loyalty to employer); *see also* section IV.A of this chapter, *infra.*

7   *See, e.g.,* Appalachian Contracting Co. v. Cox, 403 F. Supp. 176 (E.D. Tenn. 1975) (employee engaging in coal-brokering activities for own profit).

8   *See, e.g.,* Arnold's Ice Cream Co. v. Carlson, 330 F. Supp. 1185 (E.D.N.Y. 1971).

9   *Id.*

10   *See, e.g.,* Meeker v. Stuart, 188 F. Supp. 272 (D.D.C. 1960), *aff'd,* 289 F.2d 902 (D.C. Cir. 1961) (soliciting employer's customers while employed).

11   *See, e.g.,* Ralph's Grocery Co., 87 Lab. Arb. (BNA) 1140 (1986) (Darrow, Arb.) (employee purchasing materials from employer's supplier for use in employee's competing business after being warned by employer that this was improper).

12   *See, e.g.,* University of Calif, 78 Lab. Arb. (BNA) 1032 (1982) (Ross, Arb.) (employee properly terminated for entering into a contract on behalf of the employer with a firm in which her husband had a substantial financial interest not revealed to the employer).

13   *See* section III of this chapter, *supra.*

14   *See* section II of this chapter, *supra.*

15   New York Post Corp. 62 Lab. Arb. (BNA) 225 (1973) (Friedman, Arb.).

16   Forest City Publishing Co., 58 Lab. Arb. (BNA) 773, 783 (1972) (McCoy, Arb.) ("Can you bite the hand that feeds you, and insist on staying for future banquets?").

17   San Diego Gas & Elec. Co., 82 Lab. Arb. (BNA) 1039 (1983) (Johnston, Arb.).

18   *See* Thomas v. Metroflight, Inc., 814 F.2d 1506 (10th Cir. 1987) (no-spouse rule reluctantly affirmed, but court indicated that no-spouse rules in practice often result in discrimination against women and generally are unjustified).

19   Staats v. Ohio Nat'l Life Ins. Co., 620 F. Supp. 118 (W.D. Pa. 1985).

20   Rulon-Miller v. IBM, 162 Cal. App. 3d 241, 208 Cal. Rptr. 524 (1984).

21   *See, e.g.,* Inland Container Corp., 28 Lab. Arb. (BNA) 312 (1957) (Ferguson, Arb.) (altercation on employer's property while employee off-duty).

22   Baltimore Transit Co., 47 Lab. Arb. (BNA) 62 (1966) (Duff, Arb.).

23   *See* General Tel. Co., 69 Lab. Arb. (BNA) 351 (1977) (Bowles, Arb.).

24   *See* Indianapolis Power & Light Co., 88 Lab. Arb. (BNA) 1109 (1987) (Volz, Arb.) (employee misconduct at employer-sponsored basketball game).

25   Flanagan v. Munger, 890 F.2d 1557 (10th Cir. 1989).

26   Hammond v. Heritage Communications, Inc., 756 S.W.2d 152 (Ky. Ct. App. 1988).

27   *See, e.g.,* Menzie Dairy Co., 45 Lab. Arb. (BNA) 283 (1965) (Mullin, Jr., Arb.) (dairy driver-salesman's arrest warranted because the circumstances were considered detrimental to employer's customer relations).

28   *See, e.g.,* New York State Dep't of Corrections, 86 Lab. Arb. (BNA) 793 (1986) (LaManna, Arb.) (police officer's off-duty marijuana smoking and burglary involvement).

29   Menzie Dairy Co., 45 Lab. Arb. (BNA) 283 (1965) (Mullin, Jr., Arb.).

30   Michigan City Sch. Corp., 91 Lab. Arb. (BNA) 1244 (1989) (Eagle, Arb.).

31   Philadelphia Civil Serv. Comm'n v. Wojtusik, 106 Pa. Commw. 214, 525 A.2d 1255 (1987).

32   Continental Baking Co., 88 Lab. Arb. (BNA) 1142 (1987) (Statham, Arb.); *see also* Florida Power & Light Co., 88 Lab. Arb. (BNA) 1136 (1987) (Kindig, Arb.) (employee reinstated where conviction did not impair usefulness or adversely affect employer's business, employees, equipment, or operations). *But see* Genesee County, 90 Lab. Arb. (BNA) 48 (1988) (House, Arb.) (suspension of nurse in employ of Sheriff's department for shoplifting while off-duty upheld where mere presence of an employee charged with a crime had potential to harm the image of the sheriff's department).

33   City of Monmouth, 79 Lab. Arb (BNA) 345 (1982) (Harter, Arb.) (unreasonable public employment residency requirement).

34   Griggs v. Duke Power Co., 401 U.S. 424, 432 (1971).

35 *See also* NAACP v. Town of Harrison, 749 F. Supp. 1327 (D.N.J.), *aff'd*, 940 F.2d 792 (3d Cir. 1990) (residency requirement discriminated against qualified black applicants for town police, fire, clerk-typist, and laborer positions).

Workplace Privacy Audits

I. Introduction

Increasingly, employers are recognizing the potential liabilities created by the growth and expansion of employment litigation arising out of individual employee rights. Employer liability was once limited to disputes occurring under grievance arbitration procedures in collective bargaining agreements. Now, *any* adverse employment decisions by private and public sector employers can be subject to federal and state regulation,[1] as well as prolonged court litigation and costly damage awards or settlements. Employers can minimize their exposure to litigation by understanding potential liability that may arise out of the hiring process,[2] employer actions at the workplace,[3] and employer regulation of employees' activities outside the workplace.[4]

To assess their potential liability, employers must develop a system for defining current workplace privacy inter-relationships between the employer and its employees. This system also must measure any changes that occur in these relationships. One such system is the Workplace Privacy Audit. The complete workplace privacy audit comprises several stages and includes: (1) an initial questionnaire to collect background information; (2) a review of relevant employer documents; (3) discussions with management and supervisors; (4) supplemental written inquiries to verify information; and (5) a final evaluation of responses. The audit provides a standardized methodology for collecting relevant information and reviewing current procedures and policies. These two steps are keys to an evaluation of potential employer exposure and liability.

For a workplace privacy audit to be useful and accurate, employer responses must be honestly given, even though legal concerns may be raised through the identification of potential workplace privacy liability. Honest responses are essential to pinpoint and isolate problem areas so that preventive action can be taken to minimize concerns before they create employer liability. The Human Resources staff should coordinate the audit function.

This chapter reviews employer procedures for assessing the potential for workplace privacy liability. It examines the issues and concerns of workplace privacy, audit formats, analysis of audit results, and implementation of change in procedures and policies.

II. Recognizing Workplace Privacy Issues

Increased employment law protections of individual employee rights mandate that employers take preventive measures now to minimize their future litigation potential arising out of workplace privacy claims.[5] Employers must evaluate the strengths and weaknesses in their procedures and policies to identify problem areas. Some of these problem areas may be apparent, but others may require closer scrutiny to be uncovered. Employers may consider consulting legal counsel and human resources professionals to ensure that no problem areas are overlooked and that employer procedures and policies comply with applicable federal and state statutes.[6]

To identify workplace privacy issues and concerns, the employer must collect information from a variety of sources. Once collected, the information can be reported on workplace privacy audit forms for evaluation. In collecting and analyzing this information, the employer will obtain an understanding about its structure and internal organization and specific functions such as recruitment, compensation, fringe benefits, promotion and transfer policies, and discipline and terminations.

III. Workplace Privacy Audits

The audit provides a written record that identifies how the employer currently handles the issues and concerns that affect employees' privacy interests. Evaluation of audit results identifies areas of concern and helps the employer establish a plan of action to minimize its potential liability.

This chapter contains forms the employer may use to conduct a workplace privacy audit. These forms may be used individually or as a group to evaluate the privacy procedures and policies currently in place. These forms address the areas of: (1) background information; (2) recruitment, hiring, and workforce composition; (3) job descriptions, assignments, promotions, and transfers; (4) employer communications; and (5) discipline and termination.

A. Background Information Audit Form

The Background Information Audit Form solicits information regarding the employer's philosophy, products and services, and operations and growth. It also indicates the employment information currently being collected, maintained, used, and disclosed regarding each employee. Each of these employer functions has an impact on workplace privacy.

Background Information Audit Form

1. Attach an organizational chart of the employer's operations.

2. List all employer facilities, their locations, and the number of supervisory and nonsupervisory employees at each facility. Describe the function of each facility.

Facility/ Location	Nonsupervisory Employees	Supervisory Employees	Total	Function

3. For each facility, specify the number of employees represented by a union, the union's name, and the date of the
   union's recognition or certification.

Facility	Employees	Name of Union	Date of Recognition or Certification

Attach copies of current collective bargaining agreements.

4. For each facility, list each department and identify its supervisor. List all job classifications/titles and indicate the number of employees in each classification.

Facility	Department	Supervisor	Classifications/ Titles	Employees

Attach organizational charts for each facility.

5. For each facility, list the name, job title, and duties of the
   person directly responsible for employment relations, procedures, and policies and the length of time that person has
   held that position.

Facility	Name	Job Title	Duties	Time Position Held

6. Indicate whether written employer procedures and policies are used to implement the following:

                                                                    Yes No

   a. The Age Discrimination in Employment Act (ADEA)   ___ ___

   b. The Employee Retirement Insurance Security Act (ERISA)   ___ ___

   c. Fair Employment Practices (FEP) statutes   ___ ___

   d. The Fair Labor Standards Act (FLSA)   ___ ___

   e. The National Labor Relations Act (NLRA)   ___ ___

   f. The Occupational Safety and Health Act (OSHA)   ___ ___

   g. The Americans with Disabilities Act (ADA)   ___ ___

   h. Federal and state statutes regarding employee privacy   ___ ___

   i. Collection, maintenance, use, and disclosure of employment records[7]   ___ ___

Attach copies of existing procedures and policies relating to these statutes.

7. Indicate if any facilities have been reviewed or investigated by the following governmental agencies:

                                                                    Yes No

   a. The Equal Employment Opportunity Commission (EEOC)   ___ ___

   b. A state Equal Employment Opportunity Commission (EEOC)   ___ ___

   c. The Department of Labor (DOL)   ___ ___

   d. A state Wage & Hour Commission   ___ ___

   e. The National Labor Relations Board (NLRB)   ___ ___

   f. The Occupational Safety and Health Administration (OSHA)   ___ ___

   g. Any other federal or state agency[8]   ___ ___

For each affirmative answer to any of the above, indicate the following:

Facility	Date	Agency and Subject	Result

8. Indicate if any facilities have ever been subject to a conciliation or settlement agreement with:

	Yes	No
a. The Equal Employment Opportunity Commission (EEOC)	___	___
b. A state Equal Employment Opportunity Commission (EEOC)	___	___
c. The Department of Labor (DOL)	___	___
d. A state Wage & Hour Commission	___	___
e. The National Labor Relations Board (NLRB)	___	___
f. The Occupational Safety and Health Administration (OSHA)	___	___
g. Any other federal or state agency[9]	___	___

9. Have any facilities ever been a party to a court decree in a matter involving adverse employment practices? [ ] Yes [ ] No

If Yes, attach a copy of any decree.

10. Indicate if any of the following information is collected and retained regarding each employee:

	Yes	No	Time Retained
a. Full name	___	___	_____
b. Address including zip code	___	___	_____
c. Birth date	___	___	_____

d. Social Security Number ___ ___ _____

e. Race ___ ___ _____

f. Gender ___ ___ _____

g. Source of the employee's knowledge of job opening ___ ___ _____

h. Employment application ___ ___ _____

i. Hiring date ___ ___ _____

j. Occupation or job classification ___ ___ _____

k. Time and day when the employee's workweek begins ___ ___ _____

l. Hours worked each workday ___ ___ _____

m. Total hours worked each workweek ___ ___ _____

n. Regular rate of pay such as "per
hour," "per week," or "piece-
work" ___ ___ _____

o. Daily or weekly straight-time
wages ___ ___ _____

p. Total overtime compensation for
the workweek ___ ___ _____

q. Total wages paid each pay period ___ ___ _____

r. Total additions or deductions
from wages each pay period ___ ___ _____

s. Date of payment and the pay period covered by the payment ___ ___ _____

t. Date and amount of wage increase or decrease due to promotion or demotion ___ ___ _____

u. Date of any disciplinary action including termination ___ ___ _____

v. Date and description of any
work-related accidents ___ ___ _____

w. Name of contact in case of emergency ___ ___ _____

   x. Disability   ___ ___ _____

   y. Other employee information[10]   ___ ___ _____

Describe:

_____

_____

_____

11. Indicate if any of the following information is disclosed internally or to outside third parties regarding each employee:

	Yes	No	If Yes, Explain
a. Full name	___	___	_____
b. Address, including zip code	___	___	_____
c. Birth date	___	___	_____
d. Social Security Number	___	___	_____
e. Race	___	___	_____
f. Gender	___	___	_____
g. Source of the employee's knowledge of job opening	___	___	_____
h. Employment application	___	___	_____
i. Hiring date	___	___	_____
j. Occupation or job classification	___	___	_____
k. Time and day when the employee's workweek begins	___	___	_____
l. Hours worked each workday	___	___	_____
m. Total hours worked each workweek	___	___	_____
n. Regular rate of pay such as "per hour," "per week," or "piecework"	___	___	_____
o. Daily or weekly straight-time wages	___	___	_____

p. Total overtime compensation for the workweek   __ __ ____

q. Total wages paid each pay period   __ __ ____

r. Total additions or deductions from wages each pay period   __ __ ____

s. Date of payment and the pay period covered by the payment   __ __ ____

t. Date and amount of wage increase or decrease due to promotion or demotion   __ __ ____

u. Date of any disciplinary action including termination   __ __ ____

v. Date and description of any work-related accidents   __ __ ____

w. Name of contact in case of emergency   __ __ ____

x. Disability   __ __ ____

y. Other employee information   __ __ ____

Describe:

_____

_____

_____

12. Is the information listed in questions 10 and 11 maintained on a computer system? [ ] Yes [ ] No

    If Yes, identify who can access this information and the circumstances under which this information can be accessed.

Name   Reason for Disclosure

_____   _____

_____   _____

_____   _____

_____   _____

If No, how is this information maintained?

_____

_____

13. Are employees provided upon request with the records listed in questions 10 and 11? [ ] Yes [ ] No

14. Describe procedure for updating employee addresses:

_____

_____

15. Are employees provided, with each wage payment, an itemization of all deductions, dates of compensation period, employer's name, and employee's name and Social Security number? [ ] Yes [ ] No

16. Indicate if notices relating to the following statutes or subjects are posted in conspicuous places in each facility:

                                                Yes No

    a. The Age Discrimination in Employment Act (ADEA) ___ ___

    b. The Americans with Disabilities Act (ADA) ___ ___

    c. The Civil Rights Act of 1964 (Title VII) ___ ___

    d. The Employee Polygraph Protection Act ___ ___

    e. The Fair Labor Standards Act (FLSA) ___ ___

    f. The Occupational Safety and Health Act (OSHA) ___ ___

    g. Applicable state wage and working hours laws ___ ___

    h. Name of workers' compensation carrier ___ ___

    i. Unemployment benefits   __ __

    j. Other required postings of federal and state statutes   __ __

Describe:

_____

_____

If Yes, where are these notices posted? _____

17. Are EEO-1 reports filed annually? [ ] Yes [ ] No

18. Is a written Affirmative Action Program (AAP) in place in each facility? [ ] Yes [ ] No

    If Yes, attach copies of the AAPs for the past five years.

19. Is there a written fair employment practice policy? [ ] Yes [ ] No

    If Yes, attach a copy and indicate if the written policy is:

                                                                                 Yes No

    a. Included in an employee handbook   __ __

    b. Posted on employee bulletin boards   __ __

    c. Included in a newsletter, annual report, or other publication   __ __

    d. Included on all purchase orders, leases, and contracts   __ __

    e. Communicated to all recruiting sources   __ __

    f. Communicated at regularly scheduled employee meetings   __ __

    g. Communicated to manager- and supervisor-trainees   __ __

    h. Communicated to managers and supervisors   __ __

    List other places where the statement is published:

_____

_____

_____

B. Recruitment, Hiring, and Workforce Composition Audit Form

The Recruitment, Hiring, and Workforce Composition Audit form identifies the workplace privacy interests that may be infringed upon during the recruiting and hiring stages and as the employment relationship continues.

Recruitment, Hiring, and Workforce Composition Audit Form

1. List all oral and written sources in which each facility advertises for employees. Attach a copy of any advertisements used within the last year.

   _____

   _____

   _____

2. Do the oral or written advertising sources segregate advertisements by sex? [ ] Yes [ ] No

3. Do the advertisements indicate a preference for young applicants or place a limit on the years of experience which the applicants may have? [ ] Yes [ ] No

4. Do the advertisements indicate any preference, limitation, or specification based on:

	Yes	No
a. Race	___	___
b. Color	___	___
c. Religion	___	___
d. National origin	___	___
e. Disability	___	___
f. Physical condition	___	___
g. Sexual orientation	___	___

5. Do the advertisements indicate that the employer is an "Equal Opportunity Employer"? [ ] Yes [ ] No

6. List any high schools, trade schools, or colleges at which each facility recruits.

_____

_____

_____

7. Do any facilities recruit at organizations or institutions comprised solely of one sex? [ ] Yes [ ] No
   If Yes, list facilities and organizations or institutions.

_____

_____

8. Indicate if applicants are questioned about the following areas during the application process:

	Yes	No
a. Marital status	___	___
b. Number of children	___	___
c. Prior addresses	___	___
d. Religion	___	___
e. Credit rating	___	___
f. Bankruptcy record	___	___
g. Garnishment record	___	___
h. Prior arrest record	___	___
i. Prior conviction record	___	___
j. Ability to be bonded	___	___
k. Charges or complaints filed with any governmental agency	___	___
l. Workers' compensation claims	___	___
m. Union affiliations	___	___

    n. Ability to speak and/or write a foreign language   ___ ___

    o. Disabilities   ___ ___

9. Does any facility employ an outside investigator or agency to verify applicant information?[11] [ ] Yes [ ] No

10. Are investigative or consumer reports used during the hiring process?[12] [ ] Yes [ ] No

   If Yes, specify source:

   _____

   _____

   _____

11. Are applicants notified that investigative or consumer reports will be used?[13] [ ] Yes [ ] No

12. Are job qualifications in written form prior to the position being advertised? [ ] Yes [ ] No

13. Indicate if the hiring criteria for any job include a limitation on any of the following applicant characteristics:

	Yes	No
a. Race	___	___
b. National origin	___	___
c. Sex	___	___
d. Age	___	___
e. Height	___	___
f. Weight	___	___
g. Religion	___	___
h. Education	___	___
i. Place of residence	___	___

  j. Marital status   ___ ___

  k. Sexual orientation   ___ ___

  l. Pregnancy   ___ ___

  m. Disability   ___ ___

  n. Military service   ___ ___

  o. Organization memberships   ___ ___

  p. Ability to speak English   ___ ___

  q. A charge filed with any governmental
    agency   ___ ___

14. Indicate if any preference is given to applicants who are:

                      Yes No

  a. Related to present or former rank-and-file
    employees   ___ ___

  b. Related to present or former managers or
    supervisors   ___ ___

  c. Referred by present or former employees[14]   ___ ___

15. Describe the employer's policy regarding hiring relatives of present employees.[15]

  _____

  _____

16. Describe the steps used in processing job applicants.

  _____

  _____

  _____

17. Does each facility have the power to:

                      Yes No

  a. Recruit its own applicants?   ___ ___

  b. Hire new employees?   ___ ___

Specify the names and locations of individuals who have the right to hire.

     Person   Title   Location

_____

_____

_____

18. Are any physical, manual, written, verbal, or other tests used in the applicant selection process?[16] [ ] Yes [ ] No

    If Yes, attach a copy or description of each test used.

19. Are written job applications used? [ ] Yes [ ] No

    If Yes, attach copies of the applications used.

20. Are employees required to sign applications? [ ] Yes [ ] No

21. Are applicants required to take a polygraph, honesty, or similar test?[17] [ ] Yes [ ] No

22. Are applicants required to provide a photograph prior to an interview?[18] [ ] Yes [ ] No

23. Are applicants advised of the full range of job openings? [ ] Yes [ ] No

24. Is there a preference for a particular sex for any positions? [ ] Yes [ ] No

    If Yes, list positions and reasons for preference.

_____

_____

25. Are any employment limitations imposed on persons with young children? [ ] Yes [ ] No

    Describe any limitations.

_____

26. Is there a preferred age range for any positions? [ ] Yes [ ] No

If Yes, list positions and reasons for preference.

_____

_____

27. What is the policy of each facility regarding hiring pregnant applicants?

_____

_____

_____

28. Are physical examinations required after an offer of employment is extended?[19] [ ] Yes [ ] No

    If physical examinations are not required for all job categories, specify which categories carry this requirement.

    _____

    _____

29. Are alcohol or drug tests required prior to employment? [ ] Yes [ ] No

30. Is the examining physician provided with a description of the job to be performed by the employee after an offer of employment is extended? [ ] Yes [ ] No

31. Does any policy exist requiring applicants or employees to prove legal residency in a specified geographic area?[20] [ ] Yes [ ] No

    If Yes, describe policy.

    _____

    _____

32. How is legal residency verified?

    _____

33. Define the geographic area from which applicants come.

    _____

34. For each facility, provide the following information if it is readily available:

    a. Estimated minority population in the immediate labor area _____

    b. Estimated minority percentage of the workforce in the immediate labor area _____

    c. Estimated size of the minority unemployment force in the immediate labor area _____

    d. Describe the labor area used in this data.[21]

    _____

    _____

35. Are employees required to sign restrictive covenants, nondisclosure of trade secrets agreements, or noncompetition agreements?[22] [ ] Yes [ ] No

    Attach a copy of any agreement(s) and indicate when the employees are required to sign these documents—at time of hiring, after hiring, or after termination.

36. How are applicants informed that they will not be offered a position?

    _____

    _____

C. Job Descriptions, Assignments, Promotions, and Transfers Audit Form

Job Descriptions, Assignments, Promotions, and Transfers
Audit Form

1. Are written job descriptions maintained? [ ] Yes [ ] No
   If Yes, attach copies of all job descriptions.

If No, explain how employees are informed of their specific responsibilities.

_____

2. Are there any positions for which a person's physical attributes are considered; for example, weight, height, or appearance? [ ] Yes [ ] No

If Yes, list positions and reasons for limitations.

_____

_____

3. Are females excluded from any positions because of protective legislation or Company determinations regarding hours worked, type of work, or weight lifting restrictions? [ ] Yes [ ] No

If Yes, list positions and reasons for exclusion.

_____

_____

_____

4. Is there a policy regarding accommodation for employees who cannot work specified days of the week or hours of the day? [ ] Yes [ ] No

If Yes, describe policy.

_____

_____

5. Are there any jobs which employees over age 40 are unable to perform? [ ] Yes [ ] No

If Yes, list these jobs and explain why employees over age 40 cannot perform them.

_____

_____

6. Is there a minimum age for employment? [ ] Yes [ ] No

   If Yes, what is that age? _____

7. What benefits are given to non-union employees on the basis of their seniority? .

   _____

8. How is seniority determined?

   _____

   _____

   Is age or sex used in determining seniority? [ ] Yes [ ] No

   If Yes, explain use.

   _____

   _____

9. Indicate if any of the following factors are currently used to determine job assignments:

	Yes	No
a. Age	___	___
b. Sex	___	___
c. Race or ethnic origin	___	___
d. Disability	___	___
e. Union membership	___	___

   If Yes to any factor, list factor and explain its use.

   _____

   Are records made of these factors? [ ] Yes [ ] No

   If yes, where are they kept? _____

10. Indicate if any of the following factors were used in the past to determine employment in any positions, promotion, or departments:

	Yes	No
a. Age	___	___

b. Sex   ___ ___

c. Race or ethnic origin   ___ ___

d. Disability   ___ ___

e. Union membership   ___ ___

11. Is a seniority system presently maintained which is based on service during the period when certain positions, lines of progression, or departments were so segregated? [ ] Yes [ ] No

12. Are employees permitted to transfer into positions in lines of progression or departments from which they were formerly excluded? [ ] Yes [ ] No

13. Are vacant positions advertised or announced to current employees? [ ] Yes [ ] No

    If Yes, are records maintained identifying employees who apply for these positions? [ ] Yes [ ] No

14. Are records maintained reflecting the reasons for denying or awarding a job to a current employee? [ ] Yes [ ] No

15. How does the employer determine if an employee should be permitted to transfer into another position?

    _____

    _____

    _____

16. Indicate if any of the following factors are used to determine if an employee will transfer to another position:

                                                   Yes No

    a. Age   ___ ___

    b. Sex   ___ ___

    c. Race or ethnic origin   ___ ___

    d. Disability   ___ ___

    e. Union Membership   ___ ___

If Yes to any factor, explain its use.

_____

_____

17. Are any positions, lines of progression, or departments limited to persons of one sex? [ ] Yes [ ] No

18. Are supervisory personnel required to submit written decisions and reasons when employees are passed over for promotions? [ ] Yes [ ] No

19. Are employees promoted or transferred between facilities? [ ] Yes [ ] No

    If Yes, how often does this occur? _____

    _____

20. For each position, describe the training programs used and indicate any prerequisites for employee participation.

    Training Program   Prerequisites

    _____

    _____

    _____

21. Describe procedures for evaluating employee performance.

    _____

    _____

    Attach any evaluation form used.

22. How frequently are performance evaluations conducted?

    _____

23. Are performance evaluations reviewed by anyone other than the person who prepared the evaluation? [ ] Yes [ ] No

24. Describe procedures for reviewing performance evaluations with employees.

    _____

    _____

25. Describe the training that supervisors receive regarding employee performance evaluations.

_____

_____

_____

D. Employer Communications Audit Form

Employer Communications Audit Form

1. Is there an orientation program for acquainting new employees with privacy procedures and policies? [ ] Yes [ ] No

   If Yes, list the privacy subjects discussed and the documents presented to new employees.

   _____

   _____

   Attach copies of employee handbook or other documents which are given to new employees.

2. List the persons responsible for or who participate in carrying out the program.

   _____

   _____

3. Are employees required to sign an acknowledgment of receipt of an employee handbook or similar document?[23] [ ] Yes [ ] No

   If Yes, attach copy of acknowledgment.

4. When was the most recent revision of the employee handbook?

   _____

   By whom was the handbook revised?

   _____

Does the employee handbook contain a statement indicating that employment is at-will and that employment may be terminated by either the employee or the employer at any time, for any or no reason, with or without notice? [ ] Yes [ ] No

If No, how is the employee made aware of this?

_____

Is the employee required to sign a statement acknowledging and agreeing that employment is at-will? [ ] Yes [ ] No

5. Is there an employer or facility newsletter? [ ] Yes [ ] No

    If Yes, attach copies for the past year.

6. What is the employer's policy regarding employee use of bulletin boards?

    _____

    _____

7. Has the employer conducted surveys among employees during the past five years? [ ] Yes [ ] No

    If Yes, when was the last survey conducted? Who conducted the survey?

    _____

    Attach a copy of the questionnaire and the employees' responses.

8. Are there any committees composed entirely or partially of employees? [ ] Yes [ ] No

    If Yes, describe each committee's composition and purpose.

    _____

    _____

9. Are there any regularly scheduled meetings between employees and supervisors? [ ] Yes [ ] No

10. How do employees bring their privacy complaints or concerns to the attention of managers and supervisors?

_____

_____

11. What procedures are used by managers and supervisors to respond to employees' privacy concerns or complaints?

_____

_____

12. Are there any procedures by which an employee may appeal decisions of supervisors? [ ] Yes [ ] No

    If Yes, describe these procedures.

_____

_____

E. Discipline and Termination Audit Form

Discipline and Termination Audit Form

1. Are there any written rules of conduct?[24] [ ] Yes [ ] No
2. When and how are employees informed of employer rules?

_____

3. Who is responsible for enforcing employer rules?

_____

4. Do persons responsible for enforcing rules have any discretion in determining the disciplinary penalty to be imposed once it is determined that an offense has occurred? [ ] Yes [ ] No

5. Is there any procedure for progressive discipline?[25] [ ] Yes [ ] No

6. How are managers and supervisors informed of the employer's disciplinary procedure?

_____

7. How and when are employees informed of the disciplinary procedure?

_____

8. Are the disciplinary decisions made by supervisors reviewed by anyone? [ ] Yes [ ] No

9. How and when are employees informed of a decision to discipline them?

_____

10. Is an employee given an opportunity to present his or her explanation prior to being disciplined? [ ] Yes [ ] No

11. Are employees given the opportunity to discuss the reasons for disciplinary actions against them? [ ] Yes [ ] No

    If Yes, explain.

_____

12. Are employees allowed to appeal disciplinary actions to a higher level manager or panel of officials? [ ] Yes [ ] No

    If Yes, explain the appeal procedure.

_____

13. Is an employee who is being investigated to determine whether discipline is appropriate or who is being notified of a disciplinary decision permitted to have a person of his or her choice present at the investigation or notification meeting?[26] [ ] Yes [ ] No

    If Yes and there are exceptions, explain exceptions.

_____

_____

14. Indicate if any of the following measures are taken if an employee receives one or more warnings or negative evaluations:

Yes No

   a. Upward or downward vertical transfer to place the employee in a position more closely suited to his or her abilities   ___ ___

   b. Lateral transfer to alleviate possible personality conflicts between the employee and immediate supervisor or between the employee and fellow workers   ___ ___

   c. Additional employee job training   ___ ___

   d. Other   ___ ___

If Other, please describe.

_____

_____

15. Who is responsible for deciding to terminate or for informing employees of termination?

_____

16. Describe the procedure for documenting disciplinary decisions and the reasons for the decisions.

_____

17. Is age ever used as a factor in decisions to terminate employees? [ ] Yes [ ] No

If Yes, explain its use.

_____

18. Is race ever used as a factor in decisions to terminate employees? [ ] Yes [ ] No

If Yes, explain its use.

_____

_____

19. Is sex ever used as a factor in decisions to terminate employees? [ ] Yes [ ] No

If Yes, explain its use.

_____

20. Is disability ever used as a factor in decisions to terminate employees? [ ] Yes [ ] No

    If Yes, explain its use.

    _____

21. Are terminated employees allowed to appeal termination decisions to a higher level manager or panel of officials? [ ] Yes [ ] No

    If Yes, explain the appeal procedure.

    _____

22. Are employees provided with a written termination notice? [ ] Yes [ ] No

23. When are terminated employees given a final paycheck?

    _____

24. Are terminated employees eligible for severance pay? [ ] Yes [ ] No

25. Are exit interviews conducted? [ ] Yes [ ] No

    If Yes, by whom? _____

26. Are records maintained of all disciplinary actions, including terminations? [ ] Yes [ ] No

    If Yes, describe what records are maintained and where they are maintained.

    _____

    _____

27. Are copies of warnings and terminations placed in the employee's personnel file? [ ] Yes [ ] No

28. Indicate if warnings contain any of the following:

	Yes	No
a. Description of offense	___	___
b. Action necessary for improvement	___	___
c. Consequences of failure to improve	___	___

F. Implementing Audit Changes

The results of the completed workplace privacy audit will give the employer a written, comprehensive description of current policies and procedures which can be examined for potential problem areas. Once problem areas are identified, the employer can use the information on the audit forms to develop remedies to any deficiencies. To implement any changes suggested by the audit, the employer should:

1. Use the workplace privacy audit report to:

   a. Identify workplace privacy priorities

   b. Distinguish facts versus opinions

   c. Evaluate workplace privacy alternatives

   d. Assess workplace privacy vulnerabilities

   e. Identify confidentiality problems

2. Implement changes in policies and procedures through:

   a. Avoidance of overreaction

   b. Consideration of gradual versus immediate changes

   c. Publication of changes to employees

   d. Use of employee committees to provide input

   e. Consideration of overall versus specific changes

   f. Involvement of the union in discussions

   g. Provision of collective bargaining agreements in new contracts

3. Establish systems to monitor workplace privacy regarding:

   a. Compliance with fair employment practice statutes

   b. Union activities

   c. Health and safety

   d. Reporting and record keeping

   e. Management responsiveness to complaints

   f. Restrictions on information disclosure

IV. Overall Guidelines for Workplace Privacy

Workplace privacy audits should help the employer develop overall policies and procedures which protect the privacy interests of employees and limit the employer's vulnerability to litigation.[27] These policies and procedures will serve as general guidelines to prevent or minimize employer liability for privacy intrusions. Overall privacy guidelines should include:

1. consistent application of and adherence to privacy procedures and policies;

2. knowledge of employees' workplace privacy rights under applicable federal and state statutes;[28]

3. respect of employee rights to privacy and confidentiality;

4. education of management and supervisory personnel regarding applicable laws and employer procedures and policies;

5. establishment of a policy that employees refrain from commenting on or disclosing information that could affect other employees' privacy interests involving hair style, disabilities, religion, politics, spouses, sexual habits, or other sensitive areas;

6. annual review of privacy procedures and policies to ensure that they are consistent, that they conform to applicable statutes, and that they reflect the employer's philosophy;

7. avoidance of spontaneous action or action taken in anger;

8. provision of some form of due process for employees prior to implementation of adverse employment actions:

   a. Take no adverse employment action without evidence.

   b. Treat all adverse employment situations consistently.

   c. Tell the employee why the adverse employment action is being taken.

   d. Give the employee an opportunity to present counterevidence prior to a final adverse employment action.

   e. Allow the employee to review, comment on, and copy any written performance evaluations or personnel file memoranda pertinent to the adverse employment action.

   f. Establish a method for employees to appeal adverse employment actions through internal or external procedures.

   g. Make certain that appeal procedures for adverse employment actions are known and available to all employees.

Employers should be aware that workplace privacy issues and concerns can confront even the most careful, ethical, and innocent employer. Potential workplace privacy claims can be anticipated by periodically updating procedures and policies to reflect current statutory requirements and the employer's operations. At a minimum, updating procedures will safeguard employers against incurring damaging liability that may affect the employer financially, may curtail the employer's business prospects, and may interfere with the employer's relationship with its workforce.

Endnotes

1   *See* Appendix A sections III and IV for a list of federal and state statutes that regulate various employer actions regarding their employees.

2   *See, e.g.,* Green v. Missouri Pac. R.R., 523 F.2d 1290 (8th Cir. 1975) (inquiring about non-job-related convictions).

3   *See, e.g.,* Quinones v. United States, 492 F.2d 1269 (3d Cir. 1974) (release of inaccurate personnel file information).

4   *See, e.g.,* Whitney v. Greater N.Y. Corp. of Seventh-Day Adventists, 401 F. Supp. 1363 (S.D.N.Y. 1975) (termination of white person for association with blacks outside the workplace).

5   *See, e.g.,* Lewis v. Equitable Life Assurance Soc'y, 361 N.W.2d 875 (Minn. Ct. App. 1985), *aff'd in pertinent part,* 389 N.W.2d 876 (Minn. 1986) (group of employees defamed by employer's false and malicious termination reasons; $425,000 damage award).

6   *See* Appendix A sections III and IV for a list of pertinent federal and state statutes.

7   *See* Appendix A sections III and IV for a description of these and other federal and state statutes.

8   *See* Appendix A sections III and IV.

9   *See* Appendix A sections III and IV.

10   A variety of federal and state statutes regulate the types of employment information that may be collected, maintained, used, and disclosed. Regulation on the federal level includes the following statutes, *inter alia*: Privacy Act of 1974, 5 U.S.C. § 552a (1988); Fair Credit Reporting Act, 15 U.S.C. §§ 1681-1681t (1988); Civil Rights Act of 1964, 42 U.S.C. §§ 2000e-1 through 2002-17 (1988); Age Discrimination in Employment Act, 29 U.S.C. §§ 621-634 (1988); Occupational Safety and Health Act, 29 U.S.C. §§ 651-678 (1988). Regulation on the state level includes *see, e.g.,* Cal. Civ. Code § 1783 (West 1986) (California's Fair Credit Reporting Act); Cal. Lab. Code §§ 1050, 1053, 1054 (West 1971) (California's statute covering employment references); Cal. Lab. Code § 1198.5 (West 1982) (California's statute covering personnel file regulation). See Appendix A sections III and IV for additional federal and state statutes.

11   *See, e.g.,* 15 U.S.C. §§ 1681-1681t (1988) (Fair Credit Reporting Act regulating access to investigative and consumer credit reports).

12   *Id.*

13   *Id.*

14   *See, e.g.,* Sprogis v. United Air Lines, Inc., 444 F.2d 1194 (7th Cir.), *cert. denied,* 404 U.S. 991 (1971), *on remand,* 56 F.R.D. 420 (1972) (spousal policies).

15   *See, e.g.,* Scott v. Pacific Maritime Ass'n, 695 F.2d 1199 (9th Cir. 1983) (employer's granting hiring preference to children of deceased employees if they were supported solely by the deceased employee, were over 18, and applied within 30 days of the father's or mother's death or of the child reaching age 18, was neutral and not discriminatory).

16   *See, e.g.,* United States v. South Carolina, 434 U.S. 1026 (1978) (some tests favor white, middle-class backgrounds).

17   *See, e.g.,* Leibowitz v. H.A. Winston Co., 342 Pa. Super. 111, 493 A.2d 111 (1985) (employer violation of Pennsylvania's polygraph statute).

18   *See, e.g.,* EEOC Decision (January 4, 1966); Opin. Ltr. of the EEOC's General Counsel, 193-95 (January 24, 1965) (employer photographing of applicants is prohibited under fair employment practice statutes).

19   *See, e.g.,* Vocational Rehabilitation Act of 1973, 29 U.S.C. §§ 701-796i (1988); Americans with Disabilities Act, 42 U.S.C. § 12101-12213 (1991) (pre-employment physical examinations prohibited).

20   *See, e.g.,* McCarthy v. Philadelphia Civil Serv. Comm'n, 424 U.S. 645 (1976) (residency requirements necessary to serve legitimate employer interests are valid).

21   Federal and state fair employment practice statutes may require employers to provide this information. *See, e.g.,* Civil Rights Act of 1964, 42 U.S.C. §§ 2000e-1 through 2002-17 (1988).

22   *See, e.g.,* Tabs Assos., Inc. v. Brohawn, 59 Md. App. 330, 475 A.2d 1203 (1984) (future use of trade secrets).

23   *See, e.g.,* Leikvold v. Valley View Community Hosp., 141 Ariz. 544, 688 P.2d 170 (1984) (handbooks may create binding employment commitments), *contra* Reynolds Mfg. Co. v. Mendoza, 644 S.W.2d 536 (Tex. 1982) (handbooks do not create binding employment commitments).

24   *Id.*

25   "Progressive discipline" is an escalating set of steps imposing more severe discipline for each succeeding rule violation by an employee, eventually culminating in termination. These disciplinary steps may consist of an oral warning, written warning, suspension, and termination.

26   *See, e.g.,* NLRB v. J. Weingarten, Inc., 420 U.S. 251 (1975) (acknowledging private sector employee's right to union representation at meeting when an employer's investigation may reasonably result in disciplinary action).

27   *See generally* Appendix B for suggested workplace privacy policies.

28   *See* Appendix A sections III and IV for a list of pertinent federal and state statutes.

10

Human Resources' Role and Discipline

I. Introduction

To deal with the potential liabilities created by workplace privacy issues, employers must develop human resources administration and discipline strategies to identify and remedy problem areas. Until these strategies are in place, employers' actions and policies may be increasingly challenged by employees over issues of workplace privacy. This chapter reviews the issues and concerns involved in administration and employee discipline procedures as they relate to workplace privacy.

II. Human Resources' Responsibilities

A. Administration of Privacy Requirements

It is essential that the human resources staff be involved in all phases of procedures and policies that regulate privacy in the workplace, including their overall development, coordination, and administration. The human resources staff should:

1. outline general objectives and goals of procedures and policies;

2. prepare initial recommendations for procedures and policies;

3. coordinate and facilitate planning by and among supervisors and management that is necessary for the orderly accomplishment of established objectives;

4. conduct studies and analyses of the actual or potential short- and long-term effects of present or proposed workplace privacy procedures and policies;

5. conduct and coordinate the research necessary to develop and implement effective and efficient privacy procedures and policies;

6. review federal and state court decisions and statutes affecting workplace privacy procedures and policies;[1]

7. serve as the central source of collection and dissemination of ideas and information related to workplace privacy procedures and policies;

8. consult with employees, supervisors, and managers in determining the feasibility of any proposed procedures and policies;

9. continuously review the employer's progress in achieving workplace privacy goals; and

10. exercise all other functions as may be necessary to accomplish its duties regarding workplace privacy procedures and policies.

To effectively carry out these responsibilities, the human resources staff must:

1. have access to records, reports, audits, reviews, recommendations, or other necessary documents and materials;

2. initiate investigations and prepare reports relating to policy administration;

3. request information or assistance from specialized sources as needed to carry out the established responsibilities;

4. provide written notification to anyone required to produce information, documents, reports, answers, records, accounts, papers, and other necessary data and documentary evidence that is not otherwise restricted;

5. have direct and prompt access to the company's President or Chief Operating Officer when necessary for the performance of workplace privacy responsibilities; and

6. select, appoint, and employ the persons necessary for carrying out procedures and policies.

B. Administration of Workplace Information

Privacy issues in the age of computerized workplace information systems are more than just a legal concern, although vulnerability to employee litigation cannot be taken lightly.[2] Human resources administrators responsible for creating and using an effective human resources information management system must first address the privacy issues regarding employee data and its confidentiality. Information system users and all other employees must be educated on the employer's policies and procedures in handling employee data. Through this preventive action, the entire workforce will be aware of the information that is accessible and that which is restricted. Consequently, workplace privacy problems and the employer's potential liability will be minimized. This education also will enable the human resources information management system to maintain valid and useful information and to retain the support of employees and management.

No two human resource information management systems are identical because no two employers are exactly alike. Employee populations differ, as do the technology and automated procedures utilized by employers. As a result, the human resources information required and used by each employer will be unique and will necessitate an information management system that is tailored to the individual employer's needs. In general, however, the development of an effective system which accounts for privacy considerations requires determination of the following:

1. A clear definition of what is a private record

2. The type of data to be included in individual records and in the system in general

3. Which employees, supervisors, and managers will have access to the system

4. What information maintained on the system can be disclosed internally and to outside parties

To limit potential privacy liability for mishandling information in its collection, maintenance, use, or disclosure, employers should observe the following safeguards:

1. Deal with employees truthfully when discussing employment problems.

2. Do not characterize employee conduct as more or less favorable than it really is.[3]

3. Limit communications inside and outside of the workplace to information that is job-related, and disclose this data only to those who have a definite need to know.[4]

4. Collect as much job-related information as possible during the hiring process.[5]

5. Conduct exit interviews at employment separation to obtain agreements on how future reference inquiries should be handled.

6. Obtain signed releases from former employees that permit only job-related information to be disclosed during reference checks by future potential employers.

7. In the absence of a release, disclose only truthful and verifiable information to a prospective employer to avoid defamation liability.

8. Properly document adverse actions against employees because often this is the employer's best defense against litigation.

C. Infractions of Workplace Privacy

Employers must be prepared to immediately deal with any infractions of workplace privacy in a positive and constructive manner. Privacy infractions may occur with no advance warning, and employers must have in place a plan of action to resolve any problems at their inception. Examples of infractions to which employers may have to react include sexual harassment incidents, improper use of personnel files,[6] alcohol and drug testing,[7] and performance evaluations.[8] The first step in an overall plan of action to deal with privacy infractions is the creation of a complaint procedure. As the monitors of this procedure, the human resources staff should:

1. receive and investigate employee-reported complaints or information related to workplace privacy which concern violations of law, rules, or regulations, and complaints that involve a substantial or specific danger to health and safety; and

2. not take, direct others to take, recommend, or approve a personnel action against any employee as a reprisal for making a complaint or disclosing information to a federal or state administrative agency or the human resources staff.

D. Privacy Infraction Complaint Form

The following form is to be completed by the employee who has a complaint or information to report. The form will notify the human resources staff of a potential workplace privacy violation and will enable the staff to investigate and remedy the matter.

Workplace Privacy Infraction Form

Name_____ Date_____

Dept_____ Title_____ Supervisor_____

Date of Situation Prompting Complaint_____

Facts of Complaint_____

_____

_____

_____

_____

_____

_____

How do you suggest this be resolved?_____

_____

_____

_____

_____

_____

_____

_____

                              Signed _____

III. Employee Discipline and Privacy

A. Privacy Considerations

It is important for employers to implement a discipline system to deal with workplace privacy infractions. Once established, these disciplinary standards must be brought to the attention of all employees. If employees are expected to abide by workplace rules and regulations, those rules and regulations must be stated clearly in an employment handbook or other written document that is distributed to all employees. Additionally, employees should be required to sign a form acknowledging that they have received the written document and agree to abide by the rules contained in it. The signed acknowledgments should be placed in employee personnel files as a record of the employee's understanding.

Employers that compile a list of specific offenses warranting immediate termination may hinder their ability to terminate employees for other serious but unlisted misconduct. To avoid this problem, employers should make clear to employees that offenses other than those enumerated may also mandate termination.

It is important that employers carefully examine all procedural prerequisites to termination that have been established by the law. The following should be noted:

1. Employee handbooks and other directives increasingly are being treated by the courts as binding employer commitments and may represent procedural obstacles to termination.[9]

2. If a handbook sets forth either standards regarding termination or procedural requirements providing an impartial hearing or a progressive disciplinary process, the employer should be prepared to follow these commitments or be willing to risk having a termination set aside because the specified procedures have been bypassed.

3. A summary or on-the-spot termination should always be avoided. This rule should apply to every management mem-

ber, particularly front-line supervisors who should have authority only to initiate the disciplinary process.

4. Although front-line supervisors play a role in disciplinary decision making, final authority to terminate should remain with upper management and should be exercised only after all the events leading to the proposed termination have been investigated thoroughly.

5. To ensure that the disciplinary/separation process works correctly, supervisors should be properly trained in the procedures to follow and be made aware of their authority limits.

6. Considering the consequences of an improper disciplinary action, it is prudent, if not imperative, to have an impartial top management official review all such actions, particularly terminations. The person appointed to be a "final filter" should:

   a. be a respected and experienced manager with authority to uphold, reverse, or modify a recommended disciplinary action;

   b. have access to all pertinent records, including the employee's personnel file and the results of any disciplinary-related investigation; and

   c. be free to interview witnesses, consult the offending employee's supervisor, and take whatever steps are necessary to ensure that the circumstances of each case are examined thoroughly before a final termination decision is made.

7. In the more difficult disciplinary situations, legal counsel should be consulted.

B. Just Cause Standard

In levying discipline, employers should strive to be fair and consistent and should act as if their disciplinary decisions will be reviewed under the most restrictive standards.[10] Even if the employer is operating in a non-union setting, every employment action should be treated as if it were subject to the review standards present in a labor arbitration proceeding under a collective bargaining agreement—an employer should be prepared to meet a "just cause" standard to verify and defend its actions.

Most collective bargaining agreements in the private and public sectors require some form of just cause standard to sustain adverse employment actions. If this standard is not contained in a collective bargaining agreement, many arbitrators imply a just cause limitation.[11] Absent precise definitions, "just cause" may constitute any of the following factors or combination of these factors:

1. The "law of the shop," or the employer's response to a particular action developed over time

2. A consistent pattern of enforcement of rules and regulations and of making these known to all employees

3. Case histories of similar employment actions

4. Known practices of severe discipline for certain offenses because of the product manufactured or service rendered, or because of safety considerations

5. General arbitral authority derived from arbitration awards and articles

6. The arbitrator's own sense of equity and subjective judgment regarding the significance and seriousness of the incident and the weight to be given the incident, the employee's record, or the circumstances causing the employment action

7. Severity of the facts of the incident

8. Attempts made by the employer to rehabilitate the employee

9. Progressive disciplinary steps that may or may not have been taken

10. The balance between the discipline penalty and the facts of the incident

11. Whether a second chance is warranted from the employee's prior employment record[12]

In further determining the presence of just cause to validate an adverse employment action, a seven-question checklist was developed by Arbitrator Carroll R. Daugherty to assist the human resources administrator.[13] This checklist suggests several questions to help the employer or arbitrator analyze whether just cause exists for a particular disciplinary situation.

1. Was the employer's rule reasonably related to the orderly, efficient, and safe operation of the business and the performance that the employer might reasonably expect of the employee?

2. Did the employer forewarn the employee orally or in writing of the possible or probable consequences of the employee's action?

3. Prior to disciplining the employee, did the employer make an effort to discover whether the employee did in fact violate or disobey an employer rule or order?

4. Was the employer's investigation conducted fairly and objectively?

5. During the employer's investigation, did the employer's decision maker obtain substantial and compelling evidence or proof that the employee was responsible or at fault as alleged?

6. Was the degree of discipline reasonably related to the seriousness of the offense and the employee's work performance record with the employer?

7. Has the employer applied its rules, orders, policies, and penalties to all employees fairly and without discrimination?

A negative response to any question on this checklist would indicate that the employer's disciplinary action may not have been properly administered and may create employer liability for the action.

C. Discipline Procedures

Prior to administering discipline in response to any employee misconduct, the employer should review the following documents relative to each situation:

1. Performance evaluations of the offending employee

2. Warning notices previously given to employee regarding adverse employment actions

3. Personnel policies or work rules

4. Statements from witnesses of the alleged misconduct

5. Notes from interviews with these witnesses

6. Other relevant documents including complaints from other employees and customers, accident reports, work records, overtime records, timecards, and safety inspections

After these documents are examined, the employer should collect and evaluate answers to the following questions:

1. Is the employee a long-service employee?

2. Is the employee's record of promotions and salary increases inconsistent with past unsatisfactory work performance?

3. Were the employee's salary increases labeled "merit" or something else?

4. Has the employee received any commendations or awards?

At this point in determining what disciplinary action to administer, the employer should evaluate the answers to these questions:

1. What action would be consistent with treatment given other employees in similar incidents?

2. Does the information collected during investigation support the proposed disciplinary action? Can the employer prove the facts that it is using as a basis for the decision?

3. Does the articulated reason for the proposed discipline comply with the employer's personnel policies and work rules and the evidence?

4. Is there a credibility dispute? How do statements of the employer's witnesses compare to those of the employee's witnesses?

5. Does the employee's explanation raise any mitigating circumstances or compelling sympathies?

6. Should an action less severe than termination be imposed?

After the discipline or termination decision has been made, the employer must inform the employee of the decision. It is important that the employer develop specific steps to accomplish this and to protect itself from potential liability.

1. Inform the employee of the decision during a face-to-face interview.

2. Discuss openly and frankly with the employee the reasons for the discipline or termination. Explain that the reason is:

   a. legitimate and

   b. consistent with the employer's past practice in similar cases.

3. Ensure that the explanation is thorough and accurate. Whether given orally or in writing, the reasons for the decision should be consistent with the evidence.

4. Carefully document the interview and have a member of management present during the interview to verify the conversation.

5. Advise the employee of the information that will be given to prospective employers.

6. Refrain from disclosing the reasons for the discipline or termination to other employees, future employers, or third parties. This will help to deflect possible claims of invasion of privacy, defamation, or intentional infliction of emotional distress.

D. Discipline Notification Form

Once the employer determines that discipline is appropriate, it should consider whether a written notice should be given to the employee. Employers may use the following form to notify an employee of the proposed disciplinary action.

Notification of Disciplinary Action

Employee Name_____

Dept_____ Date_____

For reasons listed below, the following disciplinary action is being implemented:_____

Effective Date_____ Time_____ A.M./P.M.

Reasons_____

_____

_____

_____

Warning Against Future Misconduct_____

_____

Signed_____

Employee Acknowledgment_____

Date of Acknowledgment_____

E. Monitoring Disciplinary Actions

The employer's primary concern when developing a discipline and termination process should be the centralized control of the procedure. This permits the employer to determine its best witness if the case is litigated. This witness may be a member of the human resources staff who has knowledge of the relevant facts concerning the employee's work performance and the work performance of similarly situated employees. Using a witness with such knowledge should present the employer's case in a coherent and easy-to-follow manner. Another advantage of this strategy is that a jury may be less inclined to view the litigation as a conflict between one individual against an impersonal organization if a member of the human resources staff serves as the employer's main witness. The jury might be persuaded to view the case as a test of the credibility and fairness of the human resources official as opposed to that of the employee.

If the employer designates a human resources staff member to monitor all discipline and termination decisions, that individual should be:

1. mature;

2. responsible;

3. articulate;

4. able to convey the impression of being fair and sympathetic toward employees and their problems.

F. Employer Responsibilities Following Termination

Even after the termination process is complete, employers still have some responsibilities to their former employees. Many states have statutes that specify when employees must receive their final full pay following termination or that limit deductions that can be taken from a terminated employee's pay. State and local statutes should be reviewed before any deductions or offsets are made. Whether or not there are state or local requirements, employers should clearly state in their employee handbook or policy manual the obligations of both employer and employee at the time of employment separation.

Today more and more employers have some type of grievance or appeals procedure that allows employees to challenge disciplinary actions internally rather than through litigation. The right of terminated employees to challenge a termination decision through a formal non-union grievance process should be stated clearly in the employee handbook, and employees should be reminded of their right to use that process during the exit interview. Allowing former employees to use a review procedure within specified time limits may provide employees with another outlet for venting their frustration or telling their side of the story, and gives management a tool for correcting possible wrongs and averting litigation.

Endnotes

1   *See* Appendix A sections III and IV for a list of federal and state statutes affecting privacy in the workplace.

2   *See, e.g.,* Quinones v. United States, 492 F.2d 1269, 1278 (3d Cir. 1974) (employer has a duty to use due care in keeping and maintaining employment records).

3   *See, e.g.,* McKnight v. General Motors Corp., 705 F. Supp. 464 (E.D. Wis. 1989) (unfairly building termination case against employee through negative performance evaluations subjected employer to payment of $100,000 in compensatory damages and $500,000 in punitive damages to employee).

4   *See, e.g.,* Carney v. Memorial Hosp., 64 N.Y.2d 770, 485 N.Y.S.2d 984 (1985) (unfavorable employment reference).

5   *See, e.g.,* Pruitt v. Pavelin, 141 Ariz. 195, 685 P.2d 1347 (1984) (negligent hiring in employment of convicted forger).

6   *See, e.g.,* Quinones v. United States, 492 F.2d 1269 (3d Cir. 1974).

7   *See, e.g.,* Luck v. Southern Pac. Transp. Co., 218 Cal. App. 3d 1, 267 Cal. Rptr. 618 (1990) (private employer's random alcohol and drug testing program violated privacy rights of California Constitution where employee job duties did not relate to safety risk presented by drug and alcohol use that employer sought to eliminate).

8   *See, e.g.,* McKnight v. General Motors Corp., 705 F. Supp. 464 (E.D. Wis. 1989).

9   *See, e.g.,* Leikvold v. Valley View Community Hosp., 141 Ariz. 544, 688 P.2d 170 (1984) (handbooks may create binding employment commitments). *Contra* Reynolds Mfg. Co. v. Mendoza, 644 S.W.2d 536 (Tex. 1982) (handbooks do not create binding employment commitments).

10   *See, e.g.,* Mendez v. M.S. Walker, Inc., 26 Mass. App. Ct. 431, 528 N.E.2d 891 (1988) (employer liable for failing to verify facts that employee was actually stealing before disseminating information that employee had been terminated for theft).

11   *See* Cameron Iron Works, Inc., 25 Lab. Arb. (BNA) 295, 301 (1955) (Boles, Arb.).

12   For a general discussion of just cause, *see* FRANK ELKOURI & EDNA ELKOURI, HOW ARBITRATION WORKS 651-655 (4th ed. 1985).

13   Whirlpool Corp., 58 Lab. Arb (BNA) 421 (1972) (Daugherty, Arb.).

Appendix

A

Federal and State
Constitutional and Statutory Protections
of Workplace Privacy

I. United States Constitution

A. First Amendment

Privacy interests in speech, beliefs, and association are protected by the First Amendment. U.S. CONST. amend. I. Regarding workplace privacy, the United States Supreme Court has taken judicial notice of the "sensitivity of any human being to disclosure of information that may be taken as bearing on his or her basic competence." Detroit Edison Co. v. NLRB, 440 U.S. 301 (1979). First Amendment workplace privacy themes generally involve: (1) "patronage," in which employees are disciplined, terminated, laid off, demoted, or otherwise disciplined based solely on their political affiliation or beliefs; (2) "expressive conduct," in which employment status is adversely affected by an employee's spoken, written, or other form of expression; (3) "mixed motive," in which an adverse employment action is promoted by a combination of factors, some, but not all, involving constitutionally protected activity; or (4) Hatch Act activities in which the right of public employees to engage in partisan political activity is questioned.

Freedom and privacy of association promote the individual's ability to develop and maintain relationships that otherwise might be foregone because of the hostility that might result from disclosure of these associations. By giving an employee control over the information that is disclosed about him or her, the employee can define his or her public identity. The U.S. Supreme Court has recognized freedom of association as a right necessary to the specific guarantees of the First Amendment because freedom of speech, press, assembly, and petition frequently require group activity. NAACP v. Alabama ex rel. Patterson, 357 U.S. 449 (1958). An individual's freedom to associate often depends on the concealment of associations; in other words, the individual must prevent disclosure of information pertaining to a particular association. Mere membership in an organization absent specific advocacy of illegal conduct is constitutionally protected. United States v. Robel, 389 U.S. 258 (1967).

B. Fourth Amendment

The Fourth Amendment protects the privacy interest of seclusion from unreasonable searches and seizures. U.S. CONST. amend. IV. Because searches and seizures are possible without physical intrusion, the amendment may safeguard a broader interest in confidentiality of papers and effects (in other words, information).

This amendment is made applicable to the states through the due process clause of the Fourteenth Amendment. Its basic purpose is to protect the individual's privacy and dignity against unreasonable intrusions by the state and "all of its creatures." New Jersey v. T.L.O., 469 U.S. 325, 335-36 (1985). It has been applied to the conduct of government officials in various civil activities.

To determine whether a particular intrusion is reasonable, the individual's Fourth Amendment interests must be balanced against the promotion of legitimate governmental interests. The individual's legitimate privacy interest must be evaluated within the context in which the intrusion occurred. Once this context is established, the reasonableness of the search must be reviewed. Delaware v. Prouse, 440 U.S. 648 (1979).

C. Fifth Amendment

A privacy interest as a privilege against self-incrimination is protected by the Fifth Amendment. U.S. CONST. amend. V. The Fifth Amendment prohibits evidentiary use of documents obtained in contravention of the Fourth Amendment because it violates the Fifth Amendment's zone of privacy. Boyd v. United States, 116 U.S. 616 (1886).

This amendment may impact employees through its restrictions on collection, maintenance, use, and disclosure of information and various employment inquiries. This protection extends to each person regardless of employment status or relationship to the state and precludes the state from depriving an individual of his or her livelihood for asserting that privilege. The state is prohibited from imposing penalties or sanctions that make exercise of the right to remain silent "costly." Uniformed Sanitation Men Ass'n v. Commissioner of Sanitation, 392 U.S. 280 (1968).

D. Ninth Amendment

Workplace privacy may find applications in the Ninth Amendment's concept of fundamental rights retained by the people. U.S. Const. amend. IX. Privacy as a fundamental right could be found in the collection, maintenance, use, and disclosure of employment information, along with lifestyle regulation through a public policy violation.

E. Fourteenth Amendment

The Fourteenth Amendment protects the due process aspects of privacy. U.S. Const. amend. XIV. Due process aspects could be required in wrongful collection, use, maintenance, and disclosure of information and lifestyle regulation.

Regarding public employees, it has been found that "the root requirement" of due process is that an individual be given an opportunity for a hearing before being deprived of any significant property interest. Cleveland Bd. of Educ. v. Loudermill, 470 U.S. 532 (1985). However, something less than a full evidentiary hearing is sufficient prior to adverse administrative action.

II. State Constitutions

Through constitutional, statutory, and common-law protections, states safeguard individual privacy interests present in speech, beliefs, information, association, and lifestyle. Several states have recognized a privacy right in their state constitutions that pertain to the workplace.

See, e.g., Alaska Const. art. I, § 22; Ariz. Const. art. II, § 8; Cal. Const. art. I, § 1; Fla. Const. art. I, § 23; Haw. Const. art. I, § 5; Ill. Const. art. 6, § 12; La. Const. art. I, § 5; Mass. Gen Laws Ann.

ch. 215, § 1B; MONT. CONST. art. II, § 10; R.I. GEN. LAWS § 9-1-28.1 (1985); S.C. CONST. art. 4, § 10; WASH. CONST. art. I, § 7.

III. Federal Legislation

A. Aviation Security Improvement Act of 1990

The Aviation Security Improvement Act of 1990 requires employment investigations, including criminal history record checks, of applicants or employees in positions involving unescorted access to aircraft or an airport's secured area. 49 U.S.C. § 1357 (1992). Convictions within the prior 10 years of specified crimes, including murder, espionage, rape, kidnapping, armed robbery, or drug distribution, disqualify an individual from employment. The Act also requires the development of standards for the hiring and continued employment of airport security personnel.

B. Bankruptcy Code

Private and public sector employers are prohibited by the Bankruptcy Code from discriminating in employment against an individual because he or she: (1) is or has been in bankruptcy or (2) has been associated with a bankruptcy or debtor in bankruptcy. 11 U.S.C. § 525 (1988). This Code affects workplace privacy by protecting personal rights to free association.

C. Drug Testing

1. Drug-Free Workplace Act of 1988

The Drug-Free Workplace Act of 1988 applies to employers with a federal government contract of $25,000 or more. 41 U.S.C. §§ 701-707 (1989). Violations of the Act can result in suspension of payments, contract termination, and debarment for a period of up to five years.

The Act requires federal contractors to develop a policy statement directed to employees that includes:

1. notification that the unlawful manufacture, distribution, dispensation, possession, or use of a controlled substance is prohibited in the workplace;

2. identification of the specific actions that the employer will take against employees for violating the employer's drug policy;

3. provision that, as a condition of employment, the employee will abide by the terms of the policy and notify the employer of any criminal drug statute conviction no later than five days after the conviction is imposed.

To allow the employer to enforce this policy, each employee must be given a copy of it. Along with the policy statement, the employer must develop a drug-free awareness program which sets forth:

1. The employer's policy of maintaining a drug-free workplace

2. The dangers of workplace drug abuse

3. Available drug counseling, rehabilitation, and employee assistance programs

4. The penalties the employer may impose on the employee for drug abuse violations and convictions

The Act does not require the employer to establish an alcohol and drug testing program. This decision is left up to each employer.

2. Executive Order No. 12,546 (Drug Testing)

Executive Order No. 12,546 establishes a policy against the use of illegal drugs by federal employees, whether or not on duty. Exec. Order No. 12,546 (Sept. 15, 1986), 51 Fed. Reg. 32,889 (1986). The Order provides for drug testing programs and procedures. Federal employees are prohibited from using illegal drugs, and those who use illegal drugs are not suitable for employment by the federal government.

3. Omnibus Transportation Employee Testing Act

Alcohol and drug testing in the transportation industry was previously governed by federal regulations. *See, e.g.,* 49 C.F.R. pt. 40 (1991) (Department of Transportation regulations). With the adoption of the Omnibus Transportation Employee Testing Act in 1991, alcohol and drug testing is now required by federal statute. 49 U.S.C. § 1618a (1992). The Act covers air carriers, railroads, motor carriers, and mass transit. It requires employers to formulate policies for pre-employment, reasonable suspicion, random, and post-accident testing. Discipline up to and including termination may result from a positive test. Rehabilitation is to be made available when it is feasible.

D. Employee Polygraph Protection Act of 1988

The Employee Polygraph Protection Act of 1988 prohibits employers from requiring, requesting, causing, or suggesting that an employee take a polygraph examination. 29 U.S.C. §§ 2001-2009 (1988). This Act forbids employers from retaliating against employees who exercise their rights under it.

Exempted from the provisions of the Act are federal, state, and local government employers. Exemptions also cover national defense and federal government security contractors. For example, Department of Defense contractors and their employees may have polygraph examinations administered to them by the federal government in the performance of intelligence functions.

Private sector employers may still request that employees take polygraph examinations during an ongoing investigation of economic loss or injury involving a theft or embezzlement. However, results of the examination or the employee's refusal to take the examination must be accompanied by additional supporting evidence before an employer can commence an adverse employment action against the employee. The Act also contains similar exemptions for security and pharmaceutical employers. Employers are required to post notices at the workplace of the protections offered by the Act. Violations will subject employers to fines of up to $10,000. The Act specifically provides that it shall not preempt any state statute, local law, or provision of any negotiated collective bargaining agreement that prohibits polygraph examinations or that is more restrictive in its provisions.

E. Fair Credit Reporting Act

The Fair Credit Reporting Act (FCRA) of 1970 is considered an important federal effort to influence private sector privacy activities. 15 U.S.C. §§ 1681-1681t (1988). It regulates the actions of consumer reporting agencies in preparing credit reports and reporting credit information.

The FCRA was enacted to curtail credit agency abuses in reporting information. Prior to the FCRA, disclosure of an individual's financial status, medical history, and sexual relationships could occur to almost anyone who requested the information. This often resulted in embarrassment and humiliation. Reporting inaccurate, incomplete, or obsolete information frequently caused denial of credit, employment, or insurance. The individual generally was unaware that this information was being reported. Even if the individual was aware, no legal right existed to require correction of the reports or to remedy the harm.

The FCRA is relevant to workplace privacy because credit agencies frequently distribute their reports to employers to use in making employment decisions. If an employer requests a credit report and decides not to offer employment based on the report, the employer must inform the applicant of the credit agency's name and address. The applicant may request from the credit agency the "nature and substance" of the information maintained. The credit agency must disclose the information sources and all recipients of the report within the preceding six months. 15 U.S.C. § 1681g(a)(1) (1988). If the accuracy of any file item is disputed, that item must be reinvestigated by the credit agency. Should the reinvestigation not resolve the dispute, a counterstatement may be included in subsequent reports. When the reinvestigation results in deletion of the information or causes a dispute over the results, the credit agency must, upon request, notify designated prior recipients. 15 U.S.C. § 1681i(d) (1988).

F. Fair Employment Practice Statutes

1. Age Discrimination in Employment Act of 1967

The Age Discrimination in Employment Act of 1967 (ADEA) prohibits employers from discriminating because of age against persons over the age of 40. 29 U.S.C. §§ 621-634 (1988). It applies to all employers with 20 or more employees in industries affecting commerce, including state and local governments.

The ADEA does not impose liability on an employer for a termination based "on a factor other than age," or for "good cause." 29 U.S.C. § 623(f) (1988). Employers are permitted to discriminate based on age when age is a *bona fide* occupational qualification to observe the terms of a *bona fide* seniority system. 29 U.S.C. § 625 (1988).

2. Americans with Disabilities Act of 1990

The Americans with Disabilities Act of 1990 affects all public and private employers of 15 or more employees and all places of public accommodations and services. 42 U.S.C. §§ 12101-12213 (1992). It prohibits discrimination against qualified people with disabilities in employment, public services and transportation, public accommodations, and telecommunications services. It contains five major sections dealing with each of these areas and a miscellaneous section covering, among other things, exemptions, attorney's fees, and amendments to the Vocational Rehabilitation Act of 1973.

The Act prohibits employers from discriminating against a qualified individual with a disability regarding applications, hiring, advancement, termination, compensation, training, or other terms, conditions, or privileges of employment. The Act prohibits the use of qualification standards, employment tests, or selection criteria that tend to screen out individuals with disabilities, unless the standard is job-related. Employers are required to make reasonable accommodations to the known physical or mental limitations of an otherwise qualified individual with a disability unless it would impose an undue hardship on the employer or its business interests. To determine whether an accommodation would impose an undue hardship, the following factors are be considered:

1. The nature and cost of the accommodation
2. The size, type, and financial resources of the specific facility where the accommodation would have to be made
3. The size, type, and financial resources of the employer
4. The employer's type of operation, including the composition, structure, and functions of its workforce, and the geographic separateness and administrative or fiscal relationship between the specific facility and the employer.

3. Civil Rights Acts of 1964

The Civil Rights Act of 1964 (Title VII) prohibits discrimination based on sex, race, color, religion, and national origin by employers in hiring or firing; on compensation in terms, conditions, or privileges of employment; and in limiting, segregating, or classifying employees or applicants. 42 U.S.C. §§ 2000e-1 through 2002-17 (1988). It applies to all employers with 15 or more employees in industries affecting commerce; state and local governments; labor organizations with 15 or more members; labor organizations in industries affecting commerce; and employment agencies. Differentiation is permitted based on religion, sex, or national origin only where a "bona fide occupational qualification" for the job exists. 42 U.S.C. § 2000e-2(e) (1988).

4. Civil Rights Statutes (§§ 1981, 1983, 1985, and 1986)

Congress has enacted several civil rights statutes to give force and effect to the Thirteenth, Fourteenth, and Fifteenth Amendments to the United States Constitution. 42 U.S.C. §§ 1981, 1983, 1985, 1986 (1988). These statutes safeguard employees against procedural gaps in the Civil Rights Act of 1964 (Title VII) and offer additional remedies including compensatory and punitive damages. Jury trials are also available under certain circumstances.

Section 1981 affords a federal remedy against private acts of employment discrimination based on race. 42 U.S.C. § 1981 (1988). The U.S. Supreme Court has indicated that: "[I]t is now well settled among the federal courts of appeals—and we now join them—that § 1981 affords a federal remedy against discrimination in private employment on the basis of race." Johnson v. Railway Express Agency, Inc., 421 U.S. 454, 459-60 (1975).

Section 1983 was originally enacted as part of the Civil Rights Act of 1871. 42 U.S.C. § 1983 (1988). The statute was passed pursuant to the U.S. Constitution's Fourteenth Amendment. It reaches only persons acting "under color of" state law and does not reach purely private conduct or conduct of federal agencies and officials. There must be some state involvement in the practices challenged. Section 1983 covers discrimination based on race, color, sex, religion, national origin, and other discrimination.

Sections 1985 and 1986 provide broader coverage than either Section 1981 or 1983. 42 U.S.C. §§ 1985, 1986 (1988). Like Section 1981 they extend in some circumstances to purely private conduct where race discrimination is involved. Where there is sufficient state involvement, Sections 1985 and 1986 extend to discrimination beyond Section 1981 or even Title VII. However, Sections 1985 and 1986 cannot be used to enforce rights created solely by Title VII. Absent state action, they may apply only to employment discrimination based on race and, arguably, religion.

5. Executive Order No. 11,246 (Affirmative Action)

Executive Order No. 11,246 requires that all nonexempt federal government contracts contain provisions that contractors and subcontractors not discriminate against employees or applicants because of race, color, religion, sex, or national origin, and take affirmative action to ensure that applicants and employees are employed without regard to these factors. 3 C.F.R. § 339 (1964-1965), *reprinted as amended* in 42 U.S.C. § 2000e (1988), note issued on Sept. 24,.1965. The Executive Order also applies to federal and federally assisted construction contracts. Its principal exemption is for contracts or subcontracts which do not exceed $10,000.

6. Vocational Rehabilitation Act of 1973

The Vocational Rehabilitation Act of 1973 (Title V) has been characterized as the disabled person's civil rights act. 29 U.S.C. §§ 701-796i (1988). All federal contracts and subcontracts in excess of $2,500 must include clauses in which the contractor agrees not to discriminate and to undertake affirmative action to provide employment opportunities for the disabled. 29 U.S.C. § 793(a) (1988). Responsibility for enforcement rests with the Office of Federal Contract Compliance Programs (OFCCP) of the Department of Labor.

G. Freedom of Information Act

The Freedom of Information Act (FOIA) is based on the requirement that all federal agency documents must be publicly disclosed unless specifically exempted. 5 U.S.C. § 552 (1988). Documents described as "rules of procedure" must be published in the *Federal Register*. Final opinions or orders in adjudicated agency decisions, agency policy statements and interpretations, and staff instructions affecting the public must be made available. If the requested documents are exempted from disclosure, the agency need not make them available.

H. Hatch Act

In 1802, President Thomas Jefferson issued a circular mandating the political neutrality of federal employees. For more than one hundred years, political activities of federal employees were curtailed by various Presidential Executive Orders. Not until 1938 did Congress pass the Hatch Political Activities Act detailing which forms of political activity were prohibited for federal employees and state and local employees who are substantially funded with federal monies. 5 U.S.C. §§ 1501(5), 7324(a) (1988).

The political activity prohibitions of the Hatch Act are broad. Employees cannot "take an active part in political management or in political campaigns" or interfere with or affect an election. 5 U.S.C. §§ 1501(5), 7324a (1988). Money for political purposes can be neither received nor given between federal employees. An employee cannot "coerce the political action" of others, cannot be forced to provide "political service," and cannot be terminated for refusing to aid a campaign. Id.

I. Immigration Reform and Control Act of 1986

The Immigration Reform and Control Act of 1986 requires employers to assist in stopping illegal immigration into the United States. Pub. L. No. 99-603, 100 Stat. 3359 (1986) (codified in scattered sections of 7 U.S.C.; 8 U.S.C.; 18 U.S.C.; 20 U.S.C.; 29 U.S.C.; 42 U.S.C.). A major policy of the Act is to remove the incentive for illegal immigration by eliminating the job opportunities which draw illegal aliens to this country. Civil and criminal penalties are created for employers who knowingly hire or recruit an alien who is not permitted to work in the United States.

The Act creates an additional step in the recruitment and selection process by requiring employers to ask applicants for proof showing they are authorized to work in this country. Every employer must examine certain documents to establish identity and eligibility for employment of every person who is hired. The applicant must provide one of the following documents:

1. A United States passport

2. A United States citizenship certificate

3. A naturalization certificate

4. An unexpired foreign passport, if the passport has an appropriate, unexpired endorsement of the Attorney General authorizing the individual's employment in the United States

5. A resident alien card or other alien registration card that contains a photograph or other personal identifying information and that is evidence of employment authorization in the United States.

J. Jury Systems Improvement Act

The Jury Systems Improvement Act provides that "no employer shall discharge, threaten to discharge, intimidate, or coerce any permanent employee by reason of such employee's jury service, or the attendance or scheduled attendance in connection with such service, in any court of the United States." 28 U.S.C. § 1875 (1988). Penalties to the employer for violating the Act include: reinstatement of the employee and payment of lost wages and benefits; payment of a $1,000 fine for each violation; and payment of the employee's attorneys' fees. Employees cannot recover compensatory damages for noneconomic losses, including mental distress. See Shea v. County of Rockland, 810 F.2d 87 (2d Cir. 1987).

Although an employee may not be terminated for federal jury service, the Act does not require that the employee be paid during this service. 28 U.S.C. § 1875(c) (1988). Merely having a policy allowing jury duty service may not be sufficient to avoid employer liability. If a supervisor threatens an employee into seeking release from jury service, even in contravention of the employer's policy, it may violate the Act. The general policy will not insulate the employer from liability. See In re Adams, 421 F. Supp. 1027 (E.D. Mich. 1976).

K. Mail Tampering

Federal law prohibits any person from taking mail addressed to another person before it has been delivered with the intent "to obstruct the correspondence, or pry into the business or secrets of another." 18 U.S.C. § 1702 (1988). It is designed to protect the mails and correspondence from theft, embezzlement, obstruction, and prying. United States v. Ashford, 530 F.2d 792 (8th Cir. 1976). Mail is protected until it is physically delivered to the addressee or an authorized agent. *United States v. Gaber*, 745 F.2d 952 (5th Cir. 1984).

For employers, this statute becomes important in determining when an employee's mail is still considered statutorily protected and when privacy-related liability could result. *See United States v. Cochran*, 646 F. Supp. 7 (D. Me. 1985) (distribution of mail from university office to dormitories considered further extension of mail route). Violations carry a penalty of up to five years in prison and a fine of $2,000. 18 U.S.C. § 1708 (1989). Even absent this statute, opening of employee mail without permission may be an intrusion of privacy by affecting seclusion interests. *See Vernars v. Young*, 539 F.2d 966 (3d Cir. 1976) (unauthorized opening and reading of mail marked "personal").

L. National Labor Relations Act

The National Labor Relations Act (NLRA) was enacted to provide a method of establishing employee representation for collective bargaining purposes by eliminating coercion, restraint, or interference with employee rights. 29 U.S.C. §§ 151-168 (1988). To implement the NLRA's policies and to regulate private sector employment relations, the National Labor Relations Board (NLRB) was created. The NLRB has judicial and rule-making powers.

The NLRA applies to private sector employers and employees involved in interstate commerce. Enterprises covered by the Railway Labor Act are excluded, along with public sector employers and those engaged in agriculture.

Workplace privacy concerns can be impacted through the NLRA's right to organize and its proscriptions against illegal activity curtailing this right. Interference with right to organize can result from employer surveillance. 29 U.S.C. § 157 (1988). Refusal to bargain can result from introduction of testing or surveillance devices without consultation or bargaining with an employee representative. *See NLRB v. Katz*, 369 U.S. 736 (1962).

M. Occupational Safety and Health Act

The purpose of the Occupational Safety and Health Act of 1970 (OSHA) is to "assure so far as possible every working man and woman . . . safe and healthful working conditions." 29 U.S.C. §§ 651-678 (1988). OSHA is an attempt to reduce work-related injuries and illnesses that impose a substantial burden on interstate commerce through lost production, wage loss, medical expenses, and disability compensation payments.

N. Omnibus Crime Control and Safe Streets Act

The Omnibus Crime Control and Safe Streets Act of 1968 (Title III) regulates deliberate interceptions of wire and oral communications. 18 U.S.C. §§ 2510-2520 (1988). It provides for recovery of actual damages, punitive damages, costs, and attorneys' fees. Criminal penalties also are prescribed. Except for common carriers, employers who intercept employees' confidential communications without consent violate the Act. Bad faith or malice need not be proven to recover.

O. Privacy Act of 1974

The Privacy Act of 1974 regulates information collected, maintained, used, and disclosed by federal agencies. 5 U.S.C. § 552a (1988). It must be understood in relation to the Freedom of Information Act (FOIA) of 1966. 5 U.S.C. § 552 (1988). Individual privacy protection is mandated by the Privacy Act while the FOIA compels information disclosure held by the government.

P. Racketeer Influenced and Corrupt Organizations Act

The Racketeer Influenced and Corrupt Organizations Act (RICO) was enacted to combat the infiltration of legitimate business by organized crime. 18 U.S.C. §§ 1961-1968 (1988). RICO provides criminal penalties and civil remedies. Although enacted to thwart organized crime, its provisions reach many other activities involving fraud or business torts. RICO is to be interpreted broadly and claims have been brought against banks, insurance companies, and other legitimate businesses. *See* Sedima, S.P.R.L. v. Imrex, 473 U.S. 479 (1985).

The statute contains no definition of "organized crime," and a nexus need not exist between a RICO violation and organized crime. *See* Moss v. Morgan Stanley, Inc., 719 F.2d 5 (2d Cir. 1983). On the civil side, a RICO violation results in recovery of treble damages, attorneys' fees, and costs. *See* Williams v. Hall, 683 F. Supp. 639 (E.D. Ky. 1988) (jury award of more than $69 million to two executives who were terminated for their refusal to participate in unlawful RICO activity).

RICO's flexibility, breadth, and power make it a potential weapon in workplace privacy litigation, especially if whistle-blowing incidents are involved. It can convert many commercial torts into federal treble damages actions. *See* 18 U.S.C. § 1964(c) (1988). Federal district courts have exclusive jurisdiction over civil RICO claims. RICO statutes providing for double and treble damages, along with other relief, also exist in some states.

A terminated employee can collect RICO damages from the employer and its officers if the employee can show that the termination was in furtherance of a conspiracy to run the business through a pattern of racketeering activity. Williams v. Hall, 683 F. Supp. 639 (E.D. Ky. 1988); *contra* Morast v. Lance, 807 F.2d 926 (11th Cir. 1987) (employee terminated for reporting illegal activity had no RICO standing; however, court implied that employee would have had standing if terminated for refusing to participate in illegal activity). Recovery has been permitted where employees charged that they were terminated after refusing to participate in or cover up illegal bribes. This occurred where employees claimed that for several years their employer obtained oil from Middle East countries by bribing officials. They were terminated when they refused to participate in this conduct or the coverup. *Williams.*

Q. Whistle-blowing

1. Civil Service Reform Act

The Civil Service Reform Act of 1978 contains some protection for federal employees who "blow the whistle." 5 U.S.C. § 2302(b)(g) (1988). "Whistle-blowing" covers a broad spectrum of situations in which an employee protests, publicly or not, either the employer's or another employee's criminal, illegal, immoral, or underhanded behavior.

2. False Claims Amendment Act

The False Claims Amendment Act of 1986 strengthens the anti-fraud provisions of the False Claims Act. 31 U.S.C. §§ 3729-3733 (1991). The amended Act provides protection for whistle-blowing employees who expose fraud against the federal government by contractors and others. Any employee who is terminated, demoted, threatened, harassed, or otherwise discriminated against by his or her employer for taking lawful action under the Act can sue in federal district court for all relief necessary to make the employee whole. This relief includes reinstatement with the same seniority status the employee would have had but for the discrimination, two times the amount of back-pay, interest on the back-pay, and compensation for any special damages resulting from the discrimination, including litigation costs and reasonable attorneys' fees.

3. Whistle-blower Protection Act

The Whistle-blower Protection Act of 1989 further protects from retaliation federal employees who disclose waste and fraud at the government level. 5 U.S.C. §§ 1201-1222 (1989). The Act establishes a simpler and fairer standard for whistle-blowers in proving their case of retaliation. Whistle-blowers have the right to appeal their cases to the Merit Systems Protection Board if the Special Counsel fails or refuses to do so. The independence of the Office of Special Counsel is enhanced and the office is specifically directed to work for the benefit of whistle-blowers. The Act also gives whistle-blowers increased procedural protections and confidentiality guarantees.

IV. State Regulation ›

A. Acquired Immunodeficiency Syndrome (AIDS)

With the public's current awareness of Acquired Immunodeficiency Syndrome (AIDS), employers have become increasingly concerned with the potential problems that AIDS may present in the workplace. Some employers have taken steps to implement pre-employment and workplace testing for AIDS. Some employers have formulated AIDS testing programs that do not comport with legal restrictions affecting employee privacy. *See* Glover v. Eastern Neb. Community Office of Retardation, 686 F. Supp. 243 (D. Neb. 1988), *aff'd*, 867 F.2d 461 (8th Cir.), *cert. denied*, 493 U.S. 932 (1989).

To control or prohibit employer testing programs, various states have enacted statutes governing AIDS testing. Under some of these statutes, an employee or job applicant cannot be required to take an AIDS test as a condition of hiring, promotion, or continued employment unless the employer can show that the absence of AIDS is a *bona fide* occupational qualification (BFOQ). *See, e.g.,* FLA. STAT. ANN. § 381.606(5) (West 1988). To prove a BFOQ, an employer must show: (1) that the AIDS test is necessary to determine whether the employee can perform the job or whether that person presents a significant risk of transmitting the disease to others during the normal course of work; and (2) that there are no other reasonable means of getting this information short of requiring an AIDS test. *Id.*

See, e.g., CAL. HEALTH & SAFETY CODE §§ 199.20-.22 (West Supp. 1992); DEL. CODE ANN. tit. 16, § 1202 (1989); FLA. STAT. ANN. § 381.606(5) (West 1988); IOWA CODE § 1351.1 (1988); MICH. COMP. LAWS §§ 5131, 5133 (1989); N.Y. PUB. HEALTH LAW § 2781 (McKinney 1989); VA. CODE ANN. §§ 32.1-36.1 (Michie 1989); WIS. STAT. ANN. § 631.90 (West Supp. 1992).

B. Arrest Record Regulation

Employers may be statutorily prohibited from asking an applicant or employee about arrests. Inquiry is restricted to matters pertinent to job performance and any prosecutions of the employee resulting in convictions. California provides for a fine of $200 to $500 along with a six-month sentence for the employer or its agent who violates state statute. Massachusetts requires all employment applications to have a section informing prospective employees that they can answer "no" to questions about arrests without convictions. Other states simply prohibit employers from collecting or maintaining records regarding criminal matters not relating to convictions.

See, e.g., CAL. LAB. CODE § 432.7(a)-(b) (West Supp. 1992); CONN. GEN. STAT. §§ 31-51i (1958); GA. CODE ANN. § 35-3-34 (1982); HAW. REV. STAT. § 831-3.1(a)-(c) (Supp. 1992); MD. CODE ANN., CRIM. LAW § 740 (a)-(b) (1982); MASS. GEN. LAWS ANN. ch. 276, § 100A(4), ch. 1513 § 4, para. 9 (West Supp. 1992); MICH. COMP. LAWS § 37.2205a (Supp. 1992); MINN. STAT. § 364.03 (1980); N.Y. EXEC. LAW § 296(16) (Consol. 1982); OHIO REV. CODE ANN. §§ 2151.358, 2953.43(A)-(B) (Baldwin, 1979); OR. REV. STAT. § 181.555-(2)(a)-(b), 181.560 (1981); CRIMES AND OFFENSES PA. CONS. STAT. ANN. tit. 18, § 9125 (1982); R. I. GEN. LAWS § 28-5-7(G) (1979); VA. CODE ANN. §§ 19.2 - 392.4(a)-(c) (Michie 1950); WIS. STAT. ANN. § 111.31 (West 1992).

C. Blacklisting

Blacklisting involves preventing or attempting to prevent an individual from obtaining employment. It may arise through an oral or written communication. As a workplace privacy interest, blacklisting impacts employee speech, beliefs, information, association, and lifestyle. These privacy interests recur throughout employment as they relate to hiring, the workplace environment, and life outside the workplace. In some states, blacklisting is statutorily regulated. See, e.g., IOWA CODE ANN. §§ 730.1-.3 (West 1979). Where not statutorily regulated, blacklisting may be recognized as a tort having characteristics similar to defamation. *See, e.g.,* Austin v. Torrington Co., 611 F. Supp. 191 (D.S.C. 1985), *rev'd,* 810 F.2d 416 (4th Cir.), *cert. denied,* 484 U.S. 977 (1987) (conversation between human resources managers of two companies did not establish the necessary malice for making a blacklist).

D. Drug Testing

With the current awareness of alcohol and drug abuse, employers have become increasingly concerned with the potential problems that alcohol and drug abuse can cause in the workplace. Many employers have implemented alcohol and drug testing. Absent state guidelines regulating this testing, some employers have formulated testing programs that have not comported with legal restrictions affecting workplace privacy. To control employer testing programs, various states have recently enacted statutes governing alcohol and drug testing.

See e.g., FLA. STAT. ANN. § 112.0455(1)-(16) (West 1990); IOWA CODE ANN. § 730.5 (West Supp. 1992); KAN. STAT. ANN. § 75-4382 (1990); LA. REV. STAT. ANN. § 23-1601(10) (West Supp. 1992); ME. REV. STAT. ANN. tit. 26, § 23.1601(10)(A)-(F) (West 1990); MD. CODE ANN., HEALTH-GEN. LAW § 17-214 (1990); MINN. STAT. ANN. §§ 181.950-.957 (West Supp. 1992); MONT. CODE ANN. § 39-2-304(1)-(5) (1988); NEB. REV. STAT. §§ 48-1901 through 48-1910 (1990); OR. REV. STAT. §§ 659.225-.227 (1987); R.I. GEN. LAWS § 28-6.5-1(A)-(G) (Supp. 1992); TENN. CODE ANN. § 2-19-134 (1990); UTAH CODE ANN. §§ 34-38-1 through 34-38-15 (1988); VT. STAT. ANN. tit. 21, §§ 511-520 (1988).

E. Employment File Regulation

State statutes regulating employment files are varied—some states limit their applicability to state employees while others extend coverage to private and public sector employees. Others apply only to private sector employees.

The California Labor Code requires an employer to permit employees to inspect their personnel records, including records which have been used to determine qualification for employment, promotion, additional compensation, or termination or other disciplinary action. Employers are required to maintain personnel files where employees report to work or to make them available upon reasonable notice.

This right to inspect employee personnel files is not absolute. The California statute does not grant an employee a right to inspect any records relating to the investigation of a possible criminal offense or letters of reference maintained by the employer. The employer may impose reasonable restrictions on employee access to personnel files, including: (1) requiring the employee to submit a written request; (2) allowing inspection only by appointment; (3) allowing inspection only during regular business hours; (4) allowing inspection only on the employee's own time; (5) allowing inspection only in the presence of an employer representative; and (6) limiting the frequency of the inspections.

See, e.g., CAL. LAB. CODE § 1198.5 (West Supp. 1992); CONN. GEN. STAT. §§ 31-128a through 31-128h (Supp. 1992); D.C. CODE ANN. § 1-632.5 (1981); ME. REV. STAT. ANN. tit. 26, § 631, tit. 30 §§ 664, 2257 (Supp. 1992); MICH. COMP. LAWS §§ 423.501-.512 (Supp. 1992); OR. REV. STAT. § 652.750 (1986); PA. STAT. ANN. tit. 43, §§ 1321-1324 (Purdon's 1992); S.D. CODIFIED LAWS ANN. § 3-6A-31 (Supp. 1992); UTAH CODE ANN. §§ 67-18-1, 67-18-5 (1983); VT. STAT. ANN. tit. 1, § 317(b)(1) (Supp. 1992); and WIS. STAT. §§ 103.13(7)-(8) (West Supp. 1992).

F. Employment References

Employment reference statutes generally prohibit employer misrepresentations about former employees. The California Labor Code makes it a misdemeanor for any employer to make misrepresentations that prevent or attempt to prevent a former employee from obtaining other employment. The employer also commits

a misdemeanor if it permits one of its employees to make this
misrepresentation or if it fails to take reasonable steps to prevent
the misrepresentation from occurring. Even if criminal liability is
not established, the employer will be liable for treble damages in
a civil action for a misrepresentation.

See, e.g., CAL. LAB. CODE §§ 1050, 1053, 1054 (West 1971); CONN.
GEN. STAT. ANN. § 31-51 (West 1986); IND. CODE §§ 22-6-3-1, 22-6-
3-2 (1986); KANS. STAT. ANN. § 44-808(3) (1986); Mo. Rev. Stat. § 290.140
(1985); MONT. CODE ANN. §§ 39-2-801-084 (1985); NEV. REV. STAT.
§ 613.210 (1986).

G. Fair Credit Reporting Acts

States have enacted credit reporting acts with provisions relating to employers similar to the federal Fair Credit Reporting Act
(18 U.S.C. §§ 1681-1681t (1988)). Generally, consumers may obtain
information from credit agencies concerning reports made by an
agency to employers for employment purposes involving hiring,
termination, promotion, and retention. Some acts cover private
sector and public sector employees.

Inherent in the restrictions set forth in these statutes is a prohibition against employers sharing credit information with employees' potential creditors who contact the employers. Employers may
verify employment; however, they should disclose employment
information only where the employee has signed a written release
authorizing the disclosure. The information to be disclosed should
be clearly set forth in the release.

Even though an employer may follow the procedures set forth
in these statutes, investigative reports that are not job-related may
have a disparate impact on minority applicants. It may be shown
that minorities are denied credit more often than non-minorities.
When not job-related, refusal of employment based on these reports
may be insufficient to withstand challenge of noncompliance with
federal and state fair employment practice statutes. This could
entitle the employee to back pay and reinstatement.

See, e.g., Ariz. Rev. Stat. Ann. §§ 44-1691 through 44-1696 (West Supp. 1992); Cal. Civ. Code §§ 1785-1786.56 (West 1985); Conn. Gen. Stat. Ann. §§ 36-431 through 36-435 (West 1981 & Supp. 1992); Fla. Stat. Ann. §§ 559.55-.78 (West Supp. 1992); Kan. Stat. Ann. §§ 50-701 through 50-722 (1983); Ky. Rev. Stat. Ann. § 431.350 (Baldwin Supp. 1994); Me. Rev. Stat. Ann. tit. 10, §§ 1311-1329 (West 1964 & Supp. 1992); Md. Code Ann., Com. Law I §§ 14-201 through 14-204 (1975); Mass. Gen. Laws Ann. ch. 93, §§ 50-68 (West 1984); Mont. Code Ann. §§ 30-3-101 through 30-3-153 (1985); N.H. Rev. Stat. Ann. §§ 359-B (1984 & Supp. 1992); N.M. Stat. Ann. §§ 56-3-1 through 56-3-8 (Michie 1978); N.Y. Gen. Bus. Law §§ 380-380S (McKinney 1984 & Supp. 1992); Okla. Stat. Ann. tit. 24, §§ 81-85 (West 1951 & Supp. 1992); Tex. Rev. Stat. Ann. art. 9016 (Vernon Supp. 1987); Va. Code Ann. § 6.1-366(c) (Michie 1986).

H. Fair Employment Practice Statutes

Fair employment practice (FEP) statutes prohibiting employment discrimination are found in many states. These statutes generally forbid discrimination based on race, color, creed, national origin, sex, and disability.

Because these fair employment practice statutes were enacted in response to different state needs and political pressures they are not exactly alike. The typical fair employment practice statute contains a list of employer actions involving hiring and termination that must be exercised in a nondiscriminatory manner. Fair employment practice statutes also protect persons in the pre-employment process. They prohibit employers from making inquiries that express any limitation on hiring because of an applicant's race, color, creed, national origin, sex, or disability.

Almost all states have adopted some form of protection against discrimination of the disabled in employment. In some states only the physically disabled are protected. Other states protect those with physical and mental disabilities. What constitutes a disability varies depending on the applicable state statutes.

See, e.g., ALASKA STAT. § 18.80.220 (1986); ARIZ. REV. STAT. ANN. § 36-506 (1985); ARIZ. REV. STAT. ANN. § 41-1463(B) (1985); CAL. GOV'T CODE §§ 11135, 12900 (West 1980); COLO. REV. STAT. § 24-34-402 (1980); CONN. GEN. STAT. § 46a-60 (1986); DEL. CODE ANN. tit. 19, § 711 (1985); D.C. CODE ANN. § 1-2512 (1981); GA. CODE §§ 34-1-2 (age), 34-6A-4 (disability) (1982); HAW. REV. STAT. § 378-2 (1985); IDAHO CODE §§ 56-701, 67-5909 (1980); ILL. REV. STAT. ch. 68, §§ 2-102 (West Supp. 1987); IND. CODE § 22-9-1-2 (1986); IOWA CODE § 601A.6 (1975); KAN. STAT. ANN. § 44-1009 (1986); KY. REV. STAT. ANN. § 344.040 (Baldwin 1986); LA. REV. STAT. ANN. § 46:1721 (West 1982) (disabled only); ME. REV. STAT. ANN. tit. 5, § 4572 (Supp. 1992); MASS. GEN. LAWS ANN. ch. 151B, § 4 (West 1982); MINN. STAT. § 363.03 (1987); MO. REV. STAT. § 213.010 (Supp. 1992); MONT. CODE ANN. § 49-2-303 (1985); NEB. REV. STAT. § 48-1104 (1984); NEV. REV. STAT. § 613.330 (1986); N.H. REV. STAT. ANN. §§ 275:40, 354-A:1 (1977); N.M. STAT. ANN. § 28-1-17 (Michie 1978); N.Y. EXEC. LAW § 296 (Consol. 1983); N.C. GEN. STAT. § 143-422.2 (1985); N.D. CENT. CODE § 34-01-19 (1980); OKLA STAT. tit. 25, § 1302 (1986); OR. REV. STAT. § 659.030 (1983); OR. REV. STAT. § 659.400-.900 (1983); PA. STAT. ANN. tit. 43, §§ 951-963 (1992); R.I. GEN. LAWS § 28-5-7 (1986); S.C. CODE ANN. § 1-13-10 (Law. Co-op. 1986); S.D. CODIFIED LAWS ANN. § 20-13-10 (1979); TENN. CODE ANN. § 4-21-105 (1985); TEX. HUMAN RES. CODE ANN. § 21.001-.306 (West 1980); UTAH CODE ANN. § 34-35-6 (1987); VT. STAT. ANN. tit. 21, § 495 (1987); WASH. REV. CODE §§ 49.60.030, 49.60.180 (1982); WIS. STAT. §§ 111.31-.395 (1987); WYO. STAT. § 27-9-105 (1985).

I. Fingerprinting

Fingerprinting often is used during the initial hiring process to verify information. As a collection method, it presents employment privacy problems involving the maintenance, use, and disclosure of records that also could subsequently affect the employee's lifestyle.

Fingerprinting generally has been considered a valid collection method related more to verifying information than to compulsory

extraction of incriminating facts. Despite its primary use in verifying information, some states regulate fingerprinting to limit privacy abuses. California prohibits an employer from requiring that
an applicant or employee be fingerprinted for the purpose of furnishing information to a third party as a condition precedent to
securing or retaining employment if this information could be used
to the applicant's or employee's detriment.

See, e.g., CAL. LAB. CODE § 1051 (West 1971); N.Y. LAB. LAW
§ 201-a (Consol. 1983).

J. Highly Communicable Disease Testing

A trend seems to be developing to prohibit testing for highly
communicable diseases. However, several states explicitly require
testing in some occupations. Teachers in Illinois, Indiana, and South
Dakota are required to undergo a medical examination including
a tubercular skin test. School bus drivers must have a physical
examination in Indiana, Iowa, and Michigan. Other employees who
in various states must have physical examinations include frozen
food processing plant employees, meat and poultry workers, physical rehabilitation center employees, professional boxers, and Iowa
Department of Public Safety employees.

Many states implicitly require testing by prohibiting employment of workers in certain occupations if they are infected with a
communicable disease. These statutes generally prohibit employers
who operate food-handling or -serving establishments from employing workers infected with a communicable disease. Iowa also
prohibits hotels from employing workers with a communicable
disease.

See, CAL. GOV'T CODE § 7294.0(c)(3) (West 1986) (AIDS); FLA.
STAT. ANN. § 381.606 (West Supp. 1992); WIS. STAT. ANN. § 103.15
(West 1985) (AIDS).

K. Honesty Tests

Since the Employee Polygraph Protection Act of 1988 (29 U.S.C.
§§ 2001-2009 (1988)) went into effect, many employers have begun

using other testing techniques. Among these new techniques are paper-and-pencil honesty tests. Proponents claim that these tests validly predict honesty and screen out a propensity to violence and drug use. Opponents criticize these tests as being intrusive and asking questions that may have no relation to an employee's behavior. Currently, there is no federal regulation of honesty tests. However, certain states prohibit their use in employment situations.

See, e.g., MASS. GEN. LAWS ANN. ch. 149, § 19B (West 1990); R.I. GEN. LAWS § 28-6.1 through .4 (Supp. 1992).

L. Information Practice Acts

Certain states have comprehensive legislation concerning collection, maintenance, use, and disclosure of personal information by the government. Most are similar to the Federal Privacy Act of 1974 (5 U.S.C. § 552a (1982)) in protecting these employment privacy interests.

See e.g., ARK. CODE ANN. §§ 16-801 through 16-804 (1979); CAL. CIV. CODE §§ 1798 - 1798.78 (West 1985 & Supp. 1992); CONN. GEN. STAT. ANN. §§ 4-190 through 4-197 (West Supp. 1992); IND. CODE ANN. §§ 4-1-6-1 through 4-1-6-9 (Burns 1982 & Supp. 1992); MASS. GEN. LAWS ANN. ch. 66A (West Supp. 1992); MINN. STAT. ANN. §§ 13.01-.90 (West Supp. 1992); OHIO REV. CODE ANN. §§ 1347.01-.99 (Baldwin 1979 & Supp. 1992); UTAH CODE ANN. §§ 63-2-59 through 63-2-89 (Supp. 1992); VA. CODE ANN. §§ 2.1-377 through 2.1-386 (Michie 1950 & Supp. 1987); see also N.Y. PUB. OFF. LAW § 89 (McKinney Supp. 1992); COLO. REV. STAT. § 24-72-204 (1982 & Supp. 1992) (more limited restrictions on state agencies' personal information practices).

M. Intercept Statutes

Various states have adopted intercept statutes similar to the Omnibus Safe Streets Act of 1968 (Title III) (18 U.S.C. §§ 2510-20 (1986)). States differ on whether an employer or its agent recording a conversation with another person must obtain prior consent of all parties to the conversation or only the consent of one party. Pennsylvania prohibits any electronic recording without the consent of both parties to a conversation. Colorado grants an individual or an employer a limited right to monitor employee conversations on the employer's premises for security or business purposes without the consent of the parties if prior notice is given that monitoring might occur. Connecticut prohibits an employer from using sound or photographic equipment in areas designated for health or personal comfort.

The California Penal Code contains provisions similar to those in Title III. However, the federal extension phone exemption does not apply. Knowledge of monitoring and consent by the parties being monitored is critical to an employer's right to eavesdrop or record a communication. Accordingly, an employer should advise employees that their conversations may be monitored and obtain their written consent. The penalty for violation of California's statute is a fine up to $2,000 and/or imprisonment for up to one year.

Employers in California also are subject to the state's Labor Code which regulates the use of "spotters" posing as customers to monitor employees. This statute prohibits an employee's termination or discipline based on a spotter's report, unless a copy of the report is provided to the employee or unless the spotter is employed exclusively by that employer and the spotter conducts the entire investigation.

See, e.g., ALA. CODE §§ 13A-11-30 through 13A-11-37 (1982); ALASKA STAT. §§ 42.20.300-.340 (1983); ARIZ. REV. STAT. ANN. §§ 13-3004 through 13-3013 (1978); ARK. CODE ANN. § 41-4501 (1977); CAL. PENAL CODE §§ 630-637.3 (West 1970 & Supp. 1992); COLO. REV. STAT. §§ 18-9-301 through 18-9-305 (1978); CONN. GEN. STAT. ANN. §§ 53a-187 through 53a-189 (West 1985); DEL. CODE ANN. tit. 11, §§ 1335, 1336 (1979); D.C. CODE ANN. §§ 23-541 through 23-556 (1981); FLA. STAT. ANN. §§ 934.01 through 934.10 (West 1985); GA. CODE ANN. §§ 16-11-60 through 16-11-69 (1984); HAW. REV. STAT. § 711-1111 (1985); IDAHO CODE §§ 18-6701 through 18-6718 (1979); ILL. ANN. STAT. ch. 38, ¶¶ 14-1 through 14-9 (Smith-Hurd 1979);

IOWA CODE ANN. § 727.8 (West 1977); KAN. STAT. ANN. §§ 21-4001, 21-4002 (1981); KY. REV. STAT. ANN. §§ 526.010-.080 (Baldwin 1984); LA. REV. STAT. ANN. §§ 15:1301-15:1312 (West 1981); ME. REV. STAT. ANN. tit. 15, §§ 709-713 (West 1980); MD. CODE ANN., CRIM. LAW §§ 10-401 through 10-412 (1985); MASS. GEN. LAWS ANN. ch. 272, § 99 (West 1970); MINN. STAT. ANN. §§ 626A.01-.23 (West 1983); MONT. CODE ANN. § 45-8-213 (1985); NEB. REV. STAT. §§ 86-701-.712 (1981); NEV. REV. STAT. §§ 200.610-.690 (1984); N.H. REV. STAT. ANN. §§ 570-A:1 through 570-A:11 (1986); N.J. STAT. ANN. §§ 2A:156A-1 through 2A:156A-24 (West 1985); N.M. STAT. ANN. §§ 30-12-1 through 30-12-11 (Michie 1978); N.Y. PENAL LAW §§ 250.00-.10 (Consol. 1984); N.C. GEN. STAT. § 14-155 (1986); N.D. CENT. CODE §§ 12.1-15-02 through 12.1-15-04 (1985); OHIO REV. CODE ANN. §§ 2933.58, 4931.28 (Baldwin 1986); OKLA. STAT. ANN. tit. 13, §§ 176.1-.14 (West 1983); OR. REV. STAT. §§ 165.535-.545 (1983); PA. STAT. ANN. tit. 18, §§ 5701-5726 (1983); R.I. GEN. LAWS §§ 11-35-21 through 11-35-25 (1981); S.D. CODIFIED LAWS §§ 23A-35A-1 through 23A-35A-21 (1982); TENN. CODE ANN. §§ 39-4533, 39-3-1324, 65-21-110 (1982); TEX. PENAL CODE ANN. § 16.02 (West 1974); TEX. CRIM. PROC. CODE ANN. § 18.20 (West 1977); UTAH CODE ANN. §§ 77-23a-1 through 77-23a-11 (1982); WASH. REV. CODE ANN. §§ 9.73.030 through 9.73.140 (1981); WIS. STAT. ANN. §§ 968.27-.33 (West 1985); WYO. STAT. §§ 7-3-601 through 7-3-610 (1977).

N. Jury Duty

Various states prohibit employers from discriminating or retaliating against employees for jury service. However, the approach varies with respect to availability of a private cause of action, remedies, and the availability of punitive damages.

See, e.g., ALA. CODE § 12-16-8(a) (1986); ARIZ. REV. STAT. ANN. § 21-236 (West Supp. 1992); ARK. CODE ANN. § 39-103(b) (Michie Supp. 1992); CAL. LAB. CODE § 230 (West 1987); COLO. REV. STAT. § 13-71-118 (1973); CONN. GEN. STAT. § 51-247a (1985); FLA. STAT. ANN. § 40.271 (West Supp. 1992); HAW. REV. STAT. § 612-25 (1976);

IDAHO CODE § 2-218 (1979); ILL. ANN. STAT. ch. 78, para. 4.1 (Smith-Hurd 1987); IND. CODE ANN. § 34-4-29-1 (West 1986); KY. REV. STAT. ANN. § 29A.160 (Michie/Bobbs-Merrill 1985); LA. REV. STAT. ANN. § 23:965 (West 1985); ME. REV. STAT. ANN. tit. 14, § 1218 (West Supp. 1992); MD. CODE ANN., CTS. & JUD. PROC. § 8-105 (1984); MASS. ANN. LAWS ch. 268, § 14A (Law Co-op. 1980); MICH. COMP. LAWS ANN. § 600.1348 (West Supp. 1992); MINN. STAT. ANN. § 593.50 (West Supp. 1992); NEB. REV. STAT. § 25-1640 (1985); NEV. REV. STAT. § 6.190 (1985); N.H. REV. STAT. ANN. § 500-A:14 (1983); N.M. STAT. ANN. § 38-5-18 (Supp. 1992); N.Y. JUD. LAW § 519 (McKinney Supp. 1992); N.D. CENT. CODE § 27-09.1-17 (Supp. 1992); OHIO REV. CODE ANN. § 2313.18 (Baldwin Supp. 1992); OKLA. STAT. ANN. tit. 38, §§ 34-35 (West Supp. 1992); OR. REV. STAT. §§ 10.990-.992 (1986); JUDICIARY AND JUDICIAL PROCEDURE PA. CONS. STAT. ANN. tit. 42, § 4563 (Purdon Supp. 1992-93); S.D. CODIFIED LAWS ANN. § 16-13-41.1 (1979); TENN. CODE ANN. § 22-4-108(f)(2)(A) (Supp. 1992); TEX. CIV. PRAC. & REM. CODE ANN. § 122.001 (West 1986); UTAH CODE ANN. § 78-46-21 (Supp. 1992); VA. CODE ANN. § 18.2-465.1 (Michie Supp. 1992); VT. STAT. ANN. tit. 21, § 499(a) (1978); W. VA. CODE § 52-3-1 (Supp. 1992); WIS. STAT. ANN. § 756.25(1) (West 1981); WYO. STAT. § 1-11-401 (Supp. 1992).

O. Labor Relations Acts

1. Private Sector

States have adopted private sector labor relations acts similar to the provisions of the National Labor Relations Act (29 U.S.C. §§ 151-168 (1988)). Where a state act is patterned after the NLRA's language, decisions under the NLRA may offer guidance in interpreting the state statute. While NLRA decisions may be helpful, they are not binding on the state in interpreting its statute.

See e.g., ALA. CODE § 25-7-35 (1986); ARIZ. REV. STAT. ANN. §§ 23-1305, 23-1342 (1983); ARK. CODE ANN. § 81-202 (Michie 1976); CAL. LAB. CODE § 922 (West 1971); COLO. REV. STAT. § 8-2-102 (1974 &

Supp. 1992); CONN. GEN. STAT. ANN. § 31-105 (West 1987); GA. CODE
ANN. §§ 34-6-6, 34-6-21, 34-6-22 (1982); HAW. REV. STAT. § 377-6
(1985); IOWA CODE ANN. § 731.1 (West 1979); KAN. STAT. ANN. § 44-
808 (1986); LA. REV. STAT. ANN. § 23:983 (West 1985); MASS. GEN.
LAWS ANN. ch. 149, § 20 (West 1982); MINN. STAT. §§ 179.12, 179.18,
179.60 (1966); MISS. CODE ANN. 71-1-47 (1973); NEV. REV. STAT.
§§ 613.340, 614.080 (1986); N.H. REV. STAT. ANN. § 275.1 (1978); N.C.
GEN. STAT. §§ 95-80, 95-81 (1985); N.D. CENT. CODE § 34-01-14 (1980);
OR. REV. STAT. § 663.125 (1983); PA. STAT. ANN. tit. 43, §§ 211.1-.11
(1964 & Supp. 1992); R.I. GEN. LAW § 28-7-13 (1986); S.C. CODE ANN.
§ 41-1-20, 41-7-70 (Law. Co-op. 1986); S.D. CODIFIED LAWS ANN. § 60-
8-6 (1978); TENN. CODE ANN. § 50-1-201 (1983); TEX. CODE ANN. art.
5207(a) (Vernon 1987); UTAH CODE ANN. §§ 34-34-8, 34-34-9, 34-34-
13, 34-20-8 (1974); VA. CODE ANN. §§ 40.1-60, 40.1-61 (Michie 1986);
WYO. STAT. §§ 27-7-109, 27-7-110 (1985).

2. Public Sector

Public sector labor relations acts have been held constitutional
as an exercise of the state's police power. They do not reasonably
interfere with property rights, freedom of contract, or employees'
rights to a jury trial, nor do they constitute special legislation regulating labor.

See e.g., CONN. GEN. STAT. § 7-470(c) (1984) (municipal employ-
ees); CONN. GEN. STAT. § 10-153e(d) (1984) (teachers); DEL. CODE
ANN. tit. 14, § 4002(e) (Supp. 1992) (public school employees); DEL.
CODE ANN. tit. 19, § 1301(5) (1985) (public employees); HAW. REV.
STAT. § 89-2(5) (Supp. 1992) (public employees); Illinois Public La-
bor Relations Act § 7, ILL. REV. STAT. ch. 48, ¶ 1607 (1984) (municipal
employees); Illinois Educational Labor Relations Act § 10(a), ILL.
REV. STAT. ch. 48, ¶ 1710(a) (1984) (public school employees); IND.
CODE § 20-7.5-1-2(n) (1968) (educational employees); ME. REV. STAT.
ANN. tit. 26, § 965(1)(C) (Supp. 1992) (municipal public employees);
ME. REV. STAT. ANN. tit. 26, § 979-D(1)(E)(1) (Supp. 1992) (state
employees); ME. REV. STAT. ANN. tit. 26, § 1026(1)(C) (Supp. 1992)
(university employees); ME. REV. STAT. ANN. tit. 26, § 1285(1)(E)

(Supp. 1992) (judicial employees); MASS. GEN. LAWS ANN. ch. 150E, § 6 (West 1982) (public employees); MICH. COMP. LAWS § 423.215 (1978) (public employees); MINN. STAT. ANN. §§ 179A.06(5), 179A.07(2) (West Supp. 1992) (public employees); MONT. CODE ANN. § 39-31-305(2), (3) (1983) (public employees); N.H. REV. STAT. ANN. § 273-A:5(I) (1978) (public employees); N.M. State Personnel Board Regulations for Labor Management Relations §§ 2d, 7a (1983) (state employees); N.Y. CIV. SERV. LAW § 204(3) (McKinney 1983) (public employees); N.D. CENT. CODE 15-38.1-12(4) (1981) (teachers); OHIO REV. CODE ANN. § 4117.01(G) (Baldwin Supp. 1992) (public employees); OR. REV. STAT. § 243.650(4) (1985) (public employees); PA. STAT. ANN. tit. 43, § 1101.701 (1992) (public employees); TEX. REV. CIV. STAT. ANN. art. 5154c-1(7)(b) (West 1987) (police officers and fire-fighters); VT. STAT. ANN. tit. 21, § 1725(a) (1978) (municipal employees); WASH. REV. CODE ANN. § 41.59.030(4) (Supp. 1992) (public employees, except educational); WASH. REV. CODE ANN. § 41.59.020(2) (Supp. 1992) (educational employees); WIS. STAT. ANN. § 111.70(1)(a) (West Supp. 1992) (municipal employees); WIS. STAT. ANN. § 111.81(1) (West Supp. 1992) (state employees).

P. Medical Records Regulation

Some states have special provisions governing medical records. While most states regulate access to medical records, Maryland limits the medical questions an employer may ask employees or applicants.

The California Confidentiality of Medical Information Act restricts an employer's use and disclosure of employees' medical information. Employers must establish appropriate procedures to ensure the confidentiality of medical records and to protect the records from unauthorized use and disclosure. These procedures may include instructions regarding confidentiality to employees handling files and security systems restricting file access. California employers are prohibited from using, disclosing, or knowingly permitting employees to use or disclose medical information that the employer possesses without the affected employee having first signed an authorization. An authorization for an employer to disclose an employee's medical information is valid if it:

1. is handwritten by the person who signs it or is in typeface no smaller than 8-point type;

2. is clearly separate from any other language present on the same page and is executed by a signature which serves no purpose other than to execute the authorization;

3. is signed and dated by the employee;

4. states the name or function of the employer or person authorized to disclose the medical information;

5. states the names or functions of the persons or entities authorized to receive the medical information;

6. states the limitation, if any, on the use of the medical information by those authorized to receive it;

7. states a specific date after which the employer is no longer authorized to disclose the information; and

8. advises the person who signed the authorization of the right to receive a copy of it.

Employers are required to provide a copy of the authorization to the signer upon demand. The employer also must disclose any limitations on the use of the information to the person to whom it is communicated. The employer, however, is not liable for any unauthorized use of the medical information if it has attempted in good faith to communicate the limitations of use. An employer must honor any cancellation or modification of the authorization by the employee upon receipt of written notice of such action. If an employee refuses to execute an authorization, the employer is prohibited from discriminating in terms or conditions of employment.

Violation of California's statute which results in economic loss or personal injury to an employee is punishable as a misdemeanor and the employee may recover compensatory damages, punitive damages (not to exceed $3,000.00), attorneys' fees (up to $1,000.00), and the cost of litigation.

See e.g., CAL. CIV. CODE §§ 6.05, 56.20, 56.22, 56.23, 56.24, 56.30, 56.35 (West 1982); CONN. GEN. STAT. ANN. § 31-128C (1987); ME. REV. STAT. ANN. tit. 5, § 7070 (Supp. 1992); MD. ANN. CODE art. 100, § 95A(a)-(e) (1979); OHIO REV. CODE ANN. §§ 2953.43(A)-(B), 4113.23 (Baldwin, 1979); R.I. GEN. LAWS § 5-37.3-5(a)(4) (1979); WIS. STAT. ANN. § 103.13 (West Supp. 1992).

Q. Mini Hatch Acts

Various states have statutes similar to the federal Hatch Act (5 U.S.C. §§ 1501(5), 7324(a) (1988)) that regulate public employee political activities.

See e.g., ALASKA STAT. § 39.25.160 (1984); ARK. CODE ANN. § 21-12-304 (Michie 1976); CONN. GEN. STAT. REV. § 5-266a (Supp. 1992); HAW. REV. STAT. §§ 76-1, 76-91 (1985); IDAHO CODE § 67-5311 (Supp. 1992); ILL. REV. STAT., ch. 24-1/2, ¶ 38t (Smith-Hurd Supp. 1992); IOWA CODE ANN. § 19A.18 (West 1978); KAN. STAT. ANN. § 75-2953 (1984); KY. REV. STAT. ANN. §§ 18A.140, 18A.145 (Baldwin 1985); ME. REV. STAT. ANN. tit. 5, § 7056 (Supp. 1992); MASS. GEN. LAWS ANN. ch. 55, §§ 1-15, ch. 56, §§ 35-36 (West 1975 & Supp. 1992); MINN. STAT. ANN. § 43.28 (West 1970); MO. ANN. STAT. § 36.150 (Vernon 1987); N.H. REV. STAT. ANN. §§ 98:18, 98:19 (1977); N.Y. CIV. SERV. LAW § 106 (Consol. 1982 & Supp. 1992); N.C. GEN. STAT. §§ 126-13 through 126-15 (1987); OR. REV. STAT. § 260.432 (1983); PA. STAT. ANN. tit. 71, § 741.904 (Purdon's Supp. 1992); R.I. GEN. LAWS §§ 36-4-51 through 36-4-53 (1984); UTAH CODE ANN. § 67-19-19 (1986); W. VA. CODE § 29-6-20 (1986).

R. Polygraph and Truth-Eliciting Device Regulation

Statutes regulating the use of polygraphs and truth-eliciting devices in employment are the most numerous regarding state workplace privacy protection. These statutes are diverse and are similar to the federal Employee Polygraph Protection Act. Some prohibit polygraph use in employment. Others forbid employers to require, request or suggest, directly or indirectly, that an employee take a lie detector test. Some permit polygraph testing only with the employee's knowledge and voluntary consent.

Polygraph operators also are regulated. Some states require that operators be licensed, that they inform subjects that participation is voluntary, and that they inform the subject of the results. Operators are prohibited from making certain inquiries involving religion, labor, sexual activities, and political affiliation. Other states require only that the operator be licensed and that the operator refrain from certain inquiries unless the subject gives written consent. Still other states require only that the subject be provided a copy of the test, on which certain inquiries are prohibited, or simply that the operator be licensed.

California has separate provisions for voice stress analyzers. Maryland requires a bold-faced notice on employment applications stating that polygraph examinations cannot be used in making employment decisions.

The District of Columbia prohibits employers from administering, accepting, or using test results conducted in the District. It also provides that a violation is an unwarranted invasion of privacy and that the individual is to be compensated by tort damages. A contract or arbitration award which violates this statute's provisions is void.

Massachusetts imposes a $200 fine on the employer simply for administering a polygraph test for employment. New Jersey provides that an employer who influences, requests, or requires an employee to take a polygraph test as an employment condition is a disorderly person. Maine mandates loss of license for a polygraph examiner who gives a test for employment decisions or to prevent union organization.

The following are examples of state statutes that regulate polygraph examinations in the employment relationship: ALASKA STAT.

§ 23.10.037 (1985); CAL. LAB. CODE § 432.2 (West Supp. 1992); CONN. GEN. STAT. § 31-51(g) (1982); DEL. CODE ANN. tit. 19, § 704 (1985); D.C. CODE ANN. §§ 36-801 through 36-803 (1981); HAW. REV. STAT. § 378-21-22 (1982); IDAHO CODE § 44-903-904 (1977); IOWA CODE § 321-5-56 (1982); ME. REV. STAT. ANN. tit. 32, § 7166 (West 1985); MD. ANN. CODE art. 100, § 95 (1985); MICH. COMP. LAWS ANN. §§ 37.201-.208 (West 1985); MINN. STAT. ANN. §§ 181.75-76 (West 1987); MONT. CODE ANN. § 39-2-3034 (1982); N.J. STAT. ANN. § 2 C:40A-1 (West 1982); N.Y. LABOR LAW § 773 (McKinney 1983); OR. REV. STAT. §§ 659.225-.227 (1981); CRIMES AND OFFENSES PA. CONS. STAT. ANN. tit. 18, § 7321 (1982); R.I. GEN. LAWS §§ 28-6.1-1 through 28-6.1-4 (1987); UTAH CODE ANN. §§ 34.37-16 (1982); VT. STAT. ANN. tit. 26, § 2901 (Equity Supp. 1992); WASH. REV. CODE ANN. §§ 49.44.120-.130 (West 1986); W. VA. CODE § 21-5-5a (1985); WIS. STAT. ANN. § 111.326 (West Supp. 1992).

The following are examples of state statutes that require licensing of polygraph examiners: ARIZ. REV. STAT. ANN. § 32-2702A (1976); ILL. ANN. STAT. ch. 111, para. 2404, § 4 (Smith-Hurd 1978); ME. REV. STAT. ANN. tit. 32, § 7154 (West 1978); MICH. COMP. LAWS § 338.1708 (1976); NEV. REV. STAT. ANN. § 648.060 (Michie 1986); N.M. STAT. ANN. § 61-26-4 (Michie 1978); TENN. CODE ANN. § 62-27-106 (1982).

S. Psychological Matters

Maryland prohibits inquiries into psychological matters unless directly related to an individual's capacity to perform in a particular position. Other states have not directly prohibited this. Because inquiries of this nature are extremely personal, they may be further regulated.

See MD. ANN. CODE art. 100, §§ 95A (1985).

T. Racketeering

Several states have enacted racketeering statutes patterned after the federal Racketeer Influenced and Corrupt Organizations

Act (RICO) (18 U.S.C. §§ 1961-1968 (1988)). State remedies are some-times more flexible than federal. These remedies also may be avail-able under pendent or ancillary jurisdiction for use in connection with a federal RICO claim. All of the state statutes impose criminal sanctions, although some do not provide for private or civil relief.

See, e.g., CAL. PENAL CODE §§ 186-186.8 (West 1988); FLA. STAT. ANN. §§ 895.01-.09 (West Supp. 1992); GA. CODE ANN. §§ 16-14-1 through 16-14-15 (1984); HAW. REV. STAT. §§ 842-1 through 842-12 (1985); IDAHO CODE §§ 18-7801 through 18-7805 (1987); IND. CODE ANN. §§ 34-4-30.5-1 through 34-4-30.5-6 (Burns 1986); N.J. STAT. ANN. § 2C:41 (West 1982); OR. REV. STAT. §§ 166.715-.735 (1987); 18 PA. CONS. STAT. ANN. § 911 (1983); R.I. GEN. LAWS §§ 7-15-1 through 7-15-11 (1985); UTAH CODE ANN. §§ 76-10-1601 through 76-10-1609 (Supp. 1992); WIS. STAT. ANN. §§ 946.80-.87 (West Supp. 1992).

U. "Right to Know" Laws

Worker "right to know" laws have been enacted by several states. They generally involve workplace health and safety issues similar to the federal Occupational Safety and Health Act of 1970 (OSHA) (29 U.S.C. §§ 651-678 (1988)). These statutes require em-ployers to notify employees when they are working with specific toxic or hazardous substances.

See e.g., ALASKA STAT. § 18.60.067 (1986); CAL. LAB. CODE § 6408 (West Supp. 1992); CONN. GEN. STAT. § 31-40 (Supp. 1992); ME. REV. STAT. ANN. tit. 26, §§ 1701-1707 (Supp. 1992); MASS. GEN. LAWS. ANN. ch. 111F, § 1-21 (West Supp. 1992); MICH. STAT. ANN. § 17.50(11)(c) (Callaghan 1982); MINN. STAT. ANN. § 182.65 (West Supp. 1992); N.Y. LAB. LAW §§ 875-883 (Consol. 1983); R.I. GEN. LAWS §§ 28-21-1 through 28-21-21 (1986); WASH. REV. CODE ANN. § 49.17-220(3) (West 1981); W. VA. CODE 21-3-18 (1985); WIS. STAT. ANN. § 101.58 (West Supp. 1992).

V. Sickle Cell Anemia

Various states restrict screening for sickle cell anemia. Screen-ing for this trait may adversely affect blacks, who as a group are more prone to inheriting this disease. Florida, Louisiana, and North Carolina prohibit discrimination in employment based on this condition.

See e.g., ARIZ. REV. STAT. ANN. §§ 36-797.41 through 36-797.43 (1974 & Supp. 1992); CAL. HEALTH & SAFETY CODE §§ 320.5-324.5, 325-327 (Deering 1982); COLO. REV. STAT. §§ 23-21-201 through 23-21-204 (1973 & Supp. 1992); CONN. GEN. STAT. ANN. §§ 10-206 through 10-210 (West Supp. 1992); D.C. CODE ENCYCL. § 32-322 (West Supp. 1992); GA. CODE ANN. §§ 88-1201.1 through 88-1201.3 (Supp. 1992); ILL. ANN. STAT. ch. 40, ¶¶ 204-205 (Smith-Hurd 1987); IND. CODE ANN. §§ 16-2-5-1 through 16-2-5-9, 20-8.1-7-9.5 through 20-8.1-7-11, 31-1-1-7 (Burns 1975 & Supp. 1992); IOWA CODE ANN. §§ 141.1-.6 (West Supp. 1992); KAN. STAT. ANN. §§ 65-1,105 through 65-1,106 (1980); KY. REV. STAT. ANN. §§ 403.310-.340 (Baldwin Supp. 1992); LA. REV. STAT. ANN. §§ 40:1299 through 40:1299.4 (West 1977); LA. REV. STAT. ANN. § 17:170 (West 1982); MASS. ANN. LAWS ch. 76, §§ 15A-15B (Law Co-op. 1978); MISS. CODE ANN. §§ 41-24-1 through 41-24-5 (1972); N.J. STAT. ANN. §§ 26:5B-1 through 26:5B-4 (West Supp. 1992); N.J. STAT. ANN. § 9:14B-1 (West 1976); N.M. STAT. ANN. § 24-3-1 (Michie 1981); N.Y. EDUC. LAW §§ 903-904 (McKinney Supp. 1992); N.C. GEN. STAT. §§ 143B-188 through 143B-196 (1983); OHIO REV. CODE ANN. § 3701.131 (Baldwin 1980); S.C. CODE ANN. § 44-33-10 (Law. Co-op 1976); VA. CODE ANN. §§ 32.1-68 through 32.1-69 (Michie 1979).

W. Smoking

Smoking in the workplace is an issue of increasing concern with the growing number of legal restrictions imposed by state statutes. These state statutes have been prompted by the realization that smoking is linked to more deaths and disabilities than other workplace hazards. In workplaces where smoking and exposure to hazardous agents, such as asbestos, cotton or coal dust, or petrochemicals, compound the risks of cancer and chronic lung disease, these statutes are intended to provide a means of making the workplace healthier. However, for employees who smoke, privacy concerns arise over lifestyle regulation.

See e.g., ALASKA STAT. §§ 18.35.300, 18.35.310, 18.35.330, 18.35.340, 18.35.342, 18.35.343 (1986); CONN. GEN. STAT. ANN. § 31-40q (West 1977); FLA. STAT. ANN. §§ 386.201-.209 (West Supp. 1992); ME. REV. STAT. ANN. tit. 22, §§ 1580-A(1) through (7) (Supp. 1992); MINN. STAT. ANN. §§ 144.413-.417 (West Supp. 1992); MONT. CODE. ANN. §§ 50-40-103 through 50-40-107 (1985); NEB. REV. STAT. §§ 71-5703 through 5713 (1986); N.H. REV. STAT. ANN. §§ 155.51-.53 (1986); N.J. STAT. ANN. §§ 26:3D-24 through 26:3D-30 (West Supp. 1992); N.M. STAT. ANN. §§ 24-16-3 through 24-16-11 (Michie 1986); R.I. GEN. LAWS §§ 23-20.7-3 through 23-20.7-7 (1986); UTAH CODE ANN. §§ 76-10-101 through 76-10-110 (1986); WIS. STAT. §§ 101.123(1)-(9) (West Supp. 1992).

X. Video Display Terminals

Maine is the first and only state to enact a statute regulating the use of video display terminals (VDTs) by employees. ME. REV. STAT. ANN. tit. 26, § 251-258 (West Supp. 1992). The statute covers private and public sector employers that have 25 or more terminals at one location within the state. A VDT operator is defined as "any employee whose primary task is to operate a terminal for more than 4 consecutive hours, exclusive of breaks, on a daily basis." ME. REV. STAT. ANN. tit. 26, § 252 (West Supp. 1992).

Y. Voting

Various states permit an employee to take time off from work to vote. Generally, these require an employee to apply in advance for time off to vote; allow time off, usually two or three hours, unless the polls are open a "sufficient" time during nonworking hours; and require that the employee be paid for time off to vote. Most let the employer specify the hours the employee can take off.

See e.g., ALASKA STAT. §§ 15.25.090, 15.56.100 (1982); ARIZ. REV. STAT. ANN. §§ 1-305, 16-402 (1974 & 1984); ARK. CODE ANN. § 3-1306 (Michie 1976); CAL. ELEC. CODE § 14350 (West 1977); COLO. REV. STAT. § 1-7-102 (1980); GA. CODE ANN. § 21-2-404 (1982); HAW. REV. STAT. § 11-95 (1985); ILL. ANN. STAT. ch. 46, ¶¶ 17-4, 27-15 (Smith-Hurd 1965); IND. CODE ANN. § 3-5-4-2 (Burns 1986); IOWA CODE ANN. § 49.109 (West Supp. 1992); KAN. STAT. ANN. § 25-418 (1986); KY. REV. STAT. ANN. § 118.035 (Baldwin 1983); MD. CODE ANN., ELEC. § 24-26 (1986); MINN. STAT. ANN. § 204C.04 (West Supp. 1992); NEB. REV. STAT. § 32-1046 (1984); NEV. REV. STAT. § 293.463 (1986); N.M. STAT. ANN. § 1-12-42 (Michie 1978); N.Y. ELEC. LAW § 3-110 (Consol. 1986); OKLA. STAT. ANN. tit. 26, § 7-101 (West 1976); S.D. CODIFIED LAWS ANN. § 12-3-5 (1982); TENN. CODE ANN. § 2-1-106 (1985); UTAH CODE ANN. § 20-13-18 (1984); W. VA. CODE § 3-1-42 (1987); WIS. STAT. ANN. § 6.76 (West 1986); WYO. STAT. § 22-2-111 (1977).

Z. Whistle-blowing

Related to a workplace privacy interest in speech and association is discipline or termination arising out of a whistle-blowing incident. "Whistle-blowing" involves reporting of the employer's or a fellow employee's allegedly unlawful or improper conduct to the employer or to government authorities. Whistle-blowing can be either protective or active in nature. Protective whistle-blowing occurs when the employee reports he has been asked to commit a crime. Active whistle-blowing involves the employee seizing the initiative and disclosing the employer's activities without being asked to participate in the activities.

A California statute prohibits an employer from retaliating against an employee for disclosing information to a government or law enforcement agency where the employee has reasonable cause to believe that the information revealed a violation or non-compliance with a state or federal statute or regulation. Employers are prohibited from adopting any policies or rules preventing employee disclosure of this information. The only exceptions to these prohibitions involve information that might violate the confidentiality of the lawyer-client privilege, the physician-patient privilege, or information considered to be a trade secret.

See e.g., ARIZ. REV. STAT. ANN. § 38-532 (1985); CAL. LAB. CODE § 1102.5 (West Supp. 1992); CONN. GEN. STAT. §§ 31-51m(a)-(d), 4-61dd a-c (1987); DEL. CODE ANN. tit. 29, § 5115 (1983); 1986 FLA. LAWS ch. 233, §§ 1-8; ILL. REV. STAT. ch. 127, ¶ 63b119c.1 (Smith-Hurd 1987); IND. CODE §§ 4-15-10-1 through 4-15-10-6 (1986); IOWA CODE ANN. § 19A.19 (West 1987); KAN. STAT. ANN. § 75-2973 (1986); KY. REV. STAT. ANN. §§ 61.101, .102, .103, .990 (Baldwin 1986); LA. REV. STAT. ANN. § 3:1074.1 (West Supp. 1992); ME. REV. STAT. ANN. tit. 26, §§ 831-840 (West 1986); MD. ANN. CODE art. 64A, § 12G (1986); MICH. STAT. ANN. §§ 17.428.1-.9 (Callaghan Supp. 1992); N.H. REV. STAT. ANN. § 98-E (Supp. 1992); N.J. STAT. ANN. §§ 34:19-1 through 34:19-8 (West Supp. 1992); N.Y. LAB. LAW § 740 (McKinney 1986); OKLA. STAT. ANN. tit. 74, §§ 841.7-.20 (West Supp. 1992); OR. REV. STAT. §§ 240.316(5), 240.740 (1986); PA. STAT. ANN. tit. 43, §§ 1421-1427 (Purdon's Supp. 1992); R.I. GEN. LAWS §§ 36-15-1 through 36-15-9 (1986); TEX. HUMAN RESOURCES CODE ANN. art. 6252-16a (1986); UTAH CODE ANN. §§ 67-21-1 through 67-21-9 (1986); WASH. REV. CODE §§ 42.40.010, .020, .030, .050, .070 (1981); WIS. STAT. ANN. § 230.80, .81, .83, .85, .88 (West 1987).

AA. Wrongful Termination

The National Conference of Commissioners of Uniform State Laws has prepared a Model Employment-Termination Act. National Conference of Commissioners, Uniform Law, Commission of Model Employment Termination Act (1991)) The Model Act is intended as a model for states to use in dealing with modification of the at-will employment doctrine.

The Model Act provides for "good cause" termination for all employees employed longer than six months. Disputes are to be submitted to arbitration under the Uniform Arbitration Act. 9 U.S.C. §§ 1-16 (1988 and Supp. II. 1990)) Damages for an improper termination that the arbitrator has discretion to award include:

1. Back pay

2. Reinstatement

3. Liquidated damages not greater than a back-pay award

4. Severance for up to two years from the termination date if reinstatement is not feasible

5. Attorney's fees for the prevailing employee or employer

6. Arbitration costs

7. Punitive damages

Montana has adopted a statute, similar in scope to the one recommended by the Uniform State Law Commissioners, that has been considered constitutional. MONT. CODE ANN. §§ 39-2-901 through 39-2-914 (1988); *see also* Barnes v. Stone Container Corp., 942 F.2d 689 (9th Cir. 1991) (employee who is covered by collective bargaining agreement and files claim under Montana Wrongful Discharge from Employment Act is preempted from proceeding by federal Labor Management Relations Act); Allmaras v. Yellowstone Basin Properties, 248 Mont. 477, 812 P.2d 770 (1991) (Montana Wrongful Discharge from Employment Act does not violate any constitutional right to jury trial); Johnson v. Montana, 776 P.2d 1221 (Mont. 1989) (classifications created under Montana Wrongful Discharge from Employment Act do not violate equal protection guarantees under that state's constitution); Meech v. Hillhaven West, Inc., 776 P.2d 488 (Mont. 1989) (elimination of common-law tort actions in Montana's Wrongful Discharge from Employment Act does not violate state's constitution).

Workplace Privacy Manual

To aid the employer in evaluating the formats of workplace privacy policies suitable for its needs, this sample manual covers many of the topics that are reviewed in chapters 2 through 8. In using this manual, the employer should consult the discussions set forth in these chapters.

I. Hiring Policies

A. Arrest Record

Arrest Record Policy

Section 1. DEFINITIONS. An "arrest" indicates only that a law enforcement officer believed that probable cause existed to detain an individual for possible involvement in wrongdoing. Arrest does not indicate guilt.

A "conviction" includes a plea, verdict, or finding of guilt regardless of whether sentence is imposed by a court.

Section 2. COLLECTION. The Company will not ask an applicant or employee to disclose, through any written form or verbally, information concerning an arrest, detention or disposition of charges that did not result in conviction or information concerning a referral to and participation in any pretrial or post-trial diversion program. The Company will not seek this information from any other source.

Section 3. USE. In determining any employment condition including hiring, promotion, termination, apprenticeship, or any other training program leading to employment, the Company will not utilize as a factor any record of arrest or detention that did not result in conviction or any record regarding a referral to and participation in any pretrial or post-trial diversion program.

Section 4. EXCEPTION. The Company may ask an applicant or employee about an arrest for which the applicant or employee has been released on bail or on his or her own recognizance pending trial.

B. Credit Checks

Credit Check Policy

Section 1. DEFINITIONS.   For the purposes of this policy, the following definitions will apply:

a. *Consumer report.*   Any report containing information relating to an individual's credit record, or the manner of obtaining credit directly from a creditor of the individual or from a consumer reporting agency. A consumer report also will include information pertaining to an individual's character, general reputation, personal characteristics, or mode of living obtained through personal interviews with neighbors, friends, or associates of the subject of the report, or others with whom he or she is acquainted who may have knowledge concerning any of these items.

b. *Consumer reporting agency.*   Any person or organization who, for monetary fees or dues, regularly engages in assembling or evaluating information to be used by employers for employment purposes.

c. *Individual.*   A person who has applied for employment with or who is currently employed by the Company.

Section 2. PROCUREMENT.   The Company will request a consumer report only for legitimate employment purposes which must be job-related.

Section 3. WRITTEN PERMISSION.   The Company will procure a consumer report only after receipt of written permission from the individual.

Section 4. INFORMATION INSPECTION.   The Company will, upon request and proper identification of any individual, allow the inspection of any and all consumer reports maintained regarding that individual.

Section 5. CONFIDENTIALITY. The Company will maintain all consumer report information in strict confidence and will not disclose it absent the individual's written permission.

C. Criminal Conviction

Criminal Conviction Record Policy

Section 1. CONVICTION. A "conviction" includes a plea, verdict, or finding of guilt regardless of whether sentence is imposed by a court.

Section 2. USE OF CONVICTION RECORD. The Company may consider as a possible justification for the refusal, suspension, revocation, or termination of employment any conviction when the conviction directly relates to:

a. the applicant's potential performance in the job applied for or

b. the employee's performance in the job the employee currently holds.

Section 3. JOB-RELATEDNESS OF CONVICTION. To determine if a conviction is job-related, the Company will consider, among other things:

a. the job and its responsibilities;

b. the nature and number of convictions;

c. the facts of each conviction;

d. age at the time of the conviction;

e. the geographic location of the offense

f. the length of time between a conviction and the employment decision;

g. employment history before and after the conviction;

h. the individual's efforts at rehabilitation; and

i. any possibility that the particular conviction would prevent job performance in an acceptable, businesslike manner.

Section 4. EXCLUDED CONVICTIONS. The Company will not consider:

a. convictions which have been annulled or expunged;

b. convictions of penal offenses for which no jail sentence may be imposed; or

c. convictions of misdemeanors if the period of twenty years has elapsed since the date of conviction and if there has been no subsequent arrest or conviction.

D. Fingerprinting

Fingerprinting Policy

The Company will not require, as a condition to securing or retaining employment, that an applicant or employee be fingerprinted where fingerprints could be used to the detriment of the applicant or employee in a non-job-related situation.

E. Hiring

Hiring Policy

Section 1. PURPOSE. It is the Company's intent to hire only qualified employees. Selection will be based on qualifications, skill, training, and ambition displayed by the applicant.

Job openings not filled from within the Company's workforce will be filled by referrals, walk-ins, or advertisement respondents. Active files for recent applicants are maintained by the Human Resources Department as required by law. These will be reviewed when the Company seeks new employees. The Manager requesting additional employees will submit to the Human Resources Department a written request which identifies the position and necessary qualifications.

Section 2. GENERAL PROCEDURE. Prior to employing an individual, the Company must take certain preliminary steps to ensure uniformity of personnel practices and compliance with federal and state employment statutes. The following procedure will be followed:

a. reception of applicant;

b. preliminary interview and screening by the Human Resources Department;

c. completion of application;

d. testing of applicant;

e. interview by the prospective supervisor;

f. verification of references provided by applicant;

g. preliminary selection of qualified applicants by the Human Resources Department after consultation with the prospective manager;

h. final selection by the supervisor and Human Resources Department; and

i. hiring of selected applicant.

Section 2a. RECEPTION.   The applicant will be met in the lobby of the Human Resources Department where literature and information on the Company will be available. Each referred applicant, walk-in, or advertisement respondent should be told to initially report to this area. It is the Company's policy to treat each applicant with the same consideration given to a customer. Each applicant, whether or not hired, can spread goodwill for the Company or give it a bad name based on the treatment he or she receives. The Company's policy is to maintain a good image to continue attracting qualified applicants.

Section 2b. PRELIMINARY INTERVIEW AND SCREENING.   A short, preliminary interview of each applicant by the Human Resources Department staff will identify the most promising applicants and those who are not qualified.

Section 2c. APPLICATION.   After the preliminary interview, all applicants are given an application to complete. The questions used on this application are in compliance with federal and state fair employment practice statutes and regulations. The application also includes clauses covering falsification of records and an agreement to submit to medical testing if a job offer is made. Both clauses are signed by the applicant. The applicant is asked at this time for information required by the Immigration Reform and Control Act of 1986. If the applicant cannot comply with requirements of this Act, he or she will not be considered for employment. Once it is obtained, this information will be separated from the application.

Section 2d. SKILL TESTING.   All applicants who are approved as possible candidates, whether they are walk-ins, advertisement respondents, or referrals from employees, will be subject to skill testing. An outside agency will conduct the skill testing to ensure that the Company adheres to federal and state fair employment practice statutes which require that the overall selection process show no evidence of adverse impact on minority groups.

Section 2e. INTERVIEW WITH PROSPECTIVE MANAGER.   If an applicant's test results meet the standards set for the position, an interview with the prospective manager is scheduled. The time of the interview will be mutually convenient for both supervisor and applicant. The purpose of this interview is: (a) to assess the applicant; (b) to describe the job and working conditions to the applicant by touring the area in which he or she will work; and (c) to create goodwill for the Company whether or not the applicant is hired. To accomplish these objectives, the supervisor must be alert, perceptive, free from prejudice, even-tempered, and able to keep accurate records. Managers also must avoid any question or conduct that violates federal and state fair employment practice statutes. After the interview, the applicant will be told that he or she will be contacted by the Human Resources Department. The manager does not have the authority to offer the job to the applicant. A checklist will be given to the manager to ensure that certain points are covered during the interview. The manager will return the application with the completed interview checklist to the Human Resources Department for determination of whether to continue the hiring procedure.

Section 2f. REFERENCE VERIFICATION. If the interview proves positive, the Human Resources Department will check references with former employers, schools, and other information sources listed by the applicant. The applicant must sign a consent form to be given to previous employers who otherwise might be unwilling to provide information on the applicant.

Section 2g. PRELIMINARY SELECTION. A preliminary selection will be made by the Human Resources Department and the manager after they are satisfied that qualified applicants are available. If no qualified applicants are available, other applicants will be sought.

Section 2h. FINAL SELECTION. A final selection will be made by the prospective manager and the Human Resources Department after they are satisfied that a qualified applicant is available. All participants in the selection must agree on wages, terms, and employment conditions for the new employee.

Section 2i. HIRING OF APPLICANT.   The Human Resources Department will contact the selected applicant and offer employment. Details of the wages, terms, and employment conditions will be discussed. If the applicant accepts, the Human Resources Department will set up a time for the employee to sign in and begin the Company's orientation program.

Section 3. REJECTED APPLICANTS.   In most circumstances, a number of applicants will be interviewed for a particular position. There may be times when more than one applicant will progress through the interview procedure, but only one will be chosen. If other applicants would have been eligible for the position, these approved applicants will be retained by the Human Resources Department in a special referral file to be considered for additional openings that might occur in the same department or in other departments or shifts. As openings develop, these applicants will be referred to managers for consideration with additional new applicants as required by the manager to make a quality selection.

Section 4. APPLICABILITY.   Anyone being hired as a full-time employee is subject to this hiring policy. Employees hired on a temporary basis through outside temporary services are subject to this hiring policy.

F. Photograph Requirement

Photograph Policy

The Company will not require, as a condition to securing or retaining employment, that an applicant or employee be photographed if photographs could be used to the detriment of the applicant or employee in a non-job-related manner.

G. Reference Checks

Reference Policy

Absent the written consent of an employee or a former employee, the Company will not provide information, except name, job title, and employment dates, regarding current or former employees unless required by federal or state law or court order. All requests for employee information must be referred to the Human Resources Department. Supervisors or other employees are not permitted to respond to a reference request. Telephone inquiries will not be answered. Only written inquiries from the person seeking the information will be considered if such inquiry is on that person's letterhead with his or her name and title.

H. Immigration Requirements

Immigration Policy

The Company will not discriminate against any individual other than an unauthorized alien in decisions regarding hiring, disciplining, terminating, recruiting, or other employment actions because of that individual's national origin or, in the case of a citizen or intending citizen, because of citizenship status.

II. Workplace Policies

A. AIDS/HIV

AIDS/HIV Policy

Section 1. PURPOSE. The Company will deal with acquired immunodeficiency syndrome (AIDS) in a humanitarian and non-discriminatory manner while assuring the safety and health of all employees. The Company will educate all employees in the facts of this disease.

Section 2. NONDISCRIMINATION. The Company is committed to a responsible policy of nondiscrimination regarding AIDS. An employee infected with AIDS will be accorded the same treatment as an employee suffering from a long-term disability.

Section 3. CONFIDENTIALITY. The Company will respect all employees infected with AIDS by maintaining the confidentiality of this information.

Section 4. EMPLOYMENT. The Company will hire or continue to employ individuals who have AIDS or are suspected of having AIDS as long as these persons remain qualified to perform their jobs. (The physical demands of certain positions may necessitate deviations from this policy.) The Company will employ AIDS-infected individuals and at the same time preserve the safety and morale of all employees. According to the best medical evidence available to date, casual contact in the workplace with employees who have AIDS or who have been exposed to the AIDS virus will not result in the transmission of AIDS.

Section 5. POLICY UPDATES. The Company will remain informed of the latest medical knowledge pertaining to this disease. Should it subsequently appear that AIDS may present a danger to employees, the Company will make appropriate policy revisions.

B. Alcohol and Drug Use

Alcohol and Drug Use Policy

Section 1. PURPOSE. The Company is committed to protecting the health and safety of the public and its employees. This policy supports that commitment by maintaining an alcohol- and drug-free workplace.

Section 2. APPLICABILITY. This policy has Company-wide applicability.

Section 3. DEFINITIONS.

a. *Alcohol*. Any beverage that has an alcohol content in excess of .5% by volume.

b. *Disciplinary Action*. Action taken against an employee whom the Company has found in violation of Company policies.

c. *Drug*. Any physical or mind altering substance or any "controlled substance" or "controlled dangerous substance." These include but are not limited to any nonprescribed drug, narcotic, heroin, cocaine, or marijuana or a prescribed drug which is abused or not used as directed by a physician.

d. *Employee*. All employees regardless of position or work location.

e. *Responsible Supervisor*. The supervisor to whom the employee directly reports.

Section 4. REQUIREMENTS. Employees will not consume alcoholic beverages during regular or overtime working hours, during paid or unpaid meal periods if returning to work following the meal period, or during working hours when representing the Company away from Company facilities. Additionally, employees will not report to work under the influence of alcoholic beverages or possess alcoholic beverages on Company property.

The use, possession, sale, or purchase of other substances which may alter mental or physical capacity while on the job or on Company property is prohibited. Employees will not report to work under the influence of these substances. For a list of these substances, see Section 3c of this Policy.

The unlawful involvement with alcohol or drugs on or off the job is a serious breach of conduct. Each employee has an obligation to advise the Company of any known violations of this policy. Failure to report known violations will result in disciplinary action up to and including termination.

To protect the intent of this Policy to maintain a safe work environment free of alcohol and drugs, the Company applies this Policy to all contractors, business invitees, visitors, and guests to Company property.

Section 5. DRUG AND ALCOHOL TESTING.   To help ensure an alcohol-and drug-free workplace, the Company may search employees' work areas and employees' personal effects located on Company property. The Company also may require physical examinations and/or clinical tests of employees for the presence of alcohol or drugs during working hours:

a. if there are reasonable grounds for believing an employee is either under the influence of alcohol or drugs;

b. as part of any Company-required medical examination;

c. as a follow-up to a rehabilitation program; and

d. on a random basis where health and safety requirements so necessitate.

If the alcohol or drug test reveals positive results, the employee will be suspended pending joint evaluation by the affected supervisor, Human Resources Department, and Medical Department. Employees whose physical examinations and/or test results are positive are subject to disciplinary action up to and including termination. If the test results are negative, the matter will be closed.

All Company employees and all applicants whose assignment will make them employees will be physically examined and/or chemically tested for the presence of alcohol and drugs. The hiring process will be terminated for all applicants whose examinations and/or test results are positive. Employees who test positive will be terminated unless they seek voluntary assistance.

Section 6. VOLUNTARY ASSISTANCE.   Employees who voluntarily seek assistance on a timely basis through the Employee Assistance Program or the Company's Medical Department for an alcohol- or drug-related problem, prior to the Company identifying the problem, may do so without jeopardizing their employment status provided that prescribed treatment is followed and work performance is acceptable. In some cases temporary reassignment may be necessary.

Section 7. PRESCRIBED TREATMENT.   Employees who are undergoing prescribed medical treatment with a substance that may alter physical or mental capacity must report this to the Medical Department.

Section 8. REPORTING VIOLATIONS.   Any supervisor who observes a violation or receives a violation report must, as soon as practicable, report the information to the Human Resources Department.

Employees who observe or have knowledge of a violation by an employee or another in the workplace have an obligation to promptly report this to their supervisor and/or the Human Resources Department.

Section 9. IMMINENT THREAT TO SAFETY.   In any instance where employees feel there exists an imminent threat to safety of persons or property, they must immediately contact the responsible supervisor and/or the Human Resources Department.

Section 10. RESPONSIBLE SUPERVISOR ACTION.   Supervisors must ensure that all employees are familiar with and comply with this policy. They must notify the Human Resources Department of any known or suspected violation. When a responsible supervisor observes or receives a report of a possible violation, he or she will:

    a. confirm that the Human Resources Department has been advised;

    b. follow further directions of the Human Resources Department, which may include conducting an initial evaluation;

    c. report to the Human Resources Department the results of any initial evaluation he or she is asked to conduct. If no apparent violation has occurred, the matter will be closed;

    d. determine in conjunction with the Human Resources Department whether it is advisable or necessary to suspend an employee with or without pay or to reassign him or her pending completion of the investigation; and

    e. recommend any proposed disciplinary action and ensure that the recommendation is reviewed, approved, and implemented by the Human Resources Department.

When a supervisor observes or receives a report of a possible violation by an outside party, including contractors, business invitees, visitors or guests, he or she will:

    a. advise the individual's responsible supervisor if that individual is a contractor. If the individual is a business invitee, visitor, or guest, the supervisor will advise the sponsor of the individual's access to the facility;

    b. advise the Human Resources Department; and

    c. provide further assistance or cooperation as may be requested.

Section 11. HUMAN RESOURCES. It is the responsibility of the Human Resources Department to:

a. ensure that appropriate procedures and policies are communicated to all employees;

b. review recommended disciplinary actions and ensure the actions are in accordance and consistent with Company procedure;

c. ensure that appropriate Divisions/Departments are notified of and participate in the recommendations resulting from investigations; and

d. assemble a complete, comprehensive, and coherent file on incidents in which personnel action is taken.

Section 12. OTHER RESPONSIBILITIES. The following are other responsibilities for administration of this policy and are not intended to supersede other requirements.

a. All employees shall:

1. become informed of and comply with the policy;

2. cooperate with investigations;

3. report any known policy violation; and

4. respond immediately to any threat to the safety of person or property caused by another individual's impairment.

b. Department managers shall:

1. ensure that all subordinates are conversant with and comply with the policy and

2. review investigative reports and disciplinary action recommendations.

c. Human Resources Department shall:

1. communicate policy to all employees, including new hires;

2. arrange for alcohol and drug testing; and

3. review investigative reports and recommend disciplinary action.

d. Medical Department shall:

1. supervise physical examinations and testing for presence of alcohol or drugs and

2. apprise the Human Resources Department and the responsible supervisor of the results of any examinations or tests.

C. Confidential Information

Confidential Information Policy

From time to time an employee may have access to confidential information involving Company affairs, customers' advertising, news stories prior to their release dates, and other privileged information. Unauthorized disclosure of this information is detrimental to the Company. At no time should an employee knowingly discuss the contents of this information or remove it from the Company's premises. Confidential information must be *kept* confidential. An employee's failure to maintain confidential information may result in discipline up to and including termination.

D. Customer Solicitation

Solicitation of Customers Policy

As an employment condition, all Company customers that employees service during their employment and all prospective customers from whom employees have solicited business while in the Company's employ shall be solely the Company's customers. For a period of one year immediately following employment termination, employees will neither directly nor indirectly solicit business regarding products or services competitive with those of the Company from any of the Company's customers with whom employees had contact in the one year prior to their termination.

E. Dress and Grooming Code

Dress and Grooming Code

The Company acknowledges that the employee has a right to dress and groom as he or she chooses while at the workplace, unless the employee's dress or grooming has an adverse effect on the Company's business or the employee's health and safety.

F. Employee Assistance Programs

Employee Assistance Programs

Section 1. PURPOSE. The Company has always been concerned with the health and well-being of its employees. Out of this concern, the Company has developed an Employee Assistance Program (EAP) to aid employees with medical, emotional, or behavioral problems. Some of these problems include alcohol and drug abuse, and marital, family, gambling, legal, financial, and psychological difficulties.

Section 2. GENERAL COVERAGE. Employee effectiveness can deteriorate for many reasons. Often it is personal or family problems that affect job performance. The Company's EAP is designed to help employees with these problems, including referral to appropriate professional services. Employees or their family members who are suffering from any type of personal problem are encouraged to voluntarily seek diagnostic counseling and treatment services available under the EAP.

Section 3. ALCOHOL AND DRUG ABUSE COVERAGE. For the purposes of the EAP, alcohol and drug abuse is defined as the continuing use of alcoholic substances or drugs that definitely and repeatedly interferes with health or job performance. The Company views alcoholism and drug abuse as significant problems for the addicted employee, his or her family and co-workers, and the work environment. However, the Company recognizes alcohol and drug abuse as treatable diseases and will offer assistance to any employee who voluntarily seeks it. An employee with an alcohol or drug abuse problem will receive the same care and consideration that is extended to employees suffering from any other disease.

Section 4. JOB PERFORMANCE. The Company recognizes job performance as the principal indicator of a need for EAP services. Employees whose deteriorating job performance does not respond to normal corrective action will be referred to the EAP by the supervisor if the supervisor believes that the employee's poor job performance is caused by a medical, emotional, or behavioral problem.

Section 5. SUPERVISOR PARTICIPATION. Supervisors should understand that they are not expected to be qualified to diagnose alcoholism, drug abuse, or other personal problems or to make judgments about the causes of any behavioral problem.

Section 6. EMPLOYEE RESPONSIBILITY. The employee has a responsibility to the employer to accept any EAP diagnosis and to comply with the prescribed treatment. An employee's refusal to accept diagnosis and treatment will be handled in the same way that similar refusals are handled for other illnesses if the result of the refusal is a continued deterioration of job performance.

Section 7. CONFIDENTIALITY. All records and activities generated by the EAP will be preserved in accordance with Company policies on privacy and confidentiality of sensitive records.

G. Employee Solicitation

Solicitation of Employees Policy

As a condition of employment, employees agree that the Company has invested substantial time and effort in assembling its present workforce. For a period of one year after employment termination, employees will neither directly nor indirectly induce or solicit any of the Company's employees to leave Company employment.

H. Employment Records

Employment Records Policy

Section 1. PURPOSE.   To establish policies and procedures for the collection, maintenance, access, use, and disclosure of employee information.

Section 2. OBJECTIVES.   To provide a uniform system for the collection, maintenance, access, use, and disclosure of employee information and to preserve and protect the personal privacy of all wage and salaried employees.

Section 3. PERSONNEL RECORDS.

a. An employment record will be established for each employee upon hiring.

b. Official employment records for current employees will be maintained by the Human Resources Department.

c. Documents maintained in official employment records are classified as permanent or temporary, as defined below and in Section 6 (TYPE OF INFORMATION KEPT).

1. "Permanent information" is formal documentation of a person's current employment status and employment history. Permanent information will remain in the official employment record when an employee transfers or terminates.

2. "Temporary information" is information which does not make a significant contribution to a person's employment record or which becomes outdated or inaccurate with the passage of time. Temporary information is to be retained for four years unless otherwise indicated and then is to be removed in accordance with Section 8 (REVIEW OF RECORDS).

d. The following information is specifically prohibited from being placed in official employment records:

   1. Arrest records upon acquittal or when formal charges have been dropped

   2. Investigative material regarding a civil, criminal, or administrative investigation of alleged wrongdoing by an employee which resulted in the employee's acquittal

   3. National origin identification

   4. Racial identification, except data used in support of the Company's Affirmative Action Program

   5. Political affiliation

   6. Religious affiliation

   7. Financial information and

   8. Written criticisms of which an employee is not aware.

Section 4. RECORD ACCESS.

a. Official employment records will be secured in locked file cabinets during nonwork hours. Operating instructions for computer terminals in which records are stored will be accessible only to persons designated by the Human Resources Department, and terminals will be secured during nonwork hours.

b. Only the Human Resources Department and its designees will have access to official employment records, to data maintained in the computer system files, and to computer-produced reports.

c. The following individuals will have access to all information in official employment records and to information on the computer system when needed in the performance of their duties, provided that requests for access are made to the Human Resources Department:

1. President

2. Division heads and their designees .

3. Affirmative Action Officer

4. An employee's department director

5. An employee's immediate supervisor and those in direct chain of command above the immediate supervisor

d. Employees and persons with written permission of employees have the right to review official employment records. Reviews must be conducted in the presence of a Human Resources Department staff member at times amenable to both, and an employee may have a representative present. Employees may request copies of documents in their employment records; however, they are not permitted to alter, remove, add, or replace any documents. The Human Resources Department may charge reasonable fees when requested to provide copies of all materials contained in the official employment record or when frequent requests for copies of materials are received from the same employee.

e. Employees have a right to submit rebuttals to any material in their official employment record. Rebuttals will be acknowledged by the Human Resources Department. Rebuttals and acknowledgments will become part of the official employment record in the same permanent or temporary category as the material being rebutted. If rebuttals are submitted by inactive employees, both the acknowledgment and rebuttal will be included in the former employee's official employment record.

Section 5. RESPONSIBILITIES.

a. The Director of Human Resources is required to maintain a record of all employees and to develop standards for the establishment and maintenance of employment records.

b. Department directors are to ensure that necessary procedures and safeguards are implemented in accordance with this policy.

c. Human Resources officers will be the custodians of personnel records. Custodians will disclose and withhold employee information in accordance with this policy and will ensure that information under their control is not accessible to unauthorized persons.

d. The Human Resources Department will store and control official employment records of inactive employees until each individual's 75th birthday. At that time, the folders and all contents are to be burned or shredded.

e. The Human Resources Department will audit the implementation of this policy and review complaints and appeals arising from it.

f. The Human Resources Department will review all subpoenas and other written judicial orders seeking information.

g. All personnel having access to official employment records, to data maintained on the computer files, or to computer-produced reports, directly or through someone else, are to disclose and withhold information in accordance with this policy and are to ensure that information under their control is not accessible to unauthorized persons.

Section 6. TYPE OF INFORMATION KEPT.

a. This list does not include all information appropriate for maintenance in official employment records. Questions regarding the appropriateness of maintaining other data should be referred to the Human Resources Department. The following types of information are permanent and must be included in official employment records as long as records are maintained:

1. Latest employment application

2. Last five annual performance evaluations

3. Employee benefits records

4. Significant training records

5. Absence and leave records

6. Employee requests and Company responses concerning voluntary retirement, voluntary separation, transfer, demotion, and leaves of absence other than vacation, illness, or personal days

7. Notifications to employees regarding appointment, promotion, demotion, involuntary retirement, resignation by reason of abandonment of position, layoff, reassignment, transfer, salary changes (except general pay increases), termination, suspension, disciplinary notices, and temporary assignment to a higher job classification

8. Employee-initiated acknowledgments of temporary employment or unusual employment conditions, such as the certificate required of minors

9. Authorizations for current payroll deductions including, but not limited to, group life insurance, retirement, medical/hospital insurance, workers' compensation, federal and state withholding tax, earned income tax, union dues, credit union, and tax-sheltered annuities

10. Letters of commendation, cost reduction awards, management improvement awards, awards for excellence, professional organization or society awards, and any other form of official recognition given an employee that relates to his or her duties and responsibilities

b. The following types of information are temporary and are to be purged from official employment records in accordance with Section 7b:

1. Reference letters

2. Letters of caution, reprimand, admonishment, or warning

3. Employee confirmations of oral reprimands

4. Nonpermanent performance evaluations

5. Professional affiliations

6. Out-service and in-service training of limited significance to an employee's development

7. Records of periodic health examinations required by federal or state regulations

c. Only the following employee information may be maintained by departments not maintaining official employment records:

1. Name and home address

2. Social security number

3. Job classification and title

4. Job description, performance objectives, and performance standards

5. Data necessary to verify payrolls

6. Attendance records

7. Emergency telephone numbers

8. Copies of last five performance evaluations

d. Supervisors' or managers' notes and records on matters involving discipline or performance on specific work assignments may be maintained separately from the official employment record and are not subject to employee access.

e. If a personnel action is amended, only information concerning the amended action is to be maintained. The original personnel action and any rescinded personnel actions are to be removed from an official employment record.

Section 7. REQUEST FOR INFORMATION.

a. Requests for employment information are to be handled as follows:

   1. An employee's home address may be furnished to police or court officials upon written request showing that an indictment has been returned or a complaint, information, accusation, or other writ has been filed against the employee and the home address is needed to serve a summons, warrant, or subpoena.

   2. An employee's social security number and home address may be furnished to taxing authorities upon written request.

   3. Medical information may be furnished:

     (a) to medical personnel to aid treatment when needed by an employee who is not able to provide the information; and

     (b) to a federal or state investigative agency when requested information is required to verify adherence to regulations.

   4. Any information available to an employee from his or her own official employment record may be released to a third party upon written authorization by the employee.

   5. The Director of Human Resources is to be notified immediately of the receipt of any subpoena or other written judicial order seeking information not listed in Section 7a.1. The Human Resources Department, in conjunction with the Company's Legal Counsel, will determine the response to a subpoena or judicial order. Should a subpoena appear to be relevant to the legal proceeding and not to be overly broad in scope, the Company will, absent a compelling policy or legal reason to the contrary, make

the requested records available. However, before the
Company complies with a subpoena, the employee will
be given an opportunity to consult with a private attorney to seek to have the subpoena quashed. Should the
Human Resources Department be unable to contact the
employee, it will mail notification of the subpoena to the
employee's last known address, using certified mail with
return receipt requested.

6. Federal and state law enforcement and investigative
agencies may be provided, upon request, information
deemed under the law as a public record. Requests from
these agencies for employment information are to be
honored only if the requested information is determined
to be relevant to the investigation or audit and is within
the statutory authority of the requesting agency. Questions concerning the release of this information should
be referred to the Director of Human Resources.

7. Following the release of nonpublic information to a federal or state investigative agency due to a subpoena or
otherwise, the Human Resources Department will notify
the employee in writing of the information that was
released.

8. Replies to inquiries from a prospective employer concerning specific reasons for an employee's employment
separation are to indicate only whether the separation
was voluntary or involuntary. Particular circumstances
or issues involved in an involuntary separation are to
be disclosed only with the employee's written authorization or when authorized by the Human Resources Department.

b. Requests by employees to review official employment records will be responded to as follows:

1. Employees will be advised that they may choose to travel to the location where the official employment record is maintained. Travel expenses or unpaid leave will not be authorized for this purpose.

2. Upon request, the contents of an employee's official employment record may be duplicated and forwarded to the employee for review. The Human Resources Department will attach a signed statement to the file certifying that the entire contents of the record were copied and sent to the employee.

3. Employees may be charged reasonable fees for the cost of reproducing material in their official employment records.

Section 8. REVIEW OF RECORDS. Official employment records will be reviewed at least once every two years or when an employee transfers or is terminated. Information within the files will be maintained in chronological order. Temporary information four years old or older will be removed. Oral and written reprimands will be maintained for two years if no similar incidents occur. Employees will be notified when documents are removed from their folders and will be given ten calendar days to request these documents. Documents not needed for current or pending disciplinary or grievance actions or not requested by employees will be destroyed.

Section 9. ACCESS TO INACTIVE RECORDS. The Human Resources Department will provide access to inactive official employment records to positively identified former employees or persons with letters of authorization from former employees.

Section 10. ADMINISTRATION. The Human Resources Department will review compliance with this policy. Department directors will be advised of areas of noncompliance and any corrective action required. If any procedure in this policy conflicts with provision in a collective bargaining agreement which is otherwise lawful, the provision of the collective bargaining agreement will control.

I. Inventions

Disclosure and Assignment of Inventions Policy

As a condition of employment, employees agree to disclose to the Company any and all inventions, discoveries, improvements, trade secrets, formulas, techniques, processes, and know-how, whether or not patentable and whether or not made or conceived by them either solely or in conjunction with others during their employment, which relate to or result from the actual or anticipated business, work, or research in development of the Company, and which result, to any extent, from use of the Company's premises or property, or are suggested by any task assigned to them or any work performed by them for or on the Company's behalf. Employees acknowledge and agree that all of these inventions will be the sole property of the Company and employees hereby assign to the Company their entire rights and interests in any inventions.

J. Jury and Witness Duty

Jury and Witness Duty Policy

Upon receiving a summons to report for jury or witness duty, an employee will present the summons to his or her immediate superior on his or her next working day. The employee will be excused from employment for the day or days required in serving as a juror or witness in any court created by the United States or the State of *(State's Name)*. This will be considered an excused absence. Full-time employees will be entitled to their usual compensation less any compensation received for serving as jurors or witnesses upon written presentation to the Company indicating that they have served as a juror or witness.

K. Literature Solicitation and Distribution

Literature Solicitation and Distribution Policy: Form 1

Solicitation, distribution of literature, and trespassing by non-employees on these premises are prohibited.

Literature Solicitation and Distribution Policy: Form 2

Distribution of advertising material, handbills, or other literature in working areas of this plant is prohibited at any time.

Literature Solicitation and Distribution Policy: Form 3

Solicitation by an employee of another employee is prohibited while either the person doing the soliciting or the person being solicited is on working time. Working time is the period when an employee is required to performs his or her job duties.

L. Medical Record Collection

Medical Record Collection Policy

Section 1. AUTHORIZATION FOR COLLECTION OF MEDI-CAL INFORMATION. Each employee will be required to sign an authorization for the Company to obtain medical information from the employee. The Company will provide a copy of the completed authorization to the employee upon demand. The Company will disclose any limitations on the use of the information to the person to whom it is communicated. The Company will not be liable for any unauthorized use of the medical information if it has attempted in good faith to communicate the limitations of use. The Company will honor any cancellation or modification of the authorization by the employee upon receipt of written notice.

Section 2. LACK OF MEDICAL RECORD AUTHORIZA-TION. If an employee refuses to execute an authorization, the Company will not discriminate against the employee in terms or conditions of employment on the basis of that refusal. However, discipline or termination may be appropriate if the Company is unable to ascertain an employee's ability to perform a job function due to a physical condition because the employee refuses to release medical information. When drug or alcohol use is suspected, the Company has the right to discipline an employee based on other information available to it if the employee refuses to be tested for use of these substances.

Section 3. NO AUTHORIZATION REQUIRED. The Company is not required to obtain employee authorization for release of medical records in the following circumstances:

a. the information is compelled by judicial or administrative process;

b. the information is relevant in a lawsuit, arbitration, grievance, or other claim or challenge to which the Company and employee are parties and in which the employee has placed in issue his or her medical history, medical or physical condition, or treatment;

c. the information is necessary for administering and maintaining employee benefit and workers' compensation plans and for determining eligibility for paid and unpaid leave from work for medical reasons; and

d. the information is needed by a provider of health care.

Section 4. EMPLOYEE REQUEST FOR CORRECTION OR AMENDMENT.

a. Upon the request of an employee for correction or amendment of medical information maintained by the Company, the Company will:

    1. disclose the source of the medical information to the employee or to a person designated by the employee;

    2. make the correction or amendment within a reasonable time period if the source of the information concurs that it is inaccurate or incomplete; and

    3. establish a procedure for an employee to present supplemental information to the employer's medical record of the employee, provided that the source of the supplemental information also is included.

Medical Record Release

Section 1. RELEASE. The Company will provide medical information that it has collected or maintained regarding an employee upon the written request of the employee, former employee, or his or her designated representative. This information extends to any medical report arising out of any physical examination by a physician or other health care professional and any hospital or laboratory tests or examinations which are required by the Company as a condition of employment or arising out of any injury or disease related to the employee's employment. However, if a physician concludes that presentation of all or any part of an employee's medical record directly to the employee will result in serious medical harm to the employee, the physician will so indicate on the medical record, and a copy will be given to a physician designated in writing by the employee.

Section 2. COST REIMBURSEMENT.   The Company may require the employee, former employee, or his or her designated representative to pay the reasonable cost of furnishing medical report copies.

M. Nepotism

Nepotism Policy

Section 1. FAMILY MEMBER EMPLOYMENT. Regarding a family member of a current or former employee, the Company will not:

a. refuse to hire that individual;

b. terminate that individual from current employment; or

c. discriminate against that individual in compensation or in terms, conditions, or privileges of employment.

Section 2. CONFLICT OF INTEREST. The Company is not required to hire or continue in employment an individual if the employment would:

a. place the individual in a position of supervisory, appointment, or grievance adjustment authority over a member of the individual's family or in a position of being subject to the authority exercised by a member of the individual's family; or

b. cause the Company to disregard a *bona fide* occupational requirement reasonably necessary to the normal operation of the Company's business.

Section 3. MEMBERS OF AN INDIVIDUAL'S FAMILY. Members of an individual's family include: wife, husband, son, daughter, mother, father, brother, sister, brother-in-law, sister-in-law, son-in-law, daughter-in-law, mother-in-law, father-in-law, aunt, uncle, niece, nephew, stepparent, and stepchild.

N. Performance Evaluation

Performance Evaluation Policy

Section 1. PURPOSE.   Frequent communication with employees concerning performance is essential. Ongoing, positive communications can motivate and reinforce outstanding performance, which is the ultimate goal of the Company's performance evaluation system. Also, communications may focus attention on performance which needs improvement. Timely discussion of an unsatisfactory situation will help prevent it from becoming a major problem at a review which may come several weeks or months later. An effective performance evaluation will:

a. guide the employee into action necessary for maximum growth;

b. help the supervisor to determine the type of management guidance and development needed by the employee;

c. provide direction to assure that the employee's efforts are channeled toward specified objectives;

d. provide each supervisor with the means to analyze employee performance; and

e. result in more effective work, since employees tend to work better if they know what is expected of them and they can measure their progress.

Section 2. REQUIREMENTS.   All supervisors are required to conduct performance evaluations in accordance with the following schedule:

a. For newly hired, newly transferred, and promoted employees:

   1. the first performance evaluation will occur three (3) months after the starting date in the new position;

   2. the second performance evaluation will follow three (3) months after the first; and

3. the third and subsequent performance reviews will occur at least annually thereafter.

b. All other employees will be evaluated on an annual basis.

c. Performance appraisals in addition to these may be initiated by the supervisor if a significant deterioration or improvement in performance warrants deviation from the normal schedule.

Section 3. PROCEDURE.   The following procedure will be used to conduct performance evaluations:

a. The Human Resources Department will notify the supervisor approximately one (1) month in advance of the review date by forwarding a performance evaluation form.

b. The employee's job description is the basis for the performance evaluation. Before completing the performance evaluation, the supervisor will ensure that the job description is current. If necessary, the description will be revised to reflect any significant changes in job content.

c. In completing the performance evaluation, the supervisor will review performance of employees as set forth in the job description. Consideration will also be given to employee growth and development and performance improvements that have occurred since the last performance evaluation. This can be done readily by comparing actual accomplishments against plans made at the previous review.

d. Objective, quantifiable measures will be used whenever possible to evaluate performance, and specific examples of employee behavior which illustrate performance ratings will be noted on the performance evaluation.

e. Once the performance evaluation is completed, the supervisor must secure approval of the next management level.

f. After the appropriate approvals have been obtained, the original evaluation form should be sent to the Human Resources Department, who will verify that the form has been completely and correctly filled out.

g. When the original performance evaluation form is returned from the Human Resources Department to the supervisor, an appointment will be made with the employee to discuss the review. Reasonable advance notice will be given and the time scheduled will be adequate to allow for a full discussion. The interview itself will be conducted in privacy and without interruptions.

h. During the interview, the supervisor will explain each rating individually, using examples to illustrate why the performance rating was chosen.

i. After completing the review of past performance, the supervisor and the employee will jointly determine development plans and performance goals for the next rating period. Development plans identify specific ways the employee will try to improve deficient areas or gain additional skills. Performance goals are objective, work-oriented targets the two agree are reasonable and realistic given the employee's current performance level, expected improvement, and external factors which may affect accomplishment. The supervisor will guide, rather than dominate, this phase of the review and will encourage employee participation. Achievement of these plans and goals requires the full acceptance and support of both parties.

j. Once the interview is completed, the supervisor must secure the employee's written acknowledgment of the review and his or her written approval of the development plans and performance goals.

k. The supervisor will give the employee a photocopy of the development and goals sections of the performance evaluation form and will keep a photocopy of the sections for his or her own records. The original performance evaluation including the development and goals sections should then be sent to the Human Resources Department.

Section 4. DEFINITIONS. The following definitions will be used by the supervisor in evaluating employee performance of individual factors and on an overall basis:

a. *Marginal*. Performance of a fully trained employee does not meet acceptable level and requires improvement. An overall rating of Marginal that does not prompt improved performance could result in termination or demotion and should never result in a salary increase.

b. *Provisional*. Performance does not meet acceptable levels in all areas, but the employee is steadily improving and exhibits the potential to become proficient with continued training. A Provisional rating is often given to inexperienced new employees.

c. *Proficient/Effective*. Performance fully meets standards set for the position on a consistent basis. This should be the expected level in a position. An employee operating at this level is doing a good job.

d. *Superior*. Performance consistently exceeds standards set for the position.

e. *Outstanding*. Performance so exceeds standards for the position that the excellence of the individual's work is clearly recognized by all. This level of performance is far above the Proficient/Effective level and is normally achieved by only a small percentage of employees.

Section 5. CONFIDENTIALITY. All documents obtained as part of the performance evaluation process, including the performance evaluation, will be kept confidential and may be disclosed only to the employee or to those persons who may require the information in the course of their job-related duties.

O. Physical Examinations

Physical Examination Required

To determine medical fitness for employment, the Company may require physical examinations of employees by a Company-employed physician when it deems an examination is advisable for the health and safety of both the employee and his or her co-workers. The Company may also require applicants to undergo physical examinations by an outside physician at the Company's expense after an offer of employment has been made. Should an employee be found medically unfit to work at his or her assigned job, the Company will furnish the employee a copy of the physician's report or a physician's statement. Any applicant or employee may also be examined at his or her own expense by a self-selected physician, and the physician's report may be submitted to the Company for consideration.

Physical Examination after Accident or Sickness

Section 1. PHYSICAL EXAMINATION REQUIRED. If an employee has been absent because of accident or sickness, the Company may require a physical examination by a Company-employed physician before the employee may return to work. If it is determined by the examining physician that the sickness or accident may subject the employee to other or continued sickness or accidents, he or she will not be allowed to return to work.

Section 2. RESULT DISPUTES. Should the employee disagree with the decision of the Company's physician, he or she may be examined by a physician of his or her own choosing, provided that notification of this intent is given to the Company within three (3) calendar days after the Company has denied the right to return to work. Any costs incurred because of this examination will be paid by the employee.

If the employee's physician indicates that the employee is able to return to work, the Company must be notified in writing by the physician making the determination. The notification must be given to the Company no later than thirty (30) calendar days from the date the employee has been notified that he or she has been denied the right to return to work.

If the matter still cannot be resolved, the Company's and the employee's physicians will select a third physician to whom they will submit their respective findings. The third physician will examine the employee and make a determination concerning the employee's status. Any expense incurred by the third physician will be shared equally by the Company and the employee. The finding of the third physician will be considered by the Company in determining whether the employee should return to work.

Physical Examination Information Available to Employee's Physician

Employee's physical examinations will be arranged by the Company only when necessary and only after the employee is notified of the specific reasons for the examination. Copies of the physical examination reports and medical treatments will be maintained by the Company in its Medical Department and will be available to the employee's physician, if authorized in writing by the employee.

Confidentiality of Physical Examination Results

The Company will maintain as confidential the results of all physical examinations. Results will be furnished only to the employee's designated physician upon the employee's written authorization. It is understood by employees that the Company may use or supply physical examination results in response to subpoenas or requests to the Company by any governmental agency authorized by law to obtain these reports and in arbitration or litigation of any claim or action involving the Company.

Dispute of Physical Examination Results: Medical Arbitrator

Section 1. DEFINITION.   For the purposes of this policy, "individual" will refer to either a current Company employee or an applicant for a position with the Company.

Section 2. PHYSICAL EXAMINATIONS REQUIRED.   Before being hired, an applicant must meet certain health and physical fitness standards as determined by a physical examination by a Company-designated physician. After employment, periodic physical examinations may be offered or required to aid an employee to improve health or to enable the Company to ensure its employees' health.

Section 3. RESULTS.   Upon request, an individual will have the opportunity to discuss the results of his or her physical examination with the Company's physician. Upon the individual's request, the information will be made available to his or her personal physician.

Section 4. RESULT DISPUTES.   Should the Company's physician determine that an individual cannot perform the job applied for or currently held because of an existing medical condition, and should a dispute arise between the Company's physician and the employee's personal physician regarding this determination, a complaint may be filed by the individual with the Human Resources Department.

If the Human Resources Department cannot resolve the complaint, the individual, the Company's physician, and the individual's personal physician will exchange X-rays, laboratory test reports, and physical examination reports within ten (10) calendar days of the date the complaint was filed with the Human Resources Department.

If, after exchanging X-rays and reports, final agreement cannot be reached regarding the medical findings and conclusions, the individual may, within fourteen (14) calendar days after the exchange, refer the dispute to the Company's President who will attempt to resolve the problem by examining all available medical evidence.

If a dispute still exists regarding the individual's medical condition after review of the records by the Company's President, the dispute may be presented to an impartial medical arbitrator selected by mutual agreement of the parties in accordance with the following:

a. Within fourteen (14) calendar days following referral of the dispute to the Company's President, all X-rays and reports will be forwarded to the medical arbitrator.

b. Within fourteen (14) calendar days thereafter, the medical arbitrator will conduct whatever physical examination of the individual is deemed necessary and appropriate, and will meet with the two physicians and any additional medical experts to discuss the findings.

c. Within fourteen (14) calendar days thereafter, the medical arbitrator will submit a written determination to the Company and the individual.

d. Any of the time limits provided herein may be extended by the mutual, written agreement of the parties.

e. The charges and expenses of the medical arbitrator will be paid equally by the Company and the individual.

f. The determination of the medical arbitrator will be final and binding on the parties involved.

P. Privacy Misconduct by Employees

Privacy Misconduct Policy

The Company considers employee privacy to be paramount. The Company and its employees must ensure this. Physical intrusions of another employee's personal privacy will not be tolerated. Information will be collected, maintained, used, and disclosed with employee privacy interests protected. Only when a job-related use, Company business justification, or governmental- or court-required disclosure exists will employee privacy interests be compromised. Failure to follow this policy may result in disciplinary action up to and including termination.

Q. Religious Accommodation

Religious Accommodation Policy

The Company and its employees will not discriminate against
an employee on the basis of the employee's religious beliefs. It is
the responsibility of the affected employee to inform the Company
of any religious accommodation that is sought. The Company will
use its best efforts to accommodate the employee's religious practice
provided that no undue hardship is created for the Company or
its employees and the accommodation does not affect the safety
or health of other employees in the workplace.

R. Searches

Search Policy

The Company reserves the right to question any person entering and leaving its property and to inspect any person, locker, vehicle, package, purse, handbag, briefcase, lunchbox, or other possession carried to and from its property. This policy encompasses all Company employees.

S. Sexual Harassment

Sexual Harassment Policy

Section 1. PURPOSE.· It is the purpose of this policy to ensure a work environment free of all forms of sexual harassment or intimidation.

Section 2. POLICY. It is the Company's policy to regard sexual harassment as a very serious matter and to prohibit it in the workplace by any person and in any form.

Section 3. PROCEDURE.

a. Each supervisor has an affirmative duty to maintain his or her workplace free of sexual harassment.

b. Each supervisor will discuss this policy with all employees and assure them that they are not required to endure insulting, degrading, or exploitative sexual harassment.

c. No supervisor will threaten or insinuate, either explicitly or implicitly, that an employee's refusal to submit to sexual advances will adversely affect the employee's employment, evaluation, wages, advancement, assigned duties, shifts, career development, and other conditions of employment.

d. Other sexually harassing conduct in the workplace, whether committed by supervisors or nonsupervisory personnel, is prohibited. Such acts include but are not limited to:

   1. unwelcome sexual flirtations, advances, or propositions;

   2. verbal or written abuse of a sexual nature;

   3. graphic verbal comments about an individual's body;

   4. sexually degrading words used to describe an individual; and

   5. the display in the workplace of sexually suggestive objects or pictures.

e. Any employee who believes he or she has been sexually harassed should report the alleged act immediately to the Human Resources Department. *If the complaint involves someone in the employee's direct line of supervision, the employee should inform another manager of the complaint.* The complaint will be investigated by the Human Resources Department and the employee will be advised of the findings and conclusion.

f. There will be no discrimination or retaliation against any employee for making a sexual harassment complaint.

g. All actions taken to resolve sexual harassment complaints through internal investigations will be conducted confidentially.

h. Any supervisor, agent, or employee who is found after appropriate investigation to be guilty of sexual harassment will be subject to appropriate disciplinary action up to and including termination.

T. Smoking

Smoking Policy

Section 1. PURPOSE AND BACKGROUND. This policy is designed to promote employee health and safety and the performance of Company business. It is not intended to totally prohibit smoking on the Company's premises but does restrict smoking to certain areas.

Smoking poses a significant risk to the health of smokers and nonsmokers. It can damage sensitive technical equipment and can be a safety hazard. In sufficient concentrations, second-hand smoke can be an annoyance and potential health risk to nonsmokers and may be harmful to individuals with heart and respiratory diseases or allergies to tobacco smoke.

Smoking is a habit that involves elements of psychological and physiological addictions. Many smokers who desire to eliminate smoking from their lives require assistance. It is not a dependency that can be eliminated completely by prohibition or restriction by others. This policy is intended to assist employees in finding a reasonable accommodation between those who do not smoke and those who do, and it demonstrates the Company's desire to improve the health of all employees.

Section 2. POLICY. It is the Company's policy to respect the rights of nonsmokers and smokers in Company buildings and facilities. When these rights conflict, the Company and its employees will endeavor to find a reasonable accommodation. When an accommodation is not possible, the nonsmokers' rights will prevail.

Section 3. PROHIBITED AREAS. Smoking is not permitted:

a. in areas with sensitive equipment or computer systems or where records and supplies would be exposed to hazard from fires, ashes, or smoke;

b. in areas where combustible fumes can collect (as in garage and storage areas), areas where chemicals are used, and all other designated areas where an occupational safety or health hazard might exist;

c. in confined areas of general access, such as libraries, medical facilities, cashier waiting lines, elevators, restrooms, stairwells, copy rooms, lobbies, waiting rooms, and fitness centers;

d. in areas of Company premises which are frequently visited by customers, such as public offices and customer service areas; and

e. in other locations the Company may designate where smoking specifically is not permitted.

Section 4. WORK AREAS. In work areas where space is shared by two or more persons, an effort will be made to accommodate individual smoking preferences to the degree reasonably possible. When requested, managers and supervisors will make a reasonable attempt to separate persons who smoke from those who do not.

Employees may designate their private offices as smoking or nonsmoking areas. Visitors to private work areas should honor the employees' wishes.

In Company vehicles, including Company-sponsored van pools, smoking will be permitted only when there is no objection from one or more of the occupants.

Section 5. AREAS OF COMMON USE. Smoking will not be permitted during meetings and in enclosed locations, including conference rooms and classrooms. Breaks and appropriate access to outside areas may be scheduled to accommodate the needs of smokers.

In enclosed common-use locations, including cafeterias, dining areas, employee lounges, and auditoriums, smoking sections will be identified if there is adequate ventilation and the locations are not normally used by customers. Smoking is permitted only in these designated sections of common-use locations. Smoking is permitted in corridors. Employees and visitors are expected to honor the smoking and nonsmoking designations and to be considerate of nonsmokers in their vicinity.

U. Spousal Hiring

Spousal Hiring Policy

Each employee is entitled, if otherwise qualified, to work with his or her spouse. The Company does not discriminate against an applicant or employee regarding working conditions, workplace assignment, or other employment privileges because the spouse of that applicant or employee is also a Company employee. However, this does not apply to employment of the spouse of an employee who has the responsibility to hire, fire, or to conduct performance evaluations of the position involved. That spouse may not be hired or, if already in such a position, may be transferred or terminated.

V. Third Party Representation

Third Party Representation: Non-Union Employer

Any employee who is requested to meet with a manager or supervisor for the imposition of disciplinary action will be entitled to be accompanied by another employee of his or her choosing. The employee will receive reasonable prior notice of the topics to be discussed.

Third Party Representation: Union Employer

Prior to any discipline of an employee, the Union will be given an opportunity to discuss the matter with the Company. If an employee suspects discipline, he or she may request and will be permitted to speak privately with one union representative before being interviewed by the Company.

A member of the union bargaining unit who is requested to meet with a manager or supervisor for the imposition of disciplinary action will be entitled to be accompanied by a union representative. The employee will receive reasonable prior notice of the topics to be discussed.

W. Trade Secrets

Disclosure or Use of Trade Secrets Policy

While employed with the Company, employees will have access to and become acquainted with information of a confidential or proprietary nature. This information is or may be applicable to or related to the Company's present or future business, research, development, or investigation, or the business of any Company customer. Trade secret information includes but is not limited to devices, secret inventions, processes, compilations of information, records, specifications, and information concerning customers or vendors. Employees will not disclose any Company trade secrets directly or indirectly, or use them in any way, either during the term of their employment or any time thereafter, except as required in the course of Company employment.

X. Voting Time

Voting Time Policy

Section 1. TIME OFF. Company employees are entitled to vote at general, primary, or presidential primary elections. When registered voter-employees do not have sufficient time outside of regular working hours to vote, they may take off as much working time as will enable them to vote, when this time is added to their available voting time outside their working hours. Employees will be allowed time off for voting only at the beginning or end of their regular working shifts, whichever allows them the most free time for voting and the least time off from their regular working shift, unless otherwise mutually agreed upon by the employer and employee. Employees who are election officers may absent themselves from their work schedule on election day without being subject to demotion, suspension, or termination.

Section 2. COMPENSATION. Employees may take off as much time as will enable them to vote, however, they will be compensated for no more than two hours.

Section 3. TIME OFF NOTICE. If employees know or have reason to believe that time off is needed to vote, they must notify the Company at least five (5) working days in advance of the voting date.

Y. Whistle-blowing Protection

Whistle-blowing Policy

Section 1. PURPOSE. It is the Company's policy to follow and enforce all federal, state, and local laws applicable to it and to require its employees to do likewise. Every employee has the responsibility to assist in implementing this policy.

Section 2. REPORTING COMPANY VIOLATIONS. A violation of this policy should be reported to an employee's immediate supervisor through a written report which is signed by the employee. However, if reporting a violation to the immediate supervisor is not practical, a written, signed, and dated statement should be submitted by the employee to the Director of Human Resources so that an investigation may be undertaken.

Section 3. NO RETALIATION FOR FILING COMPLAINTS. There will be no retaliation by the Company or any of its employees against any employee who makes a good-faith report pursuant to this policy, even if investigation shows that no violation has occurred.

Section 4. CORRECTIVE ACTION. It is the responsibility of the Company to correct or prevent violations of federal, state, and local laws applicable to it. This is a legal obligation. A violation can subject the Company and its employees to publicity leading the public, customers, and the government to hold an adverse image of the Company.

Section 5. VIOLATION OF THIS POLICY. The procedures outlined herein must be followed before an employee reports alleged violations to any news medium, government agency, or other outlet. The Company should have the opportunity to conduct an investigation before outside agencies are involved, and each employee should ensure that the Company can undertake this internal investigation. Employee complaints that do not follow this procedure will constitute a policy violation. Adhering to the reporting requirements of this policy is a condition of employment.

Z. Work Performance Monitoring

Work Performance Monitoring Policy

The Company may periodically monitor or review employee work performance through the use of mechanical or electronic devices. Among the mechanical or electronic devices that the Company may use are telephone monitoring, beepers, pen registers, touch tone decoders, and diodes. These may be used to limit personal calls at the workplace, to review driver routes, or to investigate workplace problems including but not limited to theft and use of illegal drugs.

Work Performance Monitoring: Employee Authorization

I understand that as a condition of employment the Company may periodically monitor or review my work performance by using mechanical or electronic devices. Among the devices that the Company may use are telephone monitoring, beepers, pen registers, touch tone decoders, and diodes. I expressly consent to this work performance monitoring.

III. Outside the Workplace Policies

A. Conflict of Interest

Conflict of Interest Policy

Section 1. ADVERSE PECUNIARY INTEREST. No employee shall:

a. engage directly or indirectly in any business transactions or private arrangement for profit that accrues from or is based on his or her position or authority with the Company or

b. participate in the negotiation of or decision to award contracts, the settlement of any claims or charges in any contracts, the making of loans, rate fixing, guarantees, or other things of value with or for any entity in which he or she has a financial or personal interest.

Section 2. MISUSE OF INFORMATION. No employee may use, for his or her own personal gain or for the gain of others, any information obtained as a result of employment and not generally available to the public, nor may he or she disclose this information.

Section 3. MISUSE OF COMPANY FACILITIES AND EQUIPMENT. No employee may use Company equipment, supplies, or properties for personal gain for purposes other than those designated and authorized by the Company.

Section 4. OUTSIDE EMPLOYMENT. No employee may engage in or accept outside employment or render services for another unless this outside employment or service is approved in advance and in writing by the Company.

Section 5. VIOLATION. Employees who refuse or fail to comply with the policies set forth herein may be subject to disciplinary action including but not limited to reprimands, suspensions, and termination.

B. Criminal Misconduct

Criminal Misconduct Policy

Section 1. CRIMINAL MISCONDUCT CONSTITUTING A FELONY OR RELATED TO EMPLOYMENT. As soon as practicable after an employee has been formally charged with criminal misconduct which constitutes a felony under the laws of this state or is related to his or her employment, the employee will be suspended without pay. If the charge results in a conviction in a court of law, the employee may be terminated.

Section 2. CRIMINAL MISCONDUCT OTHER THAN A FELONY OR NOT RELATED TO EMPLOYMENT. As soon as practicable after an employee is formally charged with criminal misconduct other than a felony or that is not related to his or her employment, the Human Resources Department will conduct an inquiry and make a preliminary determination regarding whether or not the employee should continue to perform his or her duties pending the outcome and final determination of the investigation. (See Section 3 (INVESTIGATION) and Section 4 (FINAL DETERMINATION) of this policy.) The preliminary investigation will be conducted under the following guidelines:

a. *Purpose.* The purpose of the preliminary determination is to minimize the effect which the accusation of a crime by an employee may have upon the Company's ability to function, pending an investigation and final determination regarding the existence of sufficient reason for employee disciplinary action.

b. *Factors to be Considered in Making the Preliminary Determination.* In making the preliminary determination, the Human Resources Department will consider, among other factors:

   1. The nature, weight, and source of the accusations against the employee

2. The employee's explanation, if available

3. The nature of the employee's duties, including the discretion exercised as part of those duties

4. The relationship of the accusation to the employee's duties

5. The extent to which allowing the employee to continue in his or her position would be detrimental to the physical well-being of the employee, co-workers, or other persons

6. The extent to which the employee must deal directly with the public

7. Any undue hardship to the employee that would result from a temporary reassignment of the employee

c. *Preliminary Determination.* The preliminary determination will consist of one of the following alternatives to be implemented by the Human Resources Department:

1. Allow the employee to continue to perform duties pending the outcome and final determination of the investigation.

2. Reassign the employee to less sensitive duties within the Company pending the outcome and final determination of the investigation.

3. Suspend the employee without pay pending the outcome and final determination of the investigation.

d. *Contact with Law Enforcement Agency.* In considering the nature, weight, and source of the accusations against an employee, the Company will contact the law enforcement agency involved in the accusations to verify the charge and to obtain all available information.

e. *Employee Status.* After the preliminary determination is made, the employee will remain in the status selected by the Human Resources Department pending the outcome and final determination of the investigation as outlined in Section 3 (INVESTIGATION) and Section 4 (FINAL DETERMINA-TION) of this policy. This status will be temporary and will have no bearing on the final determination.

Section 3. INVESTIGATION. Any employee formally charged with criminal misconduct will be subject to an immediate investigation conducted by the Human Resources Department:

a. *Purpose.* The purpose of the investigation will be to deter-mine if sufficient reason exists for disciplinary action includ-ing but not limited to suspension, demotion, or termination.

b. *Conduct of Investigation.* In the investigation, all relevant facts will be promptly gathered and considered. The investigation will be completed within twelve working days. The follow-ing contacts may be a part of the investigation:

   1. *Law Enforcement Agencies.* The Human Resources Depart-ment may request the assistance of any law enforcement agency involved in the matter; however, this will not relieve the Department of the responsibility to make an independent evaluation.

   2. *Employee.* The Human Resources Department will afford the employee an opportunity to respond to the accusa-tions, to have representation during meetings relating to the investigation if representation is requested, and to submit additional information.

Section 4. FINAL DETERMINATION. After completion of the investigation, the Human Resources Department will have five (5) working days to make a final determination regarding whether the investigation's results establish sufficient reason for disciplinary action. The Company's President will review this decision and ratify the Human Resources Department's decision absent an abuse of discretion by the Department. In determining whether sufficient reason for disciplinary action exists, the Human Resources Department will consider, among other factors:

a. The nature, weight, and source of the accusations against the employee

b. The employee's explanation, if available

c. The nature of the employee's duties, including the amount of discretion exercised as part of those duties

d. The relationship of the accusation to the employee's duties

e. The extent to which allowing the employee to continue in his or her position would be detrimental to the physical well-being of the employee, co-workers, or other persons

f. The extent to which the employee must deal with the public

Where sufficient reason for disciplinary action exists, the Human Resources Department will immediately take the appropriate disciplinary action including but not limited to suspension, demotion, or termination. If, based on information available at the time of investigation, a finding of sufficient reason is not made, the employee will be notified of the disposition and will retain or be retroactively reinstated to his or her position.

C. Loyalty

Loyalty Policy

Employees will not engage directly or indirectly in any outside relationship or activity that defers or adversely affects their primary responsibilities, interests, duties, or loyalties in actively furthering the Company's business.

D. Noncriminal Misconduct

Noncriminal Misconduct Policy

Section 1. OFF-DUTY NONCRIMINAL MISCONDUCT. Employee misconduct that does not result in criminal charges and that occurs outside the workplace may result in disciplinary action up to and including termination, depending on the nature of the conduct and its adverse impact on the Company's business.

Section 2. DETERMINATION. Among other factors, the following will be considered in making any disciplinary determination for incidents involving off-duty noncriminal misconduct:

a. the nature of the misconduct;

b. the employee's explanation, if available;

c. the extent to which allowing the employee to continue in his or her position would be detrimental to the physical well-being of the employee, co-workers, or other persons;

d. the nature of the employee's job duties, including responsibility and the discretion that must be exercised as part of those duties;

e. the extent to which the employee must deal directly with the public; and

f. any undue hardship to the employee which would result from his or her temporary reassignment.

E. Outside Employment

Outside Employment Prohibited

The Company will not knowingly hire or retain any person who is otherwise employed. While employed with the Company no employee will be permitted to hold outside employment.

Outside Employment Conflict of Interest

Employees may engage in outside employment provided it does not interfere with their job performance and that it is not with an employer who competes with the Company. Employees will not use their positions with the Company to exploit outside employment interests. Employees engaged in outside employment must immediately inform their supervisor.

Outside Employment Disclosure

Employees may engage in outside employment as long as this employment is disclosed to the Company and is determined by the Company not to interfere with the employee's primary job performance. Each employee must disclose in writing all outside employment. Failure to disclose outside employment or a misrepresentation of outside employment may result in disciplinary action up to and including termination.

Outside Employment Interfering with Performance

Company employment will be considered the employee's primary employment. Prior to engaging in compensated outside employment, the employee must notify the Company and obtain written approval. Compensated outside employment will be limited to avoid impairment of employees' job performance. Should there be a conflict in employment, the supervisor and the Human Resources Department will review the situation. If the dispute cannot be resolved, the employee may be required to discontinue outside employment or be subject to employment separation.

Outside Employment Approval

Employees desiring to engage in or who currently are engaged in outside employment must provide written notification to the Company's Human Resources Department. Outside employment may not be continued or entered into without written authorization by the Company.

F. Residency

Residency Policy

Section 1. RESIDENCE.   Residence is the place or locality in which an employee lives and manifests an intent to continue to lives. Factors providing evidence of intent to maintain residency include:

a. Rent, lease, or purchase of a property that the employee has made his or her home

b. Payment of state and local taxes

c. Registration within (State's Name) of personal property including bank accounts, stocks, bonds, and automobiles

d. Possession of a current (State's Name) motor vehicle operator's license

e. Current registration to vote in (State's Name)

Section 2. APPLICATION.   Residency requirements will be as follows:

a. Persons hired will be legal residents of this state, unless residence has been waived by the Human Resources Department because of unique job requirements, and will reside within (Describe Area).

b. The Director of Human Resources, upon submission of satisfactory justification, may limit hiring to individuals who are residents of this state residing within (Describe Area).

Section 3. WAIVER.   The Director of Human Resources may waive the residency requirement if there appears to be an inadequate supply of well qualified residents within (Describe Area) available for a particular position.

C

Privacy for Consumers and Workers Act

United States House of Representatives

HR 1900

103D CONGRESS, 1ST SESSION

Congressional Quarterly's Washington Alert—Text of Bills

(Sponsor Change House)

HR 1900 Privacy for Consumers and Workers Act. To prevent abuses of electronic monitoring in the workplace.
Date Introduced: 04/28/93
Version Date: 09/14/93
Version type: Sponsor Change House
Sponsor: Williams (D-MT)
Committees: COMMITTEE ON EDUCATION AND LABOR
SECTION 1. SHORT TITLE. SEC. 2. DEFINITIONS. SEC. 3. GENERAL REQUIREMENTS. SEC. 4. NOTICE REQUIREMENTS. SEC. 5. PERIODIC OR RANDOM ELECTRONIC MONITORING. SEC. 6. REVIEW OF CONTINUOUS ELECTRONIC MONITORING. SEC. 7. EMPLOYEE REVIEW OF RECORDS. SEC. 8. USE OF DATA COLLECTED BY ELECTRONIC MONITORING. SEC. 9. PRIVACY PROTECTIONS. SEC. 10. ACCESS TO DATA. SEC. 11. PROHIBITIONS. SEC. 12. ENFORCEMENT PROVISIONS. SEC. 13. APPLICATION. SEC. 14. REGULATIONS. SEC. 15 PREEMPTION. SEC.

16. COVERAGE OF EMPLOYEES OF THE HOUSE OF REPRESEN-
TATIVES AND SENATE. SEC. 17. EFFECTIVE DATE.

   H.R. 1900

To prevent abuses of electronic monitoring in the workplace.

   =========IN THE HOUSE OF REPRESENTATIVES
   April 28, 1993

Mr. WILLIAMS (for himself, Mr. FORD of Michigan, Mr. CLAY,
Mr. MILLER of California, Mr. MURPHY, Mr. KILDEE, Mr. OW-
ENS, Mr. SAWYER, Mr. EDWARDS of California, Mr. BERMAN,
Mr. WASHINGTON, Mr. PASTOR, Mr. SOLOMON, and Mr.
SHAYS) introduced the following bill; which was referred to the
Committee on Education and Labor

   June 23, 1993

Additional sponsors: Mr. STOKES, Mr. DELLUMS, Mr. WHEAT,
Mr. BROWDER, Mr. STARK, Mrs. CLAYTON, Mr. LIPINSKI, Mr.
HOCHBRUECKNER, Mrs. UNSOELD, Ms. PELOSI, Mr. VENTO,
Mr. WAXMAN, Mr. FILNER, Mr. ROMERO-BARCELO, Mr.
SCHIFF, Ms. WOOLSEY, Mr. SKAGGS, Mr. MINETA, Mr. SPRATT,
Mr. SANGMEISTER, Mr. BONIOR, Mr. TRAFICANT, Mr. MAT-
SUI, Mr. RAVENEL, Mr. STUPAK, Mr. SPENCE, Mr. PARKER,
Mr. SLATTERY, Mr. DERRICK, Mr. BOEHLERT, Mr. VOLKMER,
Mr. INGLIS of South Carolina, Mr. DARDEN, Mr. DURBIN, Mr.
SCOTT, Mr. BEILENSON, Mr. YATES, Mr. FISH, Mr. CLYBURN,
Mr. GONZALEZ, Mr. BROWN of Ohio, Mrs. MINK, Mr. OLVER,
and Ms. VELAZQUEZ
Deleted sponsor: Ms. ENGLISH of Arizona (added May 6, 1993;
deleted June 18, 1993)

   September 14, 1993

Additional sponsors: Mr. GLICKMAN, Mr. SABO, Ms. NORTON,
Mr. MCDERMOTT, Mr. HAMBURG, Mr. BECERRA, Mr. GENE
GREEN of Texas, Mr. SCHUMER, Mr. FOGLIETTA, Mr. DE LUGO,

Mr. SERRANO, Mr. APPLEGATE, Mr. EVANS, Mr. FINGERHUT, Mr. PALLONE, Mr. PRICE of North Carolina, Mrs. LOWEY, Mr. RANGEL, Mr. DEFAZIO, Mr. FROST, Mr. SYNAR, Mr. TORRES, Mr. MCCURDY, Mr. OBERSTAR, Ms. KAPTUR, Mr. WILSON, Mr. KOPETSKI, Mr. FAZIO, Mrs. MALONEY, Mr. MCCLOSKEY, Mr. BACCHUS of Florida, Mr. GEPHARDT, Mr. NEAL of Massachusetts, Mr. JEFFERSON, Mr. BORSKI, Mrs. SCHROEDER, Mr. PETERSON of Minnesota, Mr. ACKERMAN, Mr. COOPER, Miss COLLINS of Michigan, Mr. ENGLISH of Oklahoma, Ms. BYRNE, Mr. KREIDLER, Mr. SANDERS, Mr. CRAMER, Mr. TOWNS, Mr. BRYANT, Mr. DEUTSCH, Mr. GEJDENSON, Ms. ROYBAL-AL-LARD, Mr. PENNY, Mr. STUDDS, Mr. RUSH, Ms. ESHOO, Mr. MINGE, Mr. COSTELLO, Mr. COLEMAN, and Mr. HAMILTON

==========A BILL

To prevent abuses of electronic monitoring in the workplace.

Be it enacted by the Senate and House of Representatives of the United States of America in Congress assembled,

SECTION 1. SHORT TITLE.

This Act may be cited as the "Privacy for Consumers and Workers Act".

SEC. 2. DEFINITIONS.

As used in this Act: (1) ELECTRONIC MONITORING.—(A) IN GENERAL.—Except as provided in subparagraph (C), the term "electronic monitoring" means the collection, storage, analysis, or reporting of information concerning an employee's activities by means of a computer, electronic observation and supervision, telephone service observation, telephone call accounting, or other form of visual, auditory, or computer-based technology which is conducted by any method other than direct observation by another person, including the following methods: Transfer of signs, signals, writing, images, sounds, data, or intelligence of any nature which are transmitted in whole or in part by a wire, radio electromagnetic, photoelectronic, or photo-optical system. (B) TELEPHONE CALL ACCOUNTING.—For purposes of subparagraph (A), the term "telephone call accounting" means the practice of recording the telephone numbers called by a specific telephone or group of telephones, including—(i) the telephone number from which a call is being made, (ii) the telephone number which is being called, (iii) the time when the telephone call was connected, (iv) the time when the telephone call was completed, and (v) identification of the operator, if any, who assisted in placing the telephone call, for the purpose of individual employee evaluations or the setting of production quotas or work performance expectations. (C) EXCLUSION.—The term "electronic monitoring" does not include—(i) wiretapping, or (ii) the electronic transfer of—(I) payroll data, (II) insurance and other benefit data, (III) employee job application data, or (IV) other personnel-related data which an employer may collect under section 5(a), for administrative purposes only. (2) EMPLOYEE.—The term "employee" means any current, former, or leased employee of an employer. (3) EMPLOYER.—The term "employer" means any person who—(A) is engaged in commerce, and (B) who employs employees, and includes any individual, corporation, partnership, labor organization, unincorporated association, or any other legal business, the Federal Government, any State (or political subdivision thereof), and any agent of the employer. (4) PERSONAL DATA.—The term "personal data" means any information concerning an employee which, because of name, identifying number, mark, or description, can be readily associated with a particular individual, and such term includes information contained in printouts, forms, or written analyses or evaluations. (5) PROSPECTIVE EMPLOYEE.—The term "prospective employee" means an individual who has applied for a position of employment with an employer. (6) TELEPHONE SERVICE OBSERVATION.— The term "telephone service observation" means the practice of listening to or recording telephone calls being made by, or received by, an employee in order to monitor the quality of service provided by the employee. (7) SECRETARY.—The term "Secretary" means the Secretary of Labor.

SEC. 3. GENERAL REQUIREMENTS.

(a) ENGAGING IN ELECTRONIC MONITORING.—An employer may engage in electronic monitoring of the employer's employees if—(1) the employer provides the notices required by section 4, (2) if section 5 applies, the employer complies with the requirements of such section, (3) the employer complies with section 9, and (4) the employer does not violate section 11.

(b) REVIEW AND USE.—An employer may review data obtained by electronic monitoring of the employer's employees if the employer meets the requirements of section 6 and may use such data if the employer meets the requirements of section 8.

SEC. 4. NOTICE REQUIREMENTS.

(a) SECRETARY'S NOTICE.—The Secretary shall prepare, have printed, and distribute to employers a notice which will inform employees—(1) that an employer engages in or may engage in electronic monitoring of employees and specifies the circumstances (including the monitoring and exception described in section 5) under which an employee is or is not entitled to additional notice under this section, and (2) of the rights and protections provided to employees by this Act.

Each employer who engages in electronic monitoring shall post and maintain such notice in conspicuous places on its premises where notices to employees are customarily posted.

(b) EMPLOYER'S SPECIFIC NOTICE.—Each employer shall provide to each employee who will be electronically monitored with prior written notice describing the following regarding the electronic monitoring of such employee: (1) The forms of electronic monitoring to be used. (2) The personal data to be collected. (3) The hours and days per week that electronic monitoring will occur. (4) The use to be made of personal data collected. (5) Interpretation of printouts of statistics or other records of information collected through electronic monitoring if the interpretation affects the employees. (6) Existing production standards and work performance expectations. (7) Methods for determining production standards and work performance expectations based on electronic monitoring statistics if the methods affect the employees.

The notice required by this subsection shall also include a description of the monitoring and the exception which is authorized under section 5(c)(1) to be undertaken without providing such notice.

(c) EMPLOYER'S NOTICE TO PROSPECTIVE EMPLOY-EES.—(1) IN GENERAL.—Each employer shall notify a prospective employee at the first personal interview of existing forms of electronic monitoring conducted by the employer which may affect the prospective employee if such employee is hired by the employer. (2) SPECIFIC NOTICE.—Each employer, upon request by a prospective employee or when the employer offers employment to a prospective employee, shall provide the prospective employee with the written notice described in subsection (b).

(d) CUSTOMER NOTICE.—Employers who engage in the practice of telephone service observation shall inform customers who may be subject to such observation of such practice in any recorded message used in connection with customer telephone calls. If the employer does not use such a recorded message, the employer shall prominently place in each of its customer bills a statement that the employer is engaging in such practice.

(e) PUBLIC NOTICE.—If an employer engages in electronic monitoring which may include members of the public who are not employees of the employer, the employer shall notify such individuals of such monitoring. Such notice may take the form that is reasonably calculated to reach members of the public who may be affected by such monitoring.

SEC. 5. PERIODIC OR RANDOM ELECTRONIC MONITORING.

(a) GENERAL RULE.—No employer may engage in electronic monitoring of any of the employer's employees on a periodic or random basis except as authorized by subsection (b).

(b) AUTHORITY.—(1) NEW EMPLOYEES.—An employer may engage in random and periodic monitoring of an employee of such employer if the cumulative total period of such employee's employment is not more than 60 days. (2) OTHER EMPLOYEES.— An employer may not engage in random and periodic monitoring of an employee with a cumulative employment period with such employer of at least 5 years. (3) WORK GROUPS.—An employer may engage in electronic monitoring of an employee of such employer who has a cumulative employment period with such employer of less than 5 years and who is in a work group of employees on a periodic or random basis for not more than 2 hours in any week. Except as provided in subsection (c), the section 4(b) notice to each employee within such work group for such monitoring shall be provided at least 24 hours but not more than 72 hours before engaging in such monitoring. For purposes of this subsection, the term "work group" means a group of employees employed in a single facility and engaged in substantially similar work at a common time and in physical proximity to each other.

(c) EXCEPTION TO NOTICE REQUIREMENT.—(1) IN GENERAL.—Subject to paragraph (2), if an employer has a reasonable suspicion that any employee is engaged in conduct which—(A) violates criminal or civil law or constitutes willful gross misconduct, and (B) adversely affects the employer's interests or the interests of such employer's employees, the employer may engage, on the employer's worksite, in electronic monitoring of such employee or of an area in which the actions described in subparagraphs (A) and (B) occur without providing the notice required by section 4(b) and without regard to subsection (a) or (b) of section 9. (2) STATEMENT.—Before engaging in the electronic monitoring described in paragraph (1), an employer shall execute a statement setting forth—(A) with particularity the conduct which is being monitored and the basis for the monitoring, and (B) an identification of the specific economic loss or injury to the business of the employer resulting from such conduct or the injury to the interests of such employer's employees. The employer shall sign the statement and retain it for 3 years from the date the monitoring began or until judgment is rendered in an action brought under section 12(c) by an employee affected by such monitoring, whichever is later.

SEC. 6. REVIEW OF CONTINUOUS ELECTRONIC MONITORING.

(a) REVIEW DURING MONITORING.—(1) IN GENERAL.—Except as provided in paragraph (2), no employer may review data, obtained by continuous electronic monitoring of the employer's employees, on a periodic or random basis. (2) EXCEPTION.—The following are not subject to paragraph (1): (A) the review by an employer of electronic data obtained from the use of an electronic card system, (B) the review of electronic data obtained from video monitoring (with or without an audio track) which is used to deter crime by persons and to provide evidence to law enforcement personnel, and (C) the review of data which is continuously monitored by an employer and which appears simultaneously on multiple television screens or sequentially on a single screen.

(b) REVIEW AFTER MONITORING.—An employer may review data obtained by continuous electronic monitoring of the employer's employees after the monitoring was completed only if review was limited to specific data which the employer has reason to believe contains information relevant to an employee's work.

SEC. 7. EMPLOYEE REVIEW OF RECORDS.

(a) IN GENERAL.—Except as provided in subsection (b), each employer shall provide an employee (or the employee's authorized agent) with a reasonable opportunity to review all personal data obtained by electronic monitoring of the employee.

(b) EXCEPTION.—(1) IN GENERAL.—Except as provided in paragraph (2), an employer is not required to provide an employee a reasonable opportunity to review data which are obtained by electronic monitoring described in section 5(c)(1). (2) REVIEW PERMITTED.—If—(A) the investigation by an employer with respect to which electronic monitoring described in section 5(c)(1) was conducted on an employee has been completed, or (B) disciplinary action has been initiated by an employer against the employee who was the subject of such electronic monitoring, whichever occurs first, such employer shall promptly provide such employee with an opportunity to review the personal data obtained from such electronic monitoring.

SEC. 8. USE OF DATA COLLECTED BY ELECTRONIC MONITORING.

(a) EMPLOYER ACTIONS.—An employer shall not take any action against an employee on the basis of personal data obtained by electronic monitoring of such employee unless the employer has complied with the requirements of this Act.

(b) DATA SHALL NOT BE USED AS SOLE BASIS FOR EVALUATION OR PRODUCTION QUOTAS.—(1) IN GENERAL.—Except as provided in paragraph (2), an employer shall not use quantitative data on an employee which is obtained by electronic monitoring and which records the amount of work performed by such employee within a specific time as the sole basis for—(A) individual employee performance evaluation, or (B) setting production quotas or work performance expectations. (2) EXCEPTION.—If an employee is not working at a facility of an employer and transmits the employee's work to the employer electronically, such employer may use the quantitative data described in paragraph (1) for the purposes described in subparagraphs (A) and (B) of paragraph (1) if such data is the only basis available to such employer for such purposes.

SEC. 9. PRIVACY PROTECTIONS.

(a) COLLECTION.—(1) IN GENERAL.—Except as provided in paragraph (2), no employer may intentionally collect personal data about an employee through electronic monitoring if the data are not confined to the employee's work, unless the employee is a customer of the employer at the time of the electronic monitoring. (2) EXCEPTION.—Electronic monitoring by an employer whose purpose and principal effect is to collect data about the work of an employee or to collect data on subjects who are not employees of the employer is not prohibited by paragraph (1) because it incidentally collects data which is not confined to such employee's work.

(b) PRIVATE AREAS.—NO EMPLOYER MAY ENGAGE IN ELECTRONIC MONITORING IN—(1) bathrooms, (2) locker rooms, or (3) dressing rooms,

except that if the employer has a reasonable suspicion that an employee is engaged in conduct which violates civil or criminal law and which adversely affects the employer's interests or the interests of such employer's employees, the employer may engage in electronic monitoring of such employee in a place described in paragraph (1), (2), or (3) if the employer executes, in accordance with section 5(c)(2), the statement required by such section.

(c) FIRST AMENDMENT RIGHTS.—(1) IN GENERAL.—An employer shall not intentionally engage in electronic monitoring or use or disseminate personal data obtained by electronic monitoring of an employee when the employee is exercising First Amendment rights. (2) EXCEPTION.—Electronic monitoring by an employer whose purpose and principal effect is to collect data about the work of an employee of the employer is not prohibited by paragraph (1) because it collects some incidental data concerning the exercise of an employee's First Amendment rights.

(d) DISCLOSURE LIMITATIONS.—(1) IN GENERAL.— Except as provided in paragraph (2), an employer shall not disclose personal data obtained by electronic monitoring to any person or business entity except to (or with the prior written consent of) the individual employee to whom the data pertain, unless the disclosure would be—(A) to officers and employees of the employer who have a legitimate need for the information in the performance of their duties; (B) to a law enforcement agency in connection with an investigation or prosecution; or (C) pursuant to the order of a court of competent jurisdiction. (2) EXCEPTION.—An employer may disclose to the public personal data obtained by electronic monitoring of an employee if the data contain evidence of illegal conduct by a public official or have a direct and substantial effect on public health or safety.

SEC. 10. ACCESS TO DATA.

When an employer has an immediate need for specific data and if the employee who maintains such data is not available, the employer may access such data if—(1) the data is alphanumeric and do not include data obtained by the aural or visual monitoring of employees or the interception of employee communications, (2) the data will not be used for the purpose of discipline or performance evaluation, and (3) the employer notifies the employee who maintains such data that the employer has accessed such data and provides such notice within a reasonable time after the access has occurred.

SEC. 11. PROHIBITIONS.

No employer may—(1) violate any requirement of this Act, (2) engage in video monitoring with a video camera which is not visible to the subject of the monitoring, except in the case of monitoring described in section 5(c)(1), 13(a), 13(b), or 13(c)(2), (3) interfere with, or deny the exercise or the attempted exercise by, an employee of any right provided by section 9(c), or (4) discharge, discipline, or in any manner discriminate against an employee with respect to the employee's compensation or terms, conditions, or privileges of employment because the employee (or any person acting pursuant to a request of the employee) has—(A) instituted any proceeding relating to a violation of this Act, (B) has testified or is about to testify in any such proceedings, or (C) disclosed information which the employee reasonably believes evidences a violation of this Act.

SEC. 12. ENFORCEMENT PROVISIONS.

(a)   CIVIL PENALTIES.—(1) IN GENERAL.—Subject to paragraph (2), any employer who violates any provision of this Act may be assessed a civil penalty of not more than $10,000 for each such violation. (2) CONSIDERATIONS.—In determining the amount of any penalty under paragraph (1), the Secretary shall take into account the previous record of the person in terms of compliance with this Act and the gravity of the violation. (3) ASSESSMENT AND COLLECTION.—Any civil penalty under this subsection shall be assessed by the Secretary and shall be collected in the same manner as is required by subsections (b) through (e) of section 503 of the Migrant and Seasonal Agricultural Worker Protection Act (29 U.S.C. 1853) with respect to civil penalties assessed under subsection (a) of such section.

(b)   ACTIONS BY THE SECRETARY.—The Secretary may bring an action under this section to restrain violations of this Act. The Solicitor of Labor may appear for and represent the Secretary in any litigation brought under this Act. In any action brought under this section, the district courts of the United States shall have jurisdiction, for cause shown, to issue temporary or permanent restraining orders and injunctions to require compliance with this Act, including such legal or equitable relief incident thereto as may be appropriate, including employment, reinstatement, promotion, and the payment of lost wages and benefits.

(c)   PRIVATE CIVIL ACTIONS.—(1) IN GENERAL.—An employer who violates this Act shall be liable to the employee or prospective employee affected by such violation. Such employer shall be liable for such legal or equitable relief as may be appropriate, including employment, reinstatement, promotion, and the payment of lost wages and benefits. (2) JURISDICTION.—An action to recover the liability prescribed in paragraph (1) may be maintained against the employer in any Federal or State court of competent jurisdiction by any person for or on behalf of an employee or prospective employee. (3) LIMITATION.—No such action may be commenced more than 3 years after the date—(A) the employee knew of, or (B) the employee could reasonably be expected to know of, the alleged violation. (4) COSTS.—The court shall allow the prevailing party (other than the United States) reasonable costs, including attorneys' and expert witness fees.

(d) WAIVER OF RIGHTS PROHIBITED.—The rights and procedures provided by this Act may not be waived by contract or otherwise, unless such waiver is part of a written settlement agreed to and signed by the parties to a pending action or complaint under this Act.

SEC. 13. APPLICATION.

(a) LAW ENFORCEMENT.—This Act shall not apply to electronic monitoring administered by law enforcement agencies as may otherwise be permitted in criminal investigations.

(b) WORKERS' COMPENSATION.—This Act does not apply to electronic monitoring conducted by an employer of the employer's employees in connection with an investigation of a workers' compensation claim.

(c) REQUIRED MONITORING.—(1) INTELLIGENCE.— This Act (other than sections 4(a) and 7) shall not apply to electronic monitoring conducted by or for—

(A) the intelligence community, as defined in Executive Order 12333 (or successor order), or (B) intelligence community contractors with respect to contracts that bear upon national security information, as defined by Executive Order 12356 (or successor order). (2) OTHER MONITORING.—This Act (other than sections 4(a), 4(b)(1), 4(b)(2), 4(b)(4), 7, 8, and 9) shall not apply to electronic monitoring—(A) conducted by an employer pursuant to Federal law (including regulations) governing public safety or security for public transportation, (B) conducted by an employer registered under section 6, 15, 15A, 15B, 15C, or 17A of the Securities Exchange Act of 1934 (15 U.S.C. 78 et seq.), section 8(a) of the Investment Company Act of 1940 (15 U.(a)), or sections 202(a)(11) and 203(a) of the Investment Advisers Act of 1940 (15 U.(a)(11) and 80b-3(a)), conducted by an employer or a person associated with an employer registered or exempt from such registration under sections 4d, 4e, 4k, or 4m of the Commodity Exchange Act (7 U.S.C. 6d, 6e, 6k, or 6m), conducted by a self-regulatory organization or its affiliated clearinghouse designated, registered, or exempt from registration under section 6 or 17 of such Act (7 U.S.C. 8, 21), or conducted by an employer who provides an electronic trading system or other facilities for one or more self-regulatory organizations designated, registered, or exempt from registration under section 6 or 17 of such Act (7 U.S.C. 8, 21) if such monitoring is confined to management or professional employees with significant financial responsibility which involves the use of independent judgment, (C) conducted by an employer that is a financial institution, as defined in section 20 of title 18, United States Code or subparagraph (A), (B), (C), (D), or (F) of section 5312(a)(2) of title 31, United States Code, if such monitoring is confined to management or professional employees with significant financial responsibility which involves the use of independent judgment, (D) conducted in or about a gaming or gambling facility operating under license or permit issued by a State regulatory agency and as required by State law or regulations enacted or adopted, before January 1, 1992, to deter or detect criminal activities through electronic monitoring, or (E) conducted only to the extent necessary to ensure an employee provides the notices required by the Truth in Lending Act and the regulation under such Act designated Regulation Z, the Equal Credit Opportunity Act and the regulation under such Act designated Regulation B, the Fair Credit Reporting Act, the Fair Credit Billing Act, the Fair Debt Collection Practices Act, the rule of the Federal Trade Commission on credit practices, the regulations and consent orders of the

Federal Trade Commission on unfair acts and practices, the Telephone Consumer Protection Act of 1991 and regulations under such Act, and all corresponding State laws and regulations. (3) ENFORCEMENT.—The provisions of this Act made applicable to the electronic monitoring described in paragraphs (1) and (2) shall be enforced in accordance with section 12 of this Act.

(c) THIRD PARTY.—(1) MONITORING FOR ANOTHER PERSON.—A person who engages in electronic monitoring may not perform electronic monitoring for another person unless the requirements of this Act are complied with. (2) USE OF DATA.—A person who contracts with or otherwise obtains the services of a third party to electronically monitor the employees of such person may not use the data obtained from such monitoring unless the requirements of this Act are complied with.

SEC. 14. REGULATIONS.

The Secretary shall, within 6 months after the date of the enactment of this Act, issue regulations to carry out this Act.

SEC. 15 PREEMPTION.

This Act shall not be construed to restrict, limit, or eliminate a requirement of a State or political subdivision of a State or of a collective bargaining agreement relating to electronic monitoring which is more stringent than any requirement of this Act.

SEC. 16. COVERAGE OF EMPLOYEES OF THE HOUSE OF REPRESENTATIVES AND SENATE.

(a) APPLICATION.—With the exception of section 12, this Act (including the substantive requirements of implementing regulations issued under section 14) shall apply to employees and to employing authorities.

(b) ADMINISTRATION.—(1) HOUSE OF REPRESENTATIVES.—The remedies and procedures of the Fair Employment Practices Resolution shall apply with respect to a violation of this

Act as it is made applicable by subsection (a) to employees of the employing authorities described in subsection (a)(2)(A). The Office of Fair Employment Practices may, in addition to those remedies available under the Fair Employment Practices Resolution, assess such an employing authority a civil penalty of not more than $10,000 for each violation. In determining the amount, the Office shall take into account the previous record of the employing authority involved in terms of compliance with this section and the gravity of the violation. Any such penalty collected shall be paid into the Treasury of the United States. (2) SENATE.—The remedies and procedures utilized by the Office of Senate Fair Employment Practices, established by section 303 of the Civil Rights Act of 1991, shall apply with respect to a violation of this Act as it is made applicable by subsection (a) to Senate employees of an employing authority described in subsection (g)(2)(B). The Office of Senate Fair Employment Practices may, in addition to those remedies otherwise available, assess such an employing authority a civil penalty of not more than $10,000 for each violation. In determining the amount, the Office shall take into account the previous record of the employing authority involved in terms of compliance with this section and the gravity of the violation. Any such penalty collected shall be paid into the Treasury of the United States.

(c) WAIVER OF RIGHTS PROHIBITED.—The rights and procedures provided by this Act may not be waived by contract or otherwise, unless such waiver is part of a written settlement agreed to and signed by the parties to a pending action or complaint under this Act.

(d) NOTICE.—Each employing authority shall post and keep posted in conspicuous places on its premises a notice that shall be—

(1) with respect to employing authorities described in subsection (g)(2)(A), prepared by the Office of Fair Employment Practices, and (2) with respect to employing authorities described in subsection (g)(2)(B), prepared by the Office of Senate Fair Employment Practices,

setting forth such information as each such Office considers to be appropriate to carry out this section. Such notice, at a minimum, shall provide the same information as that required under section 4(a)(1).

(e) RULEMAKING.—Subsection (b) is enacted as an exercise of the rulemaking power of the House of Representatives and the Senate, with full recognition of the right of the House of Representatives and the Senate to change its rules in the same manner, and to the same extent, as in any other rule of the House of Representatives and the Senate.

(f) ENFORCEMENT.—Notwithstanding any other provision of this Act, no officer or employee of the executive branch of the Federal Government shall have authority to administer, interpret, or enforce this section.

(g) DEFINITIONS.—For purposes of this section—(1) the term "employee" means any current, prospective, or former employee of an employing authority or any leased employee; (2) the term "employing authority"—(A) has the meaning given it in the Fair Employment Practices Resolution, except that with respect to a position on the minority staff of a committee, such term means the ranking minority member of such committee; and (B) in the case of a Senate employee, includes a head of employing office as that term is defined by section 301(c)(2) of the Civil Rights Act of 1991; and (3) the term "Fair Employment Practices Resolution" means—(A) House Resolution 558 of the One Hundredth Congress, as adopted October 4, 1988, and incorporated into rule LI of the Rules of the House of Representatives of the One Hundred Second Congress; or (B) any other provision that continues in effect the provisions of such resolution.

SEC. 17. EFFECTIVE DATE.

This Act shall take effect on 6 months after the date of the enactment of this Act, except that an employer who is engaged in

electronic monitoring on the expiration of such 6 months shall have
60 days after such expiration to provide each affected employee
with the notice required by this Act.

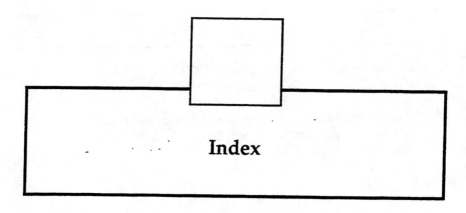

Index

B

E

F

I

R

Y

Z

About the Author

Kurt H. Decker, Esquire, is a partner with the general practice law firm of Stevens & Lee with offices in Reading, Allentown, Harrisburg, Valley Forge, and Wilkes-Barre, Pennsylvania. He earned a B.A. from Thiel College, an M.P.A. from the Pennsylvania State University, a J.D. from the School of Law at Vanderbilt University, and an L.L.M. (Labor) from the School of Law at Temple University. He serves as an Adjunct Professor of Law with the Widener School of Law in Harrisburg, Pennsylvania and as an Adjunct Professor of Industrial Relations with the Graduate School of Industrial Relations at Saint Francis College in Loretto, Pennsylvania.

Mr. Decker is the author of more than 100 articles and books dealing with employment law. Many of his writings have been cited as authority for decisions issued by federal and state courts throughout the United States. He is the author of *Employee Privacy Law and Practice; Employee Privacy Forms and Procedures, A Manager's Guide to Employee Privacy Law, Procedures, and Policies* (named one of the best business books for 1989 by the *Library Journal*); *Drafting and Revising Employment Contracts; Drafting and Revising Employment Handbooks; Drafting and Revising Employment Policies and Handbooks;* and *Covenants Not to Compete.* In 1986, he was the recipient of the Philadelphia Bar Association's Award for a series of articles on increased employer liability for employee defamation that appeared in the *Pennsylvania Law Journal-Reporter.* He serves as Editor of the *Journal of Individual Employee Rights* and is a member of the Board of Editors of the *Journal of Collective Negotiations in the Public Sector.*

Mr. Decker has represented both organized and unorganized employers in the development and implementation of their employment policies. Clients have included employers in the steel, retail, fabrication, banking, health care, and manufacturing industries, along with public sector bodies.

Mr. Decker is a member of the American and Pennsylvania Bar Associations and their respective Labor and Employment Law Sections. He is listed in *Who's Who in American Law, Who's Who in Emerging Leaders in America,* and *Who's Who in Finance and Industry.*